600

ESSENTIAL WORDS FOR THE

TOEIC*

TEST

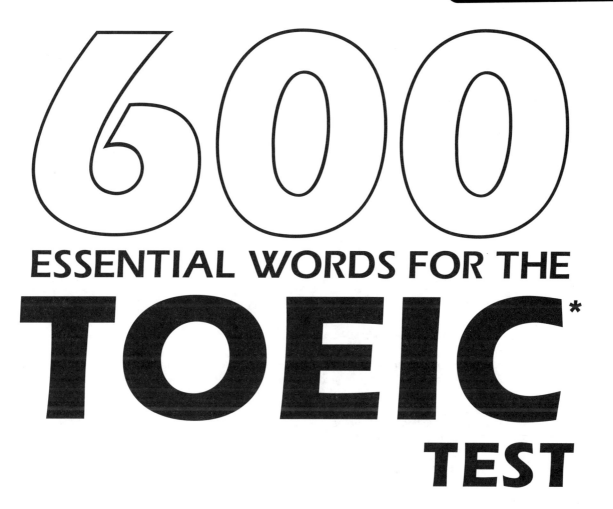

Test of English for International Communication

SECOND EDITION

Dr. Lin Lougheed

BARRON'S

All inquiries should be addressed to:
Barron's Educational Series, Inc.
250 Wireless Boulevard
Hauppauge, New York 11788
http://www.barronseduc.com

Library of Congress Catalog Card No.: 2003049553

ISBN-10: 0-7641-2024-7 (book only)

ISBN-13: 978-0-7641-7538-1 (book with CD)
ISBN-10: 0-7641-7538-6 (book with CD)

Library of Congress Cataloging-in-Publication Data
Lougheed, Lin, 1946–
    600 essential words for the TOEIC test / Lin Lougheed.—2nd ed.
        p.   cm.
    "With listening comprehension compact discs."
    Includes index.
    ISBN 0-7641-7538-6
    1. Test of English for International Communication—Study guides.   2. English language—Textbooks for foreign speakers.   3. English language—Examinations—Study guides.   4. Vocabulary—Examinations—Study guides.   I. Title: Six hundred essential words for the TOEIC test.   II. Title.

PE1128.L643   2003
428.1'076—dc21

2003049553

PRINTED IN THE UNITED STATES OF AMERICA
9 8 7

Table of Contents

What the Book Is About

The TOEIC (Test of English for International Communication) test measures the English proficiency of people working in international business or planning to use English to communicate with others. Although the test does not specifically test specialized vocabulary, the items on the exam are in specialized contexts.

This book will provide you with a basis to understand these specialized contexts that are often used on the TOEIC test. Each chapter covers a particular context that has appeared on the TOEIC test. The new words taught in each chapter are not specialized words. These words are more what is called general vocabulary. They can be used in many contexts.

However, these new words are used in a specialized context. Understanding these contexts and the words used in these contexts will help you improve your score on the TOEIC exam.

How to Use This Book

This book could also be titled *50 Days to a More Powerful Vocabulary*. There are 50 lessons. Every day, you can study one lesson. Every day you can learn 12 new words. In 50 days, you can learn 600 new words—words that will help you understand English better. And the better you understand English, the higher your TOEIC score will be.

You can sit down and in 30 minutes finish a lesson. But that is not the best way. To learn a new word, you must use it over and over. Try to spread your studying out over the whole day. Do a little bit whenever you have some free time. The 12 new words are used over and over and over in this lesson. Studying these words throughout the day will help you learn them and never forget them.

Start in the morning and look over the 12 new words and their definitions. Repeat them out loud. During the morning, read over the conversations. If you can, say the conversations out loud. The more ways you use a word (listening, speaking, reading, and writing), the better the chance you will remember it.

In the afternoon, do the exercises. In the evening, do the very last exercise. The last exercise is like a mini-test. It will tell you if you completely understood the meaning of the word and how to use it in a sentence.

Every day, do another lesson. At the end of the week, do the Word Review. I am sure you will answer every question correctly.

Most of the new words you learn in one lesson will be used again in another lesson. We recycle words just as we recycle paper. If you forget a meaning of a word, look up the word in the Word Index at the back of the book. That will tell you in which lesson you can find a definition and the pronunciation.

You will note that the order of the activities is different from that on the TOEIC test. On the TOEIC test, Listening Comprehension is first, followed by Reading. I think it is easier to learn a new word by reading it than hearing it. Consequently, I have reversed the order in each chapter. First you will *read* the word (Parts V, VI, and VII), and then you will *hear* the word (Parts I, II, III, and IV).

Strategies to Improve Your Vocabulary

The English language consists of more than 250,000 words, far more than most other languages—far more than we can include in this book. Here are some strategies that will help you remember words that you come across either in this book or in English books or magazines.

To learn a new word, of course, you first have to run across it. Therefore, you must read in English as much as you can. The best way to improve your vocabulary is to read routinely. The more you read, the more words you will encounter. The more words you run across, the more you will learn.

Once you have gotten into the habit of reading, you can systematically build your vocabulary by doing five things:

1. Analyze word parts.
2. Recognize grammatical forms.
3. Recognize word families.
4. Make your own personal dictionary.
5. Keep a daily reading log.

I. Analyze Word Parts

Many English words have Greek and Latin prefixes, roots, and suffixes. Memorizing a comprehensive list will increase your vocabulary exponentially. For example, a prefix is the part of a word that comes at the beginning of a word, like the prefix *pre-* at the beginning of the word *prefix*. The prefix *pre-* means *before*. Once you learn the meaning of this prefix, you will be able to use it to help you figure out the meaning of a new word that contains the same prefix, for example, *predetermine*, *predict*, *predecessor*.

Look at these other examples.

Prefix	re-	happens a second time
Root	circul	around
Suffix	-tion	the act of
Word	recirculation	repeating the act of motion in a circular path

Prefix	re-	happens a second time
Root	gener	bring to life
Suffix	-tion	the act of
Word	regeneration	the act of being brought to life again

Prefix	re-	happens a second time
Root	loc	place
Suffix	-tion	the act of
Word	relocation	the act of moving again to another place

By understanding that the prefix *re-* means *again*, you know that any word that begins with *re-* means something happens a second time. Students who become familiar with the most common prefixes, roots, and suffixes find that their vocabulary grows quickly. Examples of these prefixes, roots, and suffixes will be given throughout the book.

II. Recognize Grammatical Forms

Being familiar with all grammatical forms of a word helps you increase your vocabulary. Suffixes often give you a clue as to the meaning of a word and its grammatical position in a sentence. These suffixes can tell you whether the word may be a noun, verb, adjective, or adverb.

Common noun endings:

-tion	competition
-ance	deliverance
-ence	independence
-ment	government

-ism	Buddhism
-ship	friendship
-ity	community
-er	teacher
-or	doctor
-ee	attendee

Common verb endings:

-ize	memorize
-ate	refrigerate
-en	lengthen

Common adjective endings:

-y	happy
-ous	mountainous
-ious	serious
-able	capable
-al	musical
-ic	athletic
-ful	beautiful
-less	careless

Common adverb ending:

| -ly | quickly |

Learning about grammatical forms will help you identify the purpose of many words. As the endings become recognizable, they will help you figure out the meanings of new words.

Examples of these word forms will be given throughout the book.

III. Recognize Word Families

Like brothers and sisters in the same family, words can be related, too. These words have the same base but different grammatical forms. They are part of a word family. When you learn a new word, look in the dictionary for words in the same word family. Write them beside the word in your own dictionary. Make columns for nouns, verbs, adjectives, and adverbs and write down the words in the same family. For example:

verb	noun	adjective	adverb
to care	care	careful	carefully
to attend	attendance	attentive	attentively
to point	pointer	pointed	pointedly

Some members of a word family have all grammatical forms; others have just a few. Some words even have two grammatical forms of the same part of speech, but with different meanings like the nouns *attendance* and *attendee*. Examples of word families will be given throughout the book.

IV. Make Your Own Personal Dictionary

Create your own dictionary to keep track of all the new words you learn. Your own personal dictionary should look like a regular dictionary with different pages for words beginning with A, B, C, and so on.

You can photocopy the following sample dictionary page or you can use a sheet of paper to make one page for each letter of the alphabet. Put tabs on these pages and write the letter of the alphabet on the tab so you can find each letter more easily. You can add pages as necessary.

My Personal Dictionary

New word

Original sentence

_____

Definition

_____

My sentence

_____

Word forms in sentences

_____

_____

_____

_____

Word families in sentences

_____

_____

_____

_____

When you read or hear new words, you should write them in your own personal dictionary. You may even find other words in this book that you do not know. You can write these words in your personal dictionary, too. Try not to look up the meanings of these new words immediately. This will slow down your reading. Try to get the general meaning from the context. You can look up the specific meaning after you have formed a hypothesis.

Next to each word in your own personal dictionary, write a definition and make up a sentence including the word, using the dictionary as a guide. If possible, write the sentence where you originally discovered the word or a sentence whose context reminds you of the meaning.

While you are looking in the dictionary, search for words in the same word family. Write these words in your personal dictionary and make up sentences for these words, too. Notice which endings occur in each grammatical form.

Writing these sentences will help you remember the word later. It's easier to remember words when you put them in context. The more you use a word, the more likely you will remember it.

If you choose not to create your own personal dictionary, you can keep track of new words as you look them up in a regular dictionary. Take a yellow highlight pen and highlight the word you look up. At the end of the week or month, you can thumb through the dictionary and see at a glance how many words you have added to your vocabulary.

V. Keep a Daily Reading Log

It is important that you read something in English every day. You should set aside as much time as you can spare, but try to set aside at least 20 to 30 minutes every day just for reading and writing something in English. This time should not be used for reading text assigned from class or work. Select something that interests you and is appropriate for your level. It should not be too easy or too difficult. Here are samples of short passages you could read:

- the sports section of the newspaper
- an article from a popular magazine
- a chapter from a novel
- the label from an English/American product
- an advertisement in English
- Web pages on any subject in English

Try to vary the type of reading. Don't read only science journals or mystery novels. You want to build your vocabulary in a variety of areas. On the Internet, look at news sites such as *www.cnn.com*, *www.msnbc.com*, *www.abc.com*. These sites have a variety of links to many different kinds of subjects such as weather, business, sports, politics, law, technology, science and space, health, entertainment, travel, education, and many more. If you need special vocabulary for your job or course work, you could focus on these types of Web sites. But remember, the reading log should be material in addition to assigned readings.

Try to pick a time of day when your mind is alert. Don't try to study when you are tired.

Follow these steps to build a reading log.

1. Read WITHOUT stopping for about ten minutes.
   The first time you read a passage, do NOT stop to look up words. Native English readers often come across words they do not know in their reading. They get a general idea of the meaning of unknown words from the context. See if you can also get the gist of the idea without looking up the words in a dictionary.
2. Reread the passage and highlight unknown or unclear words.
   You can use a yellow highlight pen or underline the word. If you aren't permitted to write in the book, write the words down in your reading log.
3. Choose five key words.
   From all the words that you did not understand completely, select five of them for your dictionary. These should be words that kept you from understanding an entire sentence.
4. Summarize what you read.
   Write a summary about the passage you read and add it to your reading log. Summarize what you've read in approximately a three-sentence paragraph. If possible, make a copy of the passage or cut it out and paste it under the summary. If you're reading a book, write the title, pages read, and a summary of the story or argument of the book. Try to use your five new key words in your summary.

My Reading Log

Key words

Summary

_____
_____
_____
_____
_____
_____
_____
_____
_____

Key words

1._____
2._____
3._____
4._____
5._____

(Article or photocopy of article)

Key words

Summary

_____
_____
_____
_____
_____
_____
_____
_____
_____

Key words

1._____
2._____
3._____
4._____
5._____

(Article or photocopy of article)

Lesson 1

Contracts

1. **abide by** v., to comply with; to conform
   a. The two parties agreed to abide by the judge's decision.
   b. For years he has abided by a commitment to annual employee raises.

2. **agreement** n., a mutual arrangement, a contract
   a. The landlord and tenant were in agreement that the rent should be prorated to the middle of the month.
   b. According to the agreement, the caterer will also supply the flowers for the event.

3. **assurance** n., a guarantee; confidence
   a. The sales associate gave his assurance that the missing keyboard would be replaced the next day.
   b. Her self-assurance made it easy to see why she was in charge of the negotiations.

4. **cancellation** n., annulment; stopping
   a. The cancellation of her flight caused her problems for the rest of the week.
   b. The cancellation clause appears at the back of the contract.

5. **determine** v., to find out; to influence
   a. After reading the contract, I was still unable to determine if our company was liable for back wages.
   b. The skill of the union bargainers will determine whether the automotive plant will open next week.

6. **engagement** n., participation; a commitment, especially for marriage; an event
   a. The engagement begins at 7:30.
   b. The entire office was invited to her engagement party.

7. **establish** v., to institute permanently; to bring about
   a. Through her many books and interviews, Dr. Wan established herself as an authority on conflict resolution.
   b. The merger of the two companies established a powerful new corporation.

8. **obligate** v., to bind legally or morally
   a. The contractor was obligated by the contract to work 40 hours a week.
   b. I felt obligated to finish the project even though I could have exercised my option to quit.

9. **party** n., a person or group participating in an action or plan; the persons or sides concerned in a legal matter
   a. The parties agreed to a settlement in their contract dispute.
   b. The party that prepares the contract has a distinct advantage.

10. **provision** n., a measure taken beforehand; a stipulation
    a. The father made provisions for his children through his will.
    b. The contract contains a provision to deal with how payments are made if John loses his job.

11. **resolve** v., to deal with successfully; to declare; n., conviction
    a. The mediator was able to resolve the problem to everyone's satisfaction.
    b. The businessman resolved to clean out all the files by the end of the week.

12. **specific** adj., particular
    a. The customer's specific complaint was not addressed in his e-mail.
    b. In a contract, one specific word can change the meaning dramatically.

Word Families

verb	agree	If both parties agree to the terms, we can finalize the contract.
noun	agreement	As soon as the labor agreement was signed, the factory resumed production of new cars and vans.
adjective	agreeable	The parties are agreeable to the terms.

verb	assure	I assure you that our drug-testing policy is applied fairly.
noun	assurance	What assurance is there that the company will still be in business?
adverb	assuredly	He spoke assuredly, but his follow-up memo showed less conviction.

verb	cancel	The man canceled his magazine subscription and got his money back.
noun	cancellation	Writers usually receive a cancellation fee even if their articles are not published.
adjective	canceled	The canceled concert ended up costing our agency millions.

verb	obligate	The terms of the contracts obligate us to work for at least one more month.
noun	obligation	The factory managers have a legal and moral obligation to provide a safe work site.
adjective	obligatory	He finished his obligatory military service, and then joined his father on the orange farm.

verb	provide	Since the machine is very reliable, why don't we cancel the service contract they provided?
noun	provider	We must negotiate a new contract with our Internet service provider.
noun	provision	The provision for canceling the contract is in the last clause.

verb	specify	The contract specifies the percentage of raise the workers will see next year.
noun	specification	The work was done according to our specifications.
adjective	specific	We have not chosen a specific location for the reunion.

Incomplete Sentences

Choose the word that best completes the sentence.

1. The two sides were no closer to a final _____ at midnight than they were at noon.
   (A) agreement   (C) agree
   (B) agreeable   (D) agreed

2. Our union representative _____ members that our rights would be defended.
   (A) assured   (C) assuredly
   (B) assurance   (D) assure

3. If you _____ your reservation 48 hours in advance, you will not be billed.
   (A) will cancel   (C) cancellation
   (B) cancel   (D) canceled

4. I don't feel any _____ to give my boss more than two weeks notice when I leave.
   (A) oblige   (C) obliged
   (B) obligatory   (D) obligation

5. The _____ for terminating the contract were not discussed.
   (A) provide   (C) provider
   (B) provisions   (D) provisioning

6. The contract calls for the union to _____ who their bargaining representative will be.
   (A) specific   (C) specifying
   (B) specification (D) specify

Error Recognition

Choose the underlined word or phrase that should be rewritten and rewrite it.

7. When attempts at <u>resolve</u> failed, both parties, <u>determined</u> to end the conflict, <u>agreed</u> to enter into a formal
          A   B   C
   contract and promised to <u>abide by</u> the terms.
                        D

   _____

8. Both <u>parties</u> agreed that the contractor would <u>provide</u> technical assistance 24 hours a day, so it
        A   B
   was easy to <u>determination</u> that the two-day delay was not <u>acceptable</u>.
                C   D

   _____

9. We were <u>assured</u> by the cable company, before we <u>engaged</u> in a contract, that we could <u>cancellation</u> our
          A   B   C
   membership at any time with no further <u>obligations</u>.
                                        D

   _____

10. Our car insurance <u>establishments</u> the time period within which they provide assistance, <u>determines</u> the repair
                           A   B
    shops we can use, sets a fee structure for <u>payment</u>, and provides a forum for <u>resolving</u> billing errors.
                                                 C   D

    _____

Reading Comprehension

Read the following passage and write the words in the blanks below.

abide by	cancel	establishment	provide
agreement	determine	obligates	resolve
assurance	engaging	parties	specifies

Contracts are an integral part of the workplace. In simple terms, contracts are an (11.) _____ between two or more (12.) _____ that (13.) _____ terms and (14.) _____ the parties to follow them. Contracts often include the amount that a client will pay contractors and what services will be provided. For example, in your office, you may have a contract that provides (15.) _____ that your copier machine or phones will be repaired within a certain amount of time. This service can either be done off-site or at your (16.) _____. A contract often states ways to (17.) _____ if quality of work delivered is acceptable. Well-written contracts usually (18.) _____ ways to (19.) _____ problems like these when they happen. Before (20.) _____ in a contract, both parties should think carefully, as they will have to (21.) _____ the conditions specified in it. A contract usually specifies how the two parties can (22.) _____ it if either party fails to meet the terms.

LISTENING COMPREHENSION

Listen to Track 1 of the Compact Disc to hear the statements for Lesson 1

Part I Picture

Look at the picture and listen to the sentences. Choose the sentence that best describes the picture.

23. Ⓐ Ⓑ Ⓒ Ⓓ

Part II Question—Response

Listen to the question and the three responses. Choose the response that best answers the question.

24. Ⓐ Ⓑ Ⓒ   25. Ⓐ Ⓑ Ⓒ

Part III Short Conversations

Listen to the short dialogs. Then read the question and choose the best answer.

26. What is the man worried about?
    (A) A broken computer.
    (B) Being late for work.
    (C) Serving customers.
    (D) Payment in case of cancellation.

27. How do the speakers feel about the agreement?
    (A) It was well negotiated.
    (B) The lawyer's fees were too high.
    (C) Uncertain.
    (D) Fantastic.

Part IV Short Talks

Listen to the short talk. Then read the questions and choose the best answer.

28. Who is talking?
    (A) A lawyer.
    (B) An upset signer of the contract.
    (C) A secretary.
    (D) Someone who has canceled his agreement.

29. Which part of the contract are they looking at?
    (A) A cancellation clause.
    (B) The assurance of quality.
    (C) The agreement on payment.
    (D) A provision in case of bankruptcy.

Lesson 2

Words to learn

attract
compare
competition
consume
convince
currently
fad
inspiration
market
persuasion
productive
satisfaction

Marketing

1. **attract** v., to draw by appeal
   a. The display attracted a number of people at the convention.
   b. The new advertising attracts the wrong kind of customer into the store.

2. **compare** v., to examine similarities and differences
   a. Once the customer compared the two products, her choice was easy.
   b. The price for this brand is high compared to the other brands on the market.

3. **competition** n., a contest or struggle
   a. In the competition for afternoon diners, Hector's has come out on top.
   b. The company has decided not to join the growing competition for dominance in the semiconductor market.

4. **consume** v., to absorb; to use up
   a. The business plans consumed all of Fritz's attention this fall.
   b. This printer consumes more toner than the downstairs printer.

5. **convince** v., to bring to believe by argument; to persuade
   a. The salesman convinced his customer to buy his entire inventory of pens.
   b. Before a business can convince customers that it provides a quality product, it must convince its marketing staff.

6. **currently** adv., happening at the present time; now
   a. We are currently exploring plans to update the MX3 model.
   b. Currently, customers are demanding big discounts for bulk orders.

7. **fad** n., a practice followed enthusiastically for a short time; a craze
   a. The mini dress was a fad once thought to be finished, but now it is making a comeback.
   b. Classic tastes may seem boring but they have proven to resist fads.

8. **inspiration** n., a thing or person that arouses a feeling
   a. His work is an inspiration to the marketing department.
   b. Marta's high sales in Spain were an inspiration to other European reps.

9. **market** v., the course of buying and selling a product; n., the demand for a product
   a. When Omar first began making his chutneys, he marketed them door-to-door to gourmet shops.
   b. The market for brightly colored clothing was brisk last year, but it's moving sluggishly this year.

10. **persuasion** n., the power to influence; a deep conviction or belief
    a. The seminar teaches techniques of persuasion to increase sales.
    b. Under his persuasion, she returned to school for her MBA.

11. **productive** adj., constructive; high yield
    a. The unproductive sales meeting brought many staff complaints.
    b. Alonzo is excited about his productive staff.

12. **satisfaction** n., happiness
    a. Your satisfaction is guaranteed or you'll get your money back.
    b. We will print the advertisement to your satisfaction.

Word Families

verb	attract	The store's poor location did not help it attract customers.
noun	attraction	Having a clown in the toy store was a foolproof attraction for getting kids to enter.
adjective	attractive	Lou ran his store on an old-fashioned premise: quality merchandise at attractive prices.

verb	compare	She compared the prices before she made a decision.
noun	comparison	There was no comparison in the quality of the two brands.
adjective	comparable	To get an average for home costs, the agent sought prices on comparable homes.

noun	competition	Try to think of yourself as someone who leads the competition.
verb	compete	We competed against three or four other agencies to get this contract.
adjective	competitive	His competitive character made him quite successful in his department.

verb	consume	The analyst was able to consume new information quickly.
noun	consumer	The government tracks consumer spending closely.
adjective	consumable	He ran a study of the use of consumable goods.

verb	market	The sales department disagreed about how to market their newest product.
noun	marketing	A good director of marketing can find a way to sell even an unattractive product.
adjective	marketable	Once the sales manager decided to change the packaging, the product became much more marketable.

noun	satisfaction	Our highest priority is customer satisfaction.
verb	satisfy	Henri was perfectly satisfied with his new fishing rod.
adjective	satisfactory	The rods were not in satisfactory condition.

Incomplete Sentences

Choose the word that best completes the sentence.

1. Marketing specialists have conducted extensive studies of what _____ customers to a particular product.
   (A) attractive
   (B) attraction
   (C) attracts
   (D) attracting

2. Smart shoppers will _____ similar brands of an item before making a decision.
   (A) compare
   (B) comparison
   (C) comparative
   (D) comparable

3. If our work isn't to your _____, please notify us within 60 days.
   (A) satisfy
   (B) satisfactory
   (C) satisfaction
   (D) satisfied

4. Manufacturers like to know what features _____ find useful.
   (A) consumers
   (B) consume
   (C) consumption
   (D) consumable

5. Without good _____, good products can go unsold.
   (A) market
   (B) marketable
   (C) marketed
   (D) marketing

6. A careful analysis of the _____ products on the market indicated that our product lacked innovation and optional features.
   (A) compete
   (B) competing
   (C) competed
   (D) competition

Error Recognition

Choose the underlined word or phrase that should be rewritten and rewrite it.

7. George found it was more <u>productive</u> and less expensive to <u>inspiration</u> loyalty in his <u>current</u> customers
                               A   B   C
   <u>compared</u> to the cost of advertising to attract new customers.
     D

   _____

8. Joelle cannot <u>compete</u> with the prices of jewelry found in stores, but she is able to <u>persuasion</u> <u>consumers</u> that
                    A   B   C
   her handmade <u>products</u> are unique works of art.
              D

   _____

9. Adil's plan to market his soccer lessons meant <u>persuading</u> boys and girls that soccer was not a short-lived <u>fad</u>
                                             A   B
   and <u>convincing</u> parents that he offered a better service <u>comparison</u> to local soccer camps.
       C   D

   _____

10. The restaurant used an age-old <u>marketing</u> strategy of continually <u>attractive</u> new customers and <u>satisfying</u>
                                        A   B   C
    <u>current</u> customers with good food at good prices.
      D

    _____

Reading Comprehension

Read the following passage and write the words in the blanks below.

attract	consumers	fad	persuaded
compared	convince	inspire	product
competes	current	market	satisfied

Yassir is getting ready to realize his dream: opening a business that sells plants on the Internet. After completing a business plan that helped him to determine that there was demand for his (11.) _____ in the (12.) _____, Yassir is ready to start promoting his business. Having (13.) _____ the bank that there was a market—that there were consumers willing to buy plants on the Internet—he needed to find these (14.) _____.

Once he has an established base, Yassir, like other business owners, will have to continually (15.) _____ new customers. At the same time, he must make sure current customers are (16.) _____. In order to be satisfied, (17.) _____ customers must be happy with the product they receive. Yassir's job is to (18.) _____ these customers to gain their repeat business. To do this, he will have to (19.) _____ consumers that he offers a good product at a good price, especially when (20.) _____ to the businesses with which he (21.) _____. He hopes that Internet plant buyers are here to stay and not just part of a (22.) _____.

LISTENING COMPREHENSION

Listen to Track 2 of the Compact Disc to hear the statements for Lesson 2

Part I Picture

Look at the picture and listen to the sentences.
Choose the sentence that best describes the picture.

23. Ⓐ Ⓑ Ⓒ Ⓓ

Part II Question—Response

Listen to the question and the three possible responses. Choose the response that best answers the question.

24. Ⓐ Ⓑ Ⓒ   25. Ⓐ Ⓑ Ⓒ

Part III Short Conversations

Listen to the short dialogs. Then read the questions and choose the best response.

26. How will the company attract new customers?
    (A) By giving them trial products.
    (B) By giving them discounts.
    (C) By featuring happy customers in ads.
    (D) By holding an open house to promote
        products.

27. Why does the store need to be more competitive?
    (A) There's currently a recession.
    (B) Productivity has dropped lately.
    (C) There's a new competitor across the street.
    (D) New employees have little experience.

Part IV Short Talks

Listen to the short talk. Then read the questions and choose the best answer.

28. Who would listen to this talk?
    (A) Customers.
    (B) Competitors.
    (C) Students.
    (D) Salespeople.

29. What are they trying to identify?
    (A) Their weaknesses.
    (B) How to price their service.
    (C) Their strong points.
    (D) Who the competition is.

Warranties

Words to learn

characteristic
consequence
consider
cover
expiration
frequently
imply
promise
protect
reputation
require
variety

1. **characteristic** adj., revealing of individual traits; n., an individual trait
   a. The cooking pot has features characteristic of the brand, such as "heat-resistant" handles.
   b. One characteristic of the store is that it is slow in mailing refund checks.
2. **consequence** n., that which follows necessarily
   a. The consequence of not following the service instructions for your car is that the warranty is invalidated.
   b. As a consequence of not having seen a dentist for several years, Lydia had several cavities.
3. **consider** v., to think about carefully
   a. The customer considered buying the VCR until he learned that the warranty coverage was very limited.
   b. After considering all the options, Della decided to buy a used car.
4. **cover** v., to provide protection against
   a. Will my medical insurance cover this surgery?
   b. Her car insurance provided for complete coverage against collision.
5. **expiration** n., the end
   a. Have you checked the expiration date on this yogurt?
   b. We can expect that the expiration of our Japan contract will impact sales next year.
6. **frequently** adv., occurring commonly; widespread
   a. Appliances frequently come with a one-year warranty.
   b. Warranties for this kind of appliance are frequently limited in their coverage.
7. **imply** v., to indicate by inference
   a. The guarantee on the Walkman implied that all damages were covered under warranty for one year.
   b. The travel agent implied that our hotel was not in the safest part of the city, but, when pressed for details, he said the location was fine.
8. **promise** n., a pledge, a commitment; v., to pledge to do, bring about, or provide
   a. A warranty is a promise the manufacturer makes to the consumer.
   b. The sales associate promised that our new mattress would arrive by noon on Saturday.
9. **protect** v., to guard
   a. Consumer laws are designed to protect the public against unscrupulous vendors.
   b. You can protect yourself from scams by getting detailed information on the seller.
10. **reputation** n., the overall quality of character
    a. Even though the salesperson showed me a product I had never heard of, I bought it because of the good reputation of the manufacturer.
    b. The company knew that the reputation of its products was the most important asset it had.
11. **require** v., to deem necessary or essential
    a. A car warranty may require the owner to have it serviced by a certified mechanic.
    b. The law requires that each item clearly display the warranty information.
12. **variety** n., many different kinds
    a. There's a variety of standard terms that you'll find in warranties.
    b. A variety of unexpected problems appeared after the product had been on the market for about six months.

Word Families

adjective	characteristic	One characteristic of the new Lexus is its computerized seat settings.
verb	characterize	This line is characterized by its bold flavor and spicy aftertaste.
adverb	characteristically	Characteristically, she accused middle-level management of the accounting error.

verb	consider	You should consider carefully whether a product will meet your needs.
noun	consideration	After long consideration, Heloise decided that the five-year warranty would be sufficient.
adjective	considerable	The fee for the extra year of protection was a considerable expense.

verb	imply	She implied that she had graduated from Harvard.
noun	implication	What are the implications of the accident?
adjective	implicit	It is implicit in her demands that if she doesn't get the promotion, she will leave the company.

verb	protect	Juan protected the warranty by taking excellent care of his lawn mower.
noun	protection	For your own protection, you should have a warranty that provides for a replacement product.
adjective	protective	Alfredo is very protective of the condition of his car and gets all the preventive maintenance his warranty requires.

noun	reputation	The good reputation of the manufacturer inspired Maria Jose to try the new product.
adjective	reputable	Because the company had a reputable name, I did not spend sufficient time reading the details of the warranty.
adjective	reputed	The new store is reputed to carry items that are not of the highest quality.

verb	require	The warranty requires that you send the watch to an approved repair shop to have it fixed.
noun	requirement	The terms of the warranty divulge the legal requirement the manufacturer has to the consumer.
adjective	requisite	The warranty spelled out the requisite steps to take to request a replacement product.

Incomplete Sentences

Choose the word that best completes the sentence.

1. The timing belt _____ shows signs of wear after about 180,000 miles.
    (A) character
    (B) characteristic
    (C) characterize
    (D) characteristically

2. Jacques and Louisa will only _____ purchasing appliances that come with a money-back guarantee.
    (A) consideration
    (B) consider
    (C) considering
    (D) considerable

3. If there is any _____ of the director's involvement, we need to follow up swiftly and thoroughly.
    (A) imply
    (B) implicit
    (C) implicated
    (D) implication

4. The level of _____ implied by the warranty was misleading.
    (A) protect
    (B) protective
    (C) protection
    (D) protector

5. It can be very helpful to consider the _____ of the manufacturer and the merchant when making a major purchase.
    (A) reputation
    (B) reputable
    (C) reputing
    (D) reputed

6. If the appliance breaks down within two years of purchase, the manufacturer is _____ to send you a replacement at no charge.
    (A) requiring
    (B) requisite
    (C) requirement
    (D) required

Error Recognition

Choose the underlined word or phrase that should be rewritten and rewrite it.

7. Claude read the <u>required</u> warranty only to find that, while the manufacturer <u>promised</u> to repair or replace the
          A   **B**
    CD player, the <u>coverage</u> had <u>expiration</u>.
                C   **D**

    _____

8. Before buying a new appliance, compare the <u>characteristics</u> of similar products and their warranties, which
                                           A
    <u>protect</u> your purchase and <u>frequently</u> <u>various</u> from product to product.
     B   **C**   **D**

    _____

9. Bassem discovered the <u>consequent</u> of not following instructions: because he had not had the <u>required</u> service
                              A   **B**
    performed on his car, his warranty <u>coverage</u> no longer <u>protected</u> him from mechanical failure.
                                  C   **D**

    _____

10. It is especially important to <u>consideration</u> the <u>reputation</u> of a manufacturer when buying a product <u>protected</u> by
                                A   **B**   **C**
    an <u>implied</u> warranty.
       D

    _____

Reading Comprehension

Read the following passage and write the words in the blanks below.

characteristics	coverage	implies	reputations
consequences	expire	promise	required
consider	frequently	protect	vary

Warranties are a seller's (11.) _____ to stand behind its products. Most major purchases like computers or cars come with a warranty, as do smaller purchases, like stereos or other electronic housewares. Warranties are not (12.) _____ by law, but are (13.) _____ found on most products. If you are making a purchase, you should (14.) _____ the individual (15.) _____ of a warranty, as each can (16.) _____ in the amount of (17.) _____ it provides. At the minimum, warranties are required to promise that the product will do what it (18.) _____ that it will do; for example, that a blender will blend or a hair dryer will dry hair. Most warranties are good for a fixed time, then they (19.) _____. You can (20.) _____ yourself by buying products from companies with good (21.) _____ and taking good care of your new purchase. There are (22.) _____ to not taking care of a product, as most warranties require that you use the product in a certain manner.

LISTENING COMPREHENSION

Listen to Track 3 of the Compact Disc to hear the statements for Lesson 3

Part I Picture

Look at the picture and listen to the sentences.
Choose the sentence that best describes the picture.

23. Ⓐ Ⓑ Ⓒ Ⓓ

Part II Question—Response

Listen to the question and the three responses. Choose the response that best answers the question.

24. Ⓐ Ⓑ Ⓒ   25. Ⓐ Ⓑ Ⓒ

Part III Short Conversations

Listen to the short dialogs. Then read the questions and choose the best response.

26. How long is the warranty effective?
    (A) One year.
    (B) Two years.
    (C) Ten years.
    (D) The product's full life.

27. What will happen if the buyer uses an unapproved
    mechanic?
    (A) There are no consequences.
    (B) The warranty is no longer effective.
    (C) Protection is decreased by fifty percent.
    (D) The buyer gains full protection.

Part IV Short Talks

Listen to the short talk. Then read the questions and choose the best answer.

28. What is the point of the talk?
    (A) Items under warranty must be fixed.
    (B) If an item is misused, the warranty may be
        invalidated.
    (C) Machines with unusual wear are difficult to
        repair.
    (D) Customers often don't understand warranties.

29. Who is the audience for this talk?
    (A) A factory repairperson.
    (B) A customer.
    (C) Someone who rents machines.
    (D) Buyers.

Business Planning

Words to learn

address
avoid
demonstrate
develop
evaluate
gather
offer
primarily
risk
strategy
strong
substitution

1. **address** n., a formal speech; v., to direct to the attention of
   a. The article praised her address to the steering committee.
   b. Marco's business plan addresses the needs of small business owners.

2. **avoid** v., to stay clear of; to keep from happening
   a. To avoid going out of business, owners should prepare a proper business plan.
   b. Lloyd's errors in accounting could have been avoided by a business consultation with his banker.

3. **demonstrate** v., to show clearly and deliberately; to present by example
   a. Alban's business plan demonstrated that he had put a lot of thought into making his dream a reality.
   b. The professor demonstrated through a case study that a business plan can impress a lender.

4. **develop** v., to expand, progress, or improve
   a. Lily developed her ideas into a business plan by taking a class at the community college.
   b. The restaurant Wanda opened ten years ago has developed into a national chain.

5. **evaluate** v., to determine the value or impact of
   a. It's important to evaluate your competition when making a business plan.
   b. The lenders evaluated our creditability and decided to loan us money.

6. **gather** v., to accumulate; to conclude
   a. We gathered information for our plan from many sources.
   b. I gather that interest rates for small businesses will soon change.

7. **offer** n., a proposal; v., to propose; to present in order to meet a need or satisfy a requirement
   a. Devon accepted our offer to write the business plan.
   b. Jackie must offer her banker new statistics in order to encourage the bank to lend her money toward her start-up business.

8. **primarily** adv., first; most importantly
   a. We are primarily concerned with convincing the board of directors to apply for the second loan.
   b. The developers are thinking primarily of how to enter the South American market.

9. **risk** n., the chance of loss or damage
   a. The primary risk for most start-up businesses is insufficient capital.
   b. Expanding into a new market is a big risk.

10. **strategy** n., a plan of action
    a. A business plan is a strategy for running a business and avoiding problems.
    b. Let's develop a strategy for promoting our ice cream parlor.

11. **strong** adj., powerful; economically or financially sound
    a. The professor made a strong argument for the value of a good business plan.
    b. Even in a strong economic climate many businesses fail, so do your planning carefully.

12. **substitution** n., replacement
    a. Your substitution of fake names for real ones makes the document seem insincere.
    b. There is no substitution for hard work and perseverance.

Word Families

verb	avoid	It is best to avoid get-rich-quick schemes.
noun	avoidance	Your avoidance of these issues will not make them go away.
adjective	avoided	The avoided question became more important over time.

verb	demonstrate	Let me demonstrate how this computer program works.
noun	demonstration	After the lecture, there was a demonstration of new marketing techniques.
adjective	demonstrative	The densely encoded programming was demonstrative of the computer language of the era.

verb	develop	Our assignment is to develop a cogent business plan.
noun	development	The plan was under development and would not be ready for months.
noun	developer	The job developer was kept busy trying to place the recent college graduates.

verb	evaluate	Please review these articles and evaluate their usefulness for our plan.
noun	evaluation	Yoko feared the professor's evaluation of her business plan.
noun	evaluator	The independent evaluator reviewed our business plan and gave us good feedback.

verb	strategize	Instead of going into a panic, let's strategize the best way to meet the deadline.
noun	strategy	The business plan lays out a strategy for future growth.
adjective	strategic	The handout outlined the strategic points to cover in a business plan.

noun	substitution	The substitution of gasses is not so easy in this experiment.
verb	substitute	Don't try to substitute intuition for good planning.
adjective	substituted	Customers complain whenever the substituted product is of lesser value, even though we don't charge them for it.

Incomplete Sentences

Choose the word that best completes the sentence.

1. You cannot _____ learning how to use the new software as it will be needed in daily operations from now on.
   (A) avoid
   (B) avoided
   (C) avoiding
   (D) avoidance

2. I don't want to intrude, but would you like me to _____ how to use that machine?
   (A) demonstrate
   (B) demonstration
   (C) demonstrative
   (D) demonstrator

3. While you are _____ your business plan, it is a good idea to keep a resource library of valuable materials.
   (A) develop
   (B) development
   (C) developing
   (D) developer

4. After you turn in your business plan, you will receive a written _____ of your work within two weeks.
   (A) evaluator
   (B) evaluative
   (C) evaluate
   (D) evaluation

5. If we think _____, we can come up with a plan that promises success.
   (A) strategize
   (B) strategic
   (C) strategically
   (D) strategist

6. It is now legal to _____ a generic brand drug for a prescription medicine if you have the patient's consent.
   (A) substitute
   (B) substituted
   (C) substituting
   (D) substitution

Error Recognition

Choose the underlined word or phrase that should be rewritten and rewrite it.

7. By <u>addressing</u> potential problems upfront, Carlos was able to <u>demonstration</u> to his banker that he had
        A   B
   <u>gathered</u> enough information to <u>avoid</u> business failure.
     C   D

   _____

8. In a <u>risky</u> attempt to expand business, the company, whose <u>primary</u> focus was selling furniture, embarked on
      A   B
   a <u>strategy</u> that involved <u>offers</u> interior design services.
      C   D

   _____

9. Our business instructor <u>strongly</u> believes there is no <u>substitution</u> for a well-developed business plan, so all of
                           A   B
   his students were required to <u>develop</u> a plan that he would <u>evaluation</u> and give helpful criticism on.
                          C   D

   _____

10. Ms. Martinez developed her business plan by <u>addressing</u> the <u>risky</u> found in the market and <u>demonstrating</u>
                                          A   B   C
    ways to <u>avoid</u> them.
           D

    _____

Reading Comprehension

Read the following passage and write the words in the blanks below.

address	develop	offered	strategy
avoid	evaluation	primary	strength
demonstrate	gathering	risks	substitute

Every business must (11.) _____ a business plan. The business plan's (12.) _____ purpose is to improve the entrepreneur's control over the business and to help him (13.) _____ common mistakes. It is not an over-statement to say that a business will fail or succeed on the (14.) _____ of its business plan, so there is no (15.) _____ for a well-prepared plan. The business plan documents the (16.) _____ for growing the business. Think of the business plan as a road map that describes in which direction the company is going, what its goals are, and how it is going to get there.

In developing the plan, the entrepreneur will conduct research to determine a systematic and realistic (17.) _____ of the company's chances for success in the marketplace. In creating the plan, the entrepreneur must research the company's target market and define its potential. The entrepreneur must be able to prove through research that customers in the market need the good or service that is (18.) _____ and that a sufficient number of potential customers exists to support the business.

A business plan also looks at the (19.) _____ the business faces. Chief among these is competitors. The business plan must analyze the company's competition by (20.) _____ information on competitors' market share, products, and strategies. The plan should (21.) _____ what distinguishes the entrepreneur's products or services from others already in the market. It is also common for businesses to fail because the owner fails to invest or seek sufficient capital to run the business. A good business plan should (22.) _____ this issue as well.

LISTENING COMPREHENSION

Listen to Track 4 of the Compact Disc to hear the statements for Lesson 4

Part I Picture

Look at the picture and listen to the sentences. Choose the sentence that best describes the picture.

23. Ⓐ Ⓑ Ⓒ Ⓓ

Part II Question—Response

Listen to the question and the three responses. Choose the response that best answers the question.

24. Ⓐ Ⓑ Ⓒ   25. Ⓐ Ⓑ Ⓒ

Part III Short Conversations

Listen to the short dialogs. Then read the question and choose the best response.

26. How do the speakers feel about Alexa's business plan?
    (A) She has gathered too much data.
    (B) She has taken on too much risk.
    (C) She made many obvious mistakes.
    (D) She is serious-minded and cautious.

27. What is the main challenge?
    (A) Finding the right trade journals.
    (B) Understanding the competitor's market share.
    (C) Finding a substitute.
    (D) Affording trade association fees.

Part IV Short Talks

Listen to the short talk. Then read the questions and choose the best answer.

28. What is the topic of the talk?
    (A) Long-term growth plans.
    (B) An offer for a leveraged buyout.
    (C) How to minimize risk.
    (D) Where to borrow funds.

29. How will the company fund its growth?
    (A) Bank loans.
    (B) Profits.
    (C) Sale of stocks.
    (D) Owner investment.

Lesson 5

Conferences

1. **accommodate** v., to fit; to provide with something needed
   a. The meeting room was large enough to accommodate the various needs of the groups using it.
   b. Because the deadline for reserving rooms was past, the hotel manager could not accommodate our need for more rooms.

2. **arrangement** n., the plan or organization
   a. The travel arrangements were taken care of by Sara, Mr. Billings's capable assistant.
   b. The arrangement of speakers was alphabetical to avoid any hurt feelings.

3. **association** n., an organization of persons or groups having a common interest; a relationship or society
   a. Membership in a trade or professional association provides business contacts and mutual support.
   b. Local telephone companies formed an association to serve common goals, meet their common needs, and improve efficiency.

4. **attend** v., to go to; to pay attention to
   a. We expect more than 100 members to attend the annual meeting.
   b. The hotel manager attended to all our needs promptly.

5. **get in touch** v., to make contact with
   a. As soon as we arrive at the hotel, we will get in touch with the manager about the unexpected guests.
   b. The registration desk is a good central location for people to get in touch with each other.

6. **hold** v., to accommodate; to conduct
   a. This meeting room holds at least 80 people comfortably.
   b. She holds an annual seminar that is very popular.

7. **location** n., a position or site
   a. The location of the meeting was changed from the Red Room to the Green Room.
   b. Disney World was the perfect location for the annual meeting since many members could bring their families.

8. **overcrowded** adj., too crowded
   a. As soon as the guests entered the dining room for dinner, Sue Lin could see that the room would become overcrowded.
   b. To avoid being overcrowded, we limited the number of guests that members could bring.

9. **register** n., a record; v., to record
   a. According to the register, more than 250 people attended the afternoon seminar.
   b. Hotels ask all guests to register and give a home address.

10. **select** v., to choose from a group; adj., specially chosen
    a. The conference participant selected the marketing seminar from the various offerings.
    b. The winners were a select group.

11. **session** n., a meeting
    a. The morning sessions tend to fill up first, so sign up early.
    b. Due to the popularity of this course, we will offer two sessions.

12. **take part in** v., to join or participate
    a. The format for the session is very informal, which makes it easier for people to take part in the discussion.
    b. We could not get enough people to take part in the meeting, so we canceled it.

Word Families

verb	accommodate	The hotel staff was able to accommodate our many needs for the conference.
noun	accommodation	The accommodations at the hotel include swimming pool, gym, and restaurant.
adjective	accommodating	The conference center manager was extremely accommodating and tried to make our stay pleasant.

noun	arrangement	Nobody could understand the seating arrangement.
verb	arrange	We will arrange the chairs in a circle.
adjective	arranged	The arranged flowers didn't look like those we chose from the catalog.

noun	association	Any association with the former company will put us in a negative light.
verb	associate	Do you think customers will associate the failed upstart with ours?
adjective	associated	The associated costs will put this project out of our reach.

verb	attend	Gillian attended the reception for visiting ambassadors.
noun	attendee	More than 500 attendees packed the ballroom.
noun	attendance	Attendance was low for this year's annual meeting.

verb	select	Since there are overlapping workshops, participants will have to select which one most appeals to them.
noun	selection	His dinner selection of stuffed quail sounded better on the menu than it looked on the plate.
adjective	selective	The planning committee was very selective about who received invitations.

verb	register	He registered for his classes via the Internet.
noun	register	The hotel's register showed that only half the members had arrived.
noun	registration	Registration is a detail-oriented and crucial part of running any meeting.

Incomplete Sentences

Choose the word that best completes the sentence.

1. The banquet room could _____ up to 750 for dinner.
   - (A) accommodated
   - (B) accommodate
   - (C) accommodation
   - (D) accommodating

2. Helen made the final _____ for use of the conference room with the hotel's general manager.
   - (A) arranging
   - (B) arrange
   - (C) arrangement
   - (D) arranged

3. For most people, Samco is _____ with computer chip production.
   - (A) associate
   - (B) associated
   - (C) associating
   - (D) association

4. We expect that fewer guests will _____ the evening gala.
   - (A) attend
   - (B) attending
   - (C) attention
   - (D) attendance

5. The association's members were asked to _____ for the special session well in advance because space in the lecture hall was limited.
   - (A) register
   - (B) registration
   - (C) registering
   - (D) registrar

6. By adding more class _____, the staff was able to please more members.
   - (A) select
   - (B) selective
   - (C) selecting
   - (D) selections

Error Recognition

Choose the underlined word or phrase that should be rewritten and rewrite it.

7. The <u>location</u> could not hold the 50 people who <u>registration</u> for the <u>session,</u> so the room felt terribly <u>overcrowded</u>.
   A · B · C · D
   _____

8. Before <u>select</u> a site and making final <u>arrangements</u> for their annual convention, <u>associations</u> like to tour the
   A · B · C
   conference facility and <u>get in touch</u> with the site manager.
   D
   _____

9. Conference participants like to <u>take part in</u> as many <u>sessions</u> as possible, so <u>hold</u> the meetings sequentially in
   A · B · C
   adjacent <u>locations</u> can be helpful.
   D
   _____

10. When you <u>select</u> a conference site, make sure there are <u>places</u> for spouses accompanying the <u>attendance</u> to
    A · B · C
    <u>arrange</u> to visit.
    D
    _____

Reading Comprehension

Read the following passage and write the words in the blanks below.

accommodate	attending	location	select
arrangements	get in touch	overcrowded	sessions
associations	hold	register	take part in

Many (11.) _____ and organizations hold annual conferences so that their members can (12.)_____ with each other and (13.) _____ educational programs. When planning a conference, event coordinators try to have a variety of (14.) _____ so people (15.) _____ can (16.) _____ a workshop or meeting that best suits their needs. When making (17.) _____ for a conference, they look for a site that will (18.) _____ all their needs. The site should be able to (19.) _____ the number of people expected to attend, without the meeting rooms being (20.) _____. Good event coordinators tour the site before making a final decision because brochures cannot show all the necessary details. Having meetings in a fun (21.) _____ can really encourage people to (22.) _____ for the meeting.

LISTENING COMPREHENSION

Listen to Track 5 of the Compact Disc to hear the statements for Lesson 5

Part I Picture

Look at the picture and listen to the sentences. Choose the sentence that best describes the picture.

23. Ⓐ Ⓑ Ⓒ Ⓓ

Part II Question—Response

Listen to the question and the three responses. Choose the response that best answers the question.

24. Ⓐ Ⓑ Ⓒ   25. Ⓐ Ⓑ Ⓒ

Part III Short Conversations

Listen to the short dialogs. Then read the question and choose the best response.

26. Why are they having difficulty arranging a site?
    (A) It's a busy time of year.
    (B) They procrastinated.
    (C) Because of their group size.
    (D) Because the coordinator has been sick.

27. What will they do during the tour?
    (A) Choose a hotel.
    (B) Take photographs.
    (C) Attend to details.
    (D) Complain to the manager.

Part IV Short Talks

Listen to the short talk. Then read the questions and choose the best answer.

28. What is the topic of the talk?
    (A) Accommodating disabled people.
    (B) Legal responsibility for off-site events.
    (C) Arranging conferences.
    (D) Preparing convention catalogs.

29. Where are the speakers?
    (A) In a hospital.
    (B) Off site.
    (C) At a party.
    (D) At a convention center.

Word Review #1   Lessons 1–5 General Business

Choose the word that best completes the sentence.

1. Although negotiating a new contract was compli-
    cated, both parties came to an _____ that
    satisfied them.
    (A) agree
    (B) agreeable
    (C) agreement
    (D) agreeably

2. _____ conferences are a good way for
    employees to get in touch with people in similar
    organizations.
    (A) Associating
    (B) Associated
    (C) Associations
    (D) Association

3. When the family decided to open a restaurant,
    they had to find a _____ that would attract
    business.
    (A) locate
    (B) locator
    (C) locating
    (D) location

4. A _____ company will honor the terms set
    forth in its warranty.
    (A) repute
    (B) reputedly
    (C) reputation
    (D) reputable

5. The goal of marketing is to _____ customers,
    to persuade them to buy a product or service.
    (A) attract
    (B) attractive
    (C) attraction
    (D) attractiveness

6. Once both parties have agreed to a contract, they
    have also agreed to abide by every _____
    provision.
    (A) specify
    (B) specific
    (C) specification
    (D) specificity

7. Good business planning includes developing an
    overall _____, addressing likely objections, and
    demonstrating why potential buyers need the
    product or service.
    (A) strategy
    (B) strategic
    (C) strategically
    (D) strategize

8. When you register for out-of-town conferences,
    make room _____ as soon as you decide to
    attend.
    (A) accommodate
    (B) accommodations
    (C) accommodating
    (D) accommodated

9. Marketers must avoid making promises they can't
    keep while they _____ the quality of their prod-
    uct or service.
    (A) demonstrate
    (B) demonstration
    (C) demonstrative
    (D) demonstrable

10. A consultant must adhere carefully to his
    contract if he wants to _____ a good business
    reputation.
    (A) establish
    (B) establishment
    (C) established
    (D) establishing

Choose the underlined word or phrase that should be rewritten and rewrite it.

11. Any <u>association</u> should <u>inspiration</u> its members to build a <u>reputation</u> and <u>establish</u> a network of fellow workers.
         A   **B**   **C**   **D**

    _____

12. Never forget to <u>selecting</u> <u>accommodations</u> close to the <u>site</u> so you spend more time <u>taking part in</u> events and
             A   **B**   **C**   **D**
    less time commuting.

    _____

13. Marketers know that they can <u>attract</u> more customers if they <u>compare</u> favorably with the competition and
              A   **B**
    <u>convince</u> customers that their product will <u>satisfaction</u> their needs.
       C   **D**

    _____

14. <u>Agreements</u> and <u>provisions</u> in a contract are <u>developed</u> to <u>resolution</u> issues before they arise.
      A   **B**   **C**   **D**

    _____

15. My favorite part of <u>registering</u> for conferences is <u>selection</u> which <u>sessions</u> I want to <u>attend</u>.
                   A   **B**   **C**   **D**

    _____

16. When planning your business, find a <u>location</u> that <u>attracts</u> customers and <u>implications</u> success in order to
                                  A   **B**   **C**
<u>establish</u> your reputation.
D

    _____

17. Warranty <u>coverage</u> offers customers <u>assure</u> and <u>protection</u> on the <u>products</u> they buy.
               A   **B**   **C**   **D**

    _____

18. The president of the company knew that he needed to <u>attractive</u> and <u>satisfy</u> <u>consumers</u> if he wanted
                                                     A   **B**   **C**
to avoid <u>failure</u>.
         D

    _____

19. Because I am more interested in the <u>sessions</u> for which I have <u>registration</u>, the <u>location</u> of the conference is
                                         A   **B**   **C**
not of <u>primary</u> importance to me.
        D

    _____

20. Some of the best marketers are <u>inspired</u> by their belief in their <u>productive</u> and by their appreciation of the
                                   A   **B**
products <u>strengths</u> and <u>characteristics</u>.
         C   **D**

    _____

Lesson 6

Computers

Words to learn

access
allocate
compatible
delete
display
duplicate
failure
figure out
ignore
search
shut down
warning

1. **access** n., the ability or right to enter or use; v., to obtain; to gain entry
   a. You can't gain access to the files unless you know the password.
   b. We accessed the information on the company's web site.

2. **allocate** v., to designate for a specific purpose
   a. The office manager did not allocate enough money to purchase software.
   b. The software architect did not allocate enough memory for the sound card to work in your computer.

3. **compatible** adj., able to function together
   a. This operating system is not compatible with this model computer.
   b. Users of software applications want new versions to be compatible with current versions.

4. **delete** v., to remove; to erase
   a. The technicians deleted all the data on the disk accidentally.
   b. This button on the keyboard deletes the characters from the screen.

5. **display** n., what is visible on a monitor; v., to show
   a. The light on the LCD display is too weak.
   b. The accounting program displays a current balance when opened.

6. **duplicate** v., to produce something equal; to make identical
   a. I think the new word processing program will duplicate the success of the one introduced last year.
   b. Before you leave, please duplicate that file by making a copy on the CD-ROM.

7. **failure** n., an unsuccessful work or effort
   a. Your failure to inform us about the changed password cost the company a day's work.
   b. The repeated failure of her printer baffled the technician.

8. **figure out** v., to understand; to solve
   a. By examining all of the errors, the technicians figured out how to fix the problem.
   b. We figured out that it would take us at least ten minutes to download the file.

9. **ignore** v., not to notice; to disregard
   a. When the director is working at the computer, she ignores everything around her.
   b. Don't ignore the technician's advice when connecting cables.

10. **search** n., investigation; v., to look for
    a. Our search of the database produced very little information.
    b. The computer searched for all names that began with *W*.

11. **shut down** v., to turn off; to cease operations
    a. Please shut down the computer before you leave.
    b. We always shut down the air conditioning system on the weekend.

12. **warning** n., an alert to danger or problems
    a. The red flashing light gives a warning to users that the battery is low.
    b. Flashing images on a web page are designed to attract users' attention.

Word Families

noun	access	To gain access to the computer lab, all users must have a valid ID.
verb	access	Internet cafés allow you to access your web-based e-mail account.
adjective	accessible	The staff assistant always keeps the door to her office open to show she is accessible.

verb	allocate	Marla didn't allocate enough time to train the new hires on our computer systems.
noun	allocation	A different allocation of resources could certainly strengthen the R&D department.
adjective	allocated	The allocated money was never spent on new monitors.

verb	duplicate	If we work hard, we can duplicate last year's sales records for computers.
noun	duplicate	Don't worry, I have a duplicate on my hard drive.
noun	duplication	His success at our company was based on the duplication of management techniques he had used elsewhere in his career.

noun	failure	The power failure caused the system to shut down.
verb	fail	We failed to tell you that your records were deleted.
adjective	fallible	Everyone can make a mistake. Even a computer is fallible.

verb	ignore	Unfortunately, she ignored the warning about the virus.
noun	ignorance	His ignorance of this word processing program surprised everyone.
adjective	ignored	The ignored computer glitch caused the database to function improperly.

verb	warn	We were warned that our e-mail was not private.
noun	warning	The warning was written on the box.
adjective	warning	The warning signs were all there; we should have paid attention to them.

Incomplete Sentences

Choose the word that best completes the sentence.

1. In order to _____ your e-mail messages, you must type in your password.
    (A) access   (C) accessed
    (B) accessible   (D) accessibility

2. After reviewing the schedule, I realized we had not _____ enough time for the software training.
    (A) allocate   (C) allocating
    (B) allocated   (D) allocation

3. The computer staff is responsible for making sure all system files are _____.
    (A) duplication (C) duplicator
    (B) duplicated   (D) duplicate

4. _____ to examine the capabilities of the computer carefully has cost us a lot of time and money.
    (A) Fail   (C) Failed
    (B) Failure   (D) Fallible

5. She _____ the warning that the hard drive was full, and consequently they were unable to save the test data.
    (A) ignore   (C) ignoring
    (B) ignored   (D) ignorant

6. The computer will _____ you to save your work before quitting.
    (A) warning   (C) warn
    (B) warned   (D) warns

Error Recognition

Choose the underlined word or phrase that should be rewritten and rewrite it.

7. Our <u>competitors</u> learned our password and were able to <u>access</u> our computer records and <u>deletion</u> our <u>data</u>.
       A   B   C   D
    _____

8. The board <u>warned</u> us that they planned to <u>shut our department down</u>, but we <u>figured in</u> a way to <u>convince</u>
              A   B   C   D
    them that we were vital to the organization.
    _____

9. If the software is not <u>compatible</u> with the operating system, the computer may <u>fail</u> to function and <u>shut down</u>
                         A   B   C
    without <u>warn</u>.
           D
    _____

10. Our storeroom is full of <u>software</u> programs that are either <u>duplicates</u>, not <u>compatibility</u>, or those that no one
                                   A   B   C
    can <u>figure out</u> how to use.
        D
    _____

Reading Comprehension

Read the following passage and write the words in the blanks below.

access	deleted	failed	search
allocate	display	figure out	shut down
compatible	duplicate	ignore	warning

When I try to (11.) _____ my computer, a (12.) _____ pops up that says "Low Memory." From there, I can't (13.) _____ what to do. The computer won't let me (14.) _____ any of my files, so I can't (15.) _____ for those that I could delete. I've already (16.) _____ all of my (17.) _____ files, and I can't believe that my remaining files are using up so much memory. I'd be happy to (18.) _____ the computer's warning, but I have no option, since the (19.) _____ is frozen on this message. Do you think I've (20.) _____ to understand something about the operations of this computer? If you can, would you please (21.) _____ a few minutes in your busy schedule to help me solve this dilemma? As I said before, I'm sure that my software is (22.) _____ and is not the source of this problem.

LISTENING COMPREHENSION

Listen to Track 6 of the Compact Disc to hear the statements for Lesson 6

Part I Picture

Look at the picture and listen to the sentences. Choose the sentence that best describes the picture.

23. Ⓐ Ⓑ Ⓒ Ⓓ

Part II Question—Response

Listen to the question and the three responses. Choose the response that best answers the question.

24. Ⓐ Ⓑ Ⓒ   25. Ⓐ Ⓑ Ⓒ

Part III Short Conversations

Listen to the short dialogs. Then read the question and choose the best response.

26. What upsets the woman?
    (A) The war has lasted too long.
    (B) They didn't allocate enough time.
    (C) Her son is getting a bad education.
    (D) Spending on education is less than on the military.

27. What happens when the man tries to access his e-mail?
    (A) The computer shuts down.
    (B) A warning appears on the screen.
    (C) He hears a beeping noise.
    (D) The screen turns blank.

Part IV Short Talks

Listen to the short talk. Then read the questions and choose the best answer.

28. What does the speaker suggest that listeners do?
    (A) Buy his software.
    (B) Read the manual.
    (C) Figure out the program by tinkering with it.
    (D) Consult the competitor's manual to check for compatibility.

29. What problems could users face?
    (A) Their warranties could be invalidated.
    (B) Their warning systems could malfunction.
    (C) Their computers could shut down without warning.
    (D) Their manuals could be inaccurate.

Office Technology

Words to learn

affordable
as needed
be in charge of
capacity
durable
initiative
physically
provider
recur
reduction
stay on top of
stock

1. **affordable** adj., able to be paid for; not too expensive
   a. The company's first priority was to find an affordable phone system.
   b. Obviously, the computer systems that are affordable for a Fortune 500 company will not be affordable for a small company.

2. **as needed** adv., as necessary
   a. The courier service did not come every day, only as needed.
   b. The service contract states that repairs will be made on an as-needed basis.

3. **be in charge of** v., to be in control or command of
   a. He appointed someone to be in charge of maintaining a supply of paper in the fax machine.
   b. Your computer should not be in charge of you, rather you should be in charge of your computer.

4. **capacity** n., the ability to contain or hold; the maximum that something can hold or do
   a. The new conference room is much larger and has a capacity of one hundred people.
   b. The memory requirements of this software application exceed the capacity of our computers.

5. **durable** adj., sturdy, strong, lasting
   a. This printer is so durable that, with a little care, it will last another five years.
   b. These chairs are more durable than the first ones we looked at.

6. **initiative** n., the first step; an active role
   a. Employees are encouraged to take the initiative and share their ideas with management.
   b. Our technology initiative involves an exciting new database system and will help us revolutionize our customer service.

7. **physically** adv., with the senses; of the body
   a. The computer screen is making her physically sick.
   b. Physically moving your screen from one place on the desk to another can help reduce same-position-strain syndrome.

8. **provider** n., a supplier
   a. The department was extremely pleased with the service they received from the phone provider.
   b. As your health service provider, we want to make sure you are happy and satisfied with the service you are receiving.

9. **recur** v., to occur again or repeatedly
   a. The subject of decreasing sales recurs in each meeting, sometimes several times.
   b. The managers did not want that particular error to recur.

10. **reduction** n., a lessening; a decrease
    a. The outlet store gave a 20 percent reduction in the price of the shelves and bookcases.
    b. The reduction in office staff has made it necessary to automate more job functions.

11. **stay on top of** v., to know what is going on; to know the latest information
    a. In order to stay on top of her employees' progress, she arranged weekly breakfast meetings.
    b. In this industry, you must stay on top of current developments.

12. **stock** v., to keep on hand; n., a supply
    a. The employees stocked the shelves on a weekly basis.
    b. The office's stock of toner for the fax machine was quickly running out.

Word Families

adjective	affordable	Broad-band access to the Internet became more affordable at the beginning of the millennium.
verb	afford	Lucinda has taken so much leave this year that she can't afford to miss another day's work.
noun	affordability	We looked into the affordability of placing a scanner at each designer's desk.

verb	initiate	The company will initiate its new products at the beginning of the year.
noun	initiative	The manager, knowing how concerned his employees were, took the initiative to provide training for them on the new equipment.
noun	initiation	As an initiation into the sales field, Mr. Jenkins was given the most problematic customer's account.

adverb	physically	The vagrant had to be physically removed from the building.
adjective	physical	The physical presence of a computer engineer is vastly superior to telephone tech support.
noun	physique	We need a model with a proportional physique.

verb	provide	The company provides a five-year warranty on its products.
noun	provider	As your provider of network services, I promise to give you the best prices and service.
noun	provision	Our provisions of supplies should last to the end of the quarter.

verb	recur	We don't want that problem to recur every month.
noun	recurrence	Every recurrence of the same problem costs us money.
adjective	recurring	Recurring problems waste time and money.

verb	reduce	Buying in bulk can help to reduce costs.
noun	reduction	The introduction of the fax machine created a noticeable increase in phone bills.
adjective	reducible	Although our system is working at capacity, the amount of information being processed is not reducible.

Incomplete Sentences

Choose the word that best completes the sentence.

1. _____ is still a major concern for inner-city schools that want to install computers.
   (A) Afford
   (B) Affording
   (C) Affordable
   (D) Affordability

2. Hoping to repeat the success of the previous year's sales _____, the vice president held a meeting of all the managers.
   (A) initiated
   (B) initiating
   (C) initiative
   (D) initiation

3. The athlete's extraordinary _____ distracted customers from the auto itself.
   (A) physique
   (C) physical
   (C) physicality
   (D) physically

4. As promised in our last meeting, this contract _____ you with the best prices.
   (A) provide
   (B) provides
   (C) provision
   (D) provider

5. When a problem _____ frequently, it is time to reexamine the process.
   (A) recur
   (B) recurrence
   (C) recurring
   (D) recurs

6. The employee preferred to have a _____ in salary than to have to continue working with her outdated computer.
   (A) reducing
   (B) reduction
   (C) reduce
   (D) reduces

Error Recognition

Choose the underlined word or phrase that should be rewritten and rewrite it.

7. The new account manager took the <u>initiative</u> of promising to <u>stay on top of</u> orders by <u>physical</u> inspecting the
                   A   B   C
   warehouse <u>stock</u>.
           D

   _____

8. Ordering <u>as need</u> was discouraged by the <u>provider</u> who was <u>in charge of</u> maintaining a high <u>capacity</u> turnover.
          A   B   C   D

   _____

9. A plan to <u>reduce</u> the <u>physical</u> space allotted to each employee is a <u>recurs</u> idea that is usually <u>initiated</u> by a
            A   B   C   D
   new manager.

   _____

10. The company <u>initiating</u> an <u>affordable</u> new program for the division that <u>reduced</u> wastes and increased <u>capacity</u>.
                     A   B   C   D

    _____

Reading Comprehension

Read the following passage and write the words in the blanks below.

affordable	durable	physical	reduce
as needed	is in charge of	provider	stays on top of
capacity	initiates	recurring	stock

Many companies have one person or a department that (11.) _____ running the office. If you have ever worked for a company that doesn't have an office manager, you very quickly learn to appreciate the importance of the job. Who is in charge of placing orders? Who services the fax machine or printer? Who makes sure that the office is presentable for customers? Are the new conference tables and shelves (12.) _____ as well as (13.) _____?

It is the office manager's responsibility to maintain an efficient and smooth-running office. He or she looks for ways to (14.) _____ costs and minimize interruptions in the day-to-day operations. Whereas functional managers know the (15.) _____ of their employees, the office manager knows the (16.) _____ capacity of the office and the supplies and machines that are in the office.

The office manager (17.) _____ the ordering of furniture and supplies, and (18.) _____ changing office technology. Over time, he or she may notice (19.) _____ problems that require changing a service (20.) _____. Furniture and large items are ordered on an (21.) _____ basis. Other frequently used materials, such as paper, folders, and mailing materials, are on an automatic ordering schedule and a (22.) _____ of those supplies is on hand at the office.

LISTENING COMPREHENSION

Listen to Track 7 of the Compact Disc to hear the statements for Lesson 7

Part I Picture

Look at the picture and listen to the sentences. Choose the sentence that best describes the picture.

23. Ⓐ Ⓑ Ⓒ Ⓓ

Part II Question-Response

Listen to the question and the three responses. Choose the response that best answers the question.

24. Ⓐ Ⓑ Ⓒ   25. Ⓐ Ⓑ Ⓒ

Part III Short Conversations

Listen to the short dialogs. Then read the question and choose the best response.

26. What does the woman want to buy?
    (A) Office furniture.
    (B) Durable electronic equipment.
    (C) Airline tickets.
    (D) Training.

27. What is needed for all new purchases?
    (A) A receipt.
    (B) An order form.
    (C) Up-front payment.
    (D) Approval.

Part IV Short Talks

Listen to the short talk. Then read the questions and choose the best answer.

28. Why don't they order units on an as-needed basis?
    (A) They're more expensive.
    (B) The provider won't take individual orders.
    (C) Delivery time is too long.
    (D) Nobody takes the initiative to place the order.

29. What kind of provider could help them?
    (A) A less pushy provider.
    (B) A more aggressive provider.
    (C) One with better prices.
    (D) One with a web site.

Lesson 8

Office Procedures

Words to learn

appreciation
be made of
bring in
casually
code
expose
glimpse
out of
outdated
practice
reinforce
verbally

1. **appreciation** n., recognition, understanding; thanks
   (a) In appreciation of your hard work on the Castcon project, the department will hold a casual lunch party on November third.
   (b) Your appreciation of my efforts inspired me through the final stages of the construction.

2. **be made of** v., to consist of
   a. This job will really test what you are made of.
   b. People say that the negotiator has nerves made of steel.

3. **bring in** v., to hire or recruit; to cause to appear
   a. The company president wanted to bring on an efficiency consultant.
   b. The company brought in a new team of project planners.

4. **casually** adv., informally
   (a) On Fridays, most employees dress casually.
   (b) Martin spoke casually, as if he were chatting with friends.

5. **code** n., rules of behavior
   a. The new employees observed the unwritten code of conduct in their first week on the job.
   b. Even the most traditional companies are changing their dress code to something less formal.

6. **expose** v., to make aware; to give experience
   a. Mergers require that employees be exposed to different business practices.
   b. The new hires' week in each department exposed them to the various functions in the company.

7. **glimpse** n., a quick look
   a. The secretary caught a glimpse of her new boss as she was leaving the office.
   b. After one year with the company, he still felt as though he had only a glimpse of the overall operations.

8. **out of** adj., no longer having, missing
   a. Orders should be placed before you run out of the supplies.
   b. The presenter ran out of time before he reached his conclusion.

9. **outdated** adj., obsolete; not currently in use
   a. The purpose of the seminar is to have employees identify outdated methods and procedures.
   b. Before you do a mailing, make sure that none of the addresses is outdated.

10. **practice** n., method of doing something; v., to repeat in order to learn
    a. The manager had started her practice of weekly breakfast meetings more than twenty years ago.
    b. Bill practiced answering the telephone until he was satisfied.

11. **reinforce** v., to strengthen, support
    a. The financial officer's unconventional method of analyzing data was reinforced by the business journal article.
    b. Employees reinforced their learning with practice in the workplace.

12. **verbally** adv., in spoken form
    (a) She verbally reprimanded the new hire in front of his entire team.
    (b) The guarantee was made only verbally.

Word Families

noun	appreciation	In appreciation for your hard work, we are giving you a top-priority project.
verb	appreciate	We appreciate the time that you have put into this project, but we need to see more positive results.
adjective	appreciated	The intern felt appreciated, like a member of the team.

noun	code	The programmer spent three days searching for the bug in his code.
adjective	coded	Their web page contained a coded message for insiders.
verb	code	If we code the password into each user's ID number, can users avoid one step for logging on?

verb	expose	As a matter of company policy, we try to expose all managers to the challenging work of telephone sales through hands-on experience.
noun	exposure	Exposure to the elements will corrode the container for the sensor.
adjective	exposed	Mr. Lee was exposed to Chinese business practices during his three-year assignment as a manager in Beijing.

noun	practice	He was surprised at the difference in office practices from one local office to another.
verb	practice	All managers are expected to practice caution in their spending until the end of the year.
adjective	practical	We need a practical solution to this common problem.

verb	reinforce	The practical training reinforced the theoretical studies.
noun	reinforcement	If reinforcement is needed, you have the support of the executive committee.
gerund	reinforcing	Reinforcing the preferred way of selling the product was one of their job requirements.

adverb	verbally	No employees should be verbally reprimanded in front of their peers.
verb	verbalize	Well-established procedures are often difficult to verbalize.
adjective	verbal	The company operated on a practice of verbal and not written contracts.

Incomplete Sentences

Choose the word that best completes the sentence.

1. Ms. Handa was unable to express her _____ for all that her colleagues had done for her.
   (A) appreciation   (C) appreciating
   (B) appreciated   (D) appreciates

2. The programmer is _____ the message so that it's not accessible to everyone.
   (A) code   (C) coded
   (B) coding   (D) coder

3. It looks like this disk was _____ to intense heat, because it's warped and pocked.
   (A) expose   (C) exposing
   (B) exposed   (D) exposure

4. The _____ of answering each telephone call on the third ring requires a dedicated receptionist.
   (A) practices   (C) practiced
   (B) practical   (D) practice

5. Human Resources tries to _____ employees' understanding by offering workshops twice a year.
   (A) reinforce   (C) reinforced
   (B) reinforcing   (D) reinforcement

6. Senior employees are often asked to _____ office procedures.
   (A) verbally   (C) verbal
   (B) verbalize   (D) verbalizing

Error Recognition

Choose the underlined word or phrase that should be rewritten and rewrite it.

7. Although the dress <u>code</u> used to be very <u>formal</u>, it has become much more <u>casually</u> as the executives
   A   B   C
   <u>were exposed to</u> the local business atmosphere.
   D

   _____

8. In an effort to <u>expose</u> and improve some of our <u>outdated</u> operations, we have <u>brought in</u> a consultant to help
   A   B   C
   us improve the <u>practical</u> of the R&D department.
   D

   _____

9. The manager tried to <u>reinforce</u> the idea that it was much easier to be given a <u>verbal</u> warning when they were
   A   B
   running <u>out of</u> stock on an item than a written <u>warn</u>.
   C   D

   _____

10. The manager who was <u>brought in</u> to supervise the project <u>had been exposure to</u> a less <u>casual</u> style of man-
    A   B   C
    agement that we felt was <u>outdated</u>.
    D

   _____

Reading Comprehension

Read the following passage and write the words in the blanks below.

appreciation	casually	made of	practices
been exposed to	code	out of	reinforced
brought in	glimpse	outdated	verbalize

How many employees show any (11.) _____ for their corporate culture? How many executives appreciate what their corporate culture is and what it is (12.) _____? It is often (13.) _____ by the office procedures and routines that have been established over the years. A manager made her mark twenty years ago by dressing (14.) _____, thereby forever changing the dress (15.) _____. A director bought from the competition when he ran (16.) _____ stock and the practice soon became standard. These examples add to a company's culture.

Good employees know what the standard procedures are. This is an important element in recruiting new employees, as well as training workers. When training workers, it is often important to have them read the procedures, write their reactions, and (17.) _____ their opinions to these practices. This promotes a sense of cooperation between those who establish the (18.) _____ and those who must follow them.

Employees who have been with a company for many years may not be able to identify (19.) _____ practices because they haven't (20.) _____ anything else. What happens when a department needs an extra hand? Is a "temp" (21.) _____, or is someone borrowed from another department? The new recruits often ask the questions that allow more senior employees to get a (22.) _____ of the corporate culture.

LISTENING COMPREHENSION

Listen to Track 8 of the Compact Disc to hear the statements for Lesson 8

Part I Picture

Look at the picture and listen to the sentences. Choose the sentence that best describes the picture.

23. Ⓐ Ⓑ Ⓒ Ⓓ

Part II Question—Response

Listen to the question and the three responses. Choose the response that best answers the question.

24. Ⓐ Ⓑ Ⓒ   25. Ⓐ Ⓑ Ⓒ

Part III Short Conversations

Listen to the short dialogs. Then read the question and choose the best response.

26. What will the woman tell the man about?
    (A) Hiring policies.
    (B) Company practices.
    (C) How to make a schedule.
    (D) The employee's communication problems.

27. How do the speakers feel about the attorney?
    (A) She is naïve and simplistic.
    (B) She is experienced.
    (C) She is difficult to work with.
    (D) She never has any energy.

Part IV Short Talks

Listen to the short talk. Then read the questions and choose the best answer.

28. Who is the speaker?
    (A) A software trainer.
    (B) A hardware salesman.
    (C) A new computer owner.
    (D) A scientist from R&D.

29. What will they do today?
    (A) Choose new software.
    (B) Review their computer skills.
    (C) Hire a specialist.
    (D) Take apart the CPU.

Lesson 9

Electronics

Words to learn

disk
facilitate
network
popularity
process
replace
revolution
sharp
skill
software
store
technically

1. **disk** n., an object used to store digital information
   a. The head of the optical disk reader was dirty.
   b. Rewritable compact disks are more expensive than read-only CDs.

2. **facilitate** v., to make easier
   a. The computer program facilitated the scheduling of appointments.
   b. The director tried to facilitate the transition to the new policy by meeting with all staff who would be affected.

3. **network** v., to connect; to broadcast; n., an interconnected group or system over a radio or TV; to engage in informal communication
   a. The recent graduate networked with her mother's coworkers.
   b. We set up a new network in my office to share files.

4. **popularity** n., the state of being widely admired, sought, or accepted
   a. After the new commercials began running, the popularity of the batteries increased significantly.
   b. This brand of computers is extremely popular among college students.

5. **process** v., to put through a series of actions or prescribed procedure; n., a series of operations or actions to bring about a result
   a. I've processed the data I collected and have gotten some interesting results.
   b. There is a process for determining why your computer is malfunctioning.

6. **replace** v., to put back in a former place or position; to take the place of
   a. I've replaced the hard drive that was malfunctioning.
   b. We have been looking for three months and we've found no one who can replace our former administrator.

7. **revolution** n., a sudden or momentous change in a situation; a single complete cycle
   a. We see a revolution in the computer field almost every day.
   b. My CD player is broken; the disk cannot make a complete revolution around the magnet.

8. **sharp** adj., abrupt or acute; smart
   a. There was a sharp decline in calls to the help desk after we upgraded each employee's computer.
   b. The new employee proved how sharp she was when she mastered the new program in a few days.

9. **skill** n., a developed ability
   a. The software developer has excellent technical skills and would be an asset to our software programming team.
   b. Salman's job as designer of electronic tools makes good use of his manual dexterity skills.

10. **software** n., the programs for a computer
    a. This software allows me to integrate tables and spreadsheets into my reports.
    b. Many computers come pre-loaded with software.

11. **store** v., to keep
    a. You can store more data on a zip drive.
    b. We store the master disks in the fireproof safe.

12. **technically** adv., with specialized skill or knowledge
    a. Technically speaking, the virus infected only script files.
    b. The office was finally up-to-speed technically.

Word Families

verb	popularize	The Internet has popularized last-minute travel.
noun	popularity	The popularity of the product was extremely short-lived, and it soon disappeared from the store shelves.
adjective	popular	The new computer program was extremely popular, and people asked for it at all the stores.

verb	replace	I replaced your music CDs that I borrowed from your desk last week.
noun	replacement	A replacement for this damaged computer will not be cheap.
adjective	replaceable	That hard disk is not easily replaceable.

verb	revolutionized	Using diamond has revolutionized the pressure sensor industry during the last decade.
noun	revolution	The revolution in electronics technology has allowed products such as phones to get smaller and more portable.
adjective	revolutionary	The Internet is revolutionary in how it has changed the way we communicate.

noun	skill	Her marketing skills inspired Jason to return to school for his MBA.
adjective	skilled	Our carpenters are skilled in everything from cabinetry to furniture making.
adverb	skillfully	He negotiates so skillfully that both parties end up feeling that they've gotten what they wanted.

verb	store	He stored too much information on the hard drive, making the computer sluggish.
noun	store	The store's inventory has to be entered manually into the database.
noun	storage	The storage closet is where you will find all our office supplies.

adverb	technically	Technically, she was fired from her job.
adjective	technical	The computer can only be repaired by someone with technical knowledge.
noun	technicality	After we go over these minor technicalities, the agreement will be set.

Incomplete Sentences

Choose the word that best completes the sentence.

1. The _____ of the new computer network was apparent among the employees after only a few months.
   (A) popular
   (B) popularize
   (C) popularity
   (D) population

2. We will _____ all of our outdated software with the newest versions.
   (A) replacement
   (B) replaced
   (C) replaceable
   (D) replace

3. There is a _____ approach to software design integration that all the big software developers are currently learning.
   (A) revolutionized
   (B) revolutionary
   (C) revolution
   (D) revolt

4. While Fabio's _____ with computers surpasses the technicians, he is unable to communicate his personal needs to the office manager.
   (A) skill
   (B) skilled
   (C) skillful
   (D) skillfully

5. The hard disk can _____ up to 25 gigabytes of data.
   (A) stores
   (B) storage
   (C) store
   (D) storing

6. The newspaper article on the development of new fiber-optic cables was so full of _____ language that nobody could understand it.
   (A) technical
   (B) technically
   (C) technicality
   (D) technique

Error Recognition

Choose the underlined word or phrase that should be rewritten and rewrite it.

7. The popular new software, which facilitated the process of learning new functions on an as-needed basis, had
      A   B   C
   been sharp reduced in price.
        D

   _____

8. Anyone with a B.S. in computer science should have the technical and organizational skills to manage the
                                     A   B
   network and install any softwares package that we buy.
     C   D

   _____

9. Having computer networks has revolutionary not only how information is stored, but also how it can be
               A   B   C
   processed.
     D

   _____

10. Instead of replacing your disk drive, you might take advantage of another technologically that allows you to
            A   B   C
    store data at a remote site.
     D

    _____

Reading Comprehension

Read the following passage and write the words in the blanks below.

disks	popular	revolutionize	software
facilitated	processing	sharply	storage
networks	replace	skills	technical

By the mid 1980s, virtually all U.S. businesses owned at least one computer. Prices of computers declined (11.) _____ over the next few years, resulting in a surge in popularity. At the same time, offices started to rely on (12.) _____, which (13.) _____ the sharing and processing of data. Such data (14.) _____ was made possible by improvements in both the hardware and software industries.

More recently, data storage (15.) _____ have undergone their own revolution. Because of (16.) _____ advancements, the (17.) _____ capacity of a compact disc increased significantly.

In addition, manufacturers of (18.) _____ offer competitive upgrades to (19.) _____ competitors' products.

Virtually all office workers today are trained in the most (20.) _____ word processing software.

Computers repeatedly (21.) _____ the workplace, and everyone, no matter how accomplished he or she is with other (22.) _____, needs to stay abreast of major trends in computer development.

LISTENING COMPREHENSION

Listen to Track 9 of the Compact Disc to hear the statements for Lesson 9

Part I Picture

Look at the picture and listen to the sentences. Choose the sentence that best describes the picture.

23. Ⓐ Ⓑ Ⓒ Ⓓ

Part II Question–Response

Listen to the question and the three responses. Choose the response that best answers the question.

24. Ⓐ Ⓑ Ⓒ   25. Ⓐ Ⓑ Ⓒ

Part III Short Conversations

Listen to the short dialogs. Then read the question and choose the best response.

26. What do we know about the speakers' relationship?
    (A) The man is senior.
    (B) The woman is a new employee.
    (C) They're doing research together.
    (D) The woman has been at the company longer than the man.

27. Why can't the woman retrieve her file?
    (A) She doesn't know how.
    (B) She forgot its name.
    (C) It was accidentally deleted.
    (D) She can't remember where it's stored.

Part IV Short Talks

Listen to the short talk. Then read the questions and choose the best answer.

28. What is the speaker's opinion of the process of downloading software?
    (A) Anyone can do it.
    (B) It requires technical skills.
    (C) It's easiest if you download from a remote server.
    (D) It's time-consuming.

29. Who is the intended audience for this talk?
    (A) Computer technicians.
    (B) Network managers.
    (C) New computer users.
    (D) Software writers.

Lesson 10

Correspondence

Words to learn

assemble
beforehand
complication
courier
express
fold
layout
mention
petition
proof
register
revise

1. **assemble** v., to put together; to bring together
   a. Her assistant copied and assembled the documents.
   b. The mail room clerk read the directions before assembling the parts to the new postage printer.

2. **beforehand** adv., in advance, in anticipation
   a. To speed up the mailing, we should prepare the labels beforehand.
   b. The goods could have been shipped today had they faxed the order beforehand.

3. **complication** n., difficulty, complex situation
   a. She will have to spend two more days in the hospital due to complications during the surgery.
   b. Complications always arise when we try to cover too many topics in one letter.

4. **courier** n., a messenger, an official delivery person
   a. We hired a courier to deliver the package.
   b. The courier service will clear the goods through customs.

5. **express** adj., fast and direct
   a. It's important that this document be there tomorrow, so please send it express mail.
   b. Express mail costs more than regular mail service, but it is more efficient.

6. **fold** v., to bend paper
   a. Fold the letter into three parts before stuffing it into the envelope.
   b. Don't fold the document if it doesn't fit the envelope.

7. **layout** n., a format; the organization of material on a page
   a. We had to change the layout when we changed the size of the paper.
   b. The layout for the new brochure was submitted by the designer.

8. **mention** n., something said or written; v., to refer to
   a. There was no mention of the cost in the proposal.
   b. You should mention in the letter that we can arrange for mailing the brochures as well as printing them.

9. **petition** n., a formal, written request; v., to make a formal request
   a. The petition was photocopied and distributed to workers who will collect the necessary signatures.
   b. We petitioned the postal officials to start delivering mail twice a day in business areas.

10. **proof** v., to look for errors; n., evidence
    a. This letter was not proofed very carefully; it is full of typing mistakes.
    b. In order to get the rebate, you must send in proof of purchase.

11. **register** v., to record, to track; n., a record
    a. You can register this mail for an additional $2.20.
    b. Everybody needs to sign the register before entering the mail room.

12. **revise** v., to rewrite
    a. The brochure was revised several times before it was sent to the printer.
    b. We will need to revise the form letter since our address has changed.

Word Families

verb	complicate	Don't try to complicate things by making two-sided copies; single-sided will do.
noun	complication	There are a few complications with your layout, but they can be easily solved.
adjective	complicated	The revisions in the document made it more complicated, rather than simpler.

noun	mention	The mention of layoffs made us worry.
verb	mention	As I mentioned in my note to you, you should try to be less wordy and more concise in your writing.
adjective	mentionable	No one considered the mediocre design a mentionable achievement.

noun	petition	In order to be valid, the contents of the petition need to be printed at the top of each page that will contain signatures.
verb	petition	The welders petitioned the factory to install air conditioning.
noun	petitioners	The petitioners spent the night outside of the courthouse.

verb	proof	It is your responsibility to proof your own work before sending it out.
noun	proofreader	The proofreader did not find the errors.
gerund	proofing	Proofing a document is best done by starting at the end and reading backward.

verb	register	Register this letter and bring back the receipt.
noun	registration	Registration for the seminar can be done by fax.
adjective	registered	Always get a receipt for registered mail.

verb	revise	After you revise the document, give it a new name so that we will still have access to both drafts.
adjective	revised	His revised memo was easier to read.
noun	revision	You may have to do three or four full revisions to this document before it is acceptable.

Incomplete Sentences

Choose the word that best completes the sentence.

1. I don't want to _____ matters, but have you considered using color to make your brochure stand out?
   (A) complicate   (C) complicated
   (B) complication   (D) complicating

2. It's worth _____ in the memo that we've finished the draft of the proposal.
   (A) mentionable   (C) mentions
   (B) mentioning   (D) mentioned

3. The signatures on the _____ weren't all legible because rain had caused the ink to run.
   (A) petition   (C) petitioners
   (B) petitioning   (D) petitioned

4. To send out business letters without _____ them is unprofessional.
   (A) proofing   (C) proofreader
   (B) proof   (D) proofread

5. The mail room is rarely asked to send letters by _____ mail.
   (A) registers   (C) register
   (B) registered   (D) registration

6. After each _____, you need to reread what you've written and note your suggestions for changes.
   (A) revise   (C) revision
   (B) revised   (D) will revise

Error Recognition

Choose the underlined word or phrase that should be rewritten and rewrite it.

7. The manager sent the <u>letter</u> by <u>express</u> mail, but he neglected to have it <u>proof</u> <u>beforehand.</u>
   　　　　　　　　A　　　　　　B　　　　　　　　　　　　　　　　　　　　　　　C　　　　D
   _____

8. The letter was <u>revision</u>, then <u>folded</u> with the <u>petition</u>, and sent by <u>express</u> mail.
   　　　　　　　　　A　　　　　　　　B　　　　　　　C　　　　　　　　　　　D
   _____

9. You <u>mentioned</u> that the word processing program was <u>revised</u>, but it is still extremely <u>complication</u> and
   　　　　A　　　　　　　　　　　　　　　　　　　　　　　B　　　　　　　　　　　　　　　　　C
   I couldn't run the program without reading the manual <u>beforehand.</u>
   　　　　　　　　　　　　　　　　　　　　　　　　　　　　　　　D
   _____

10. The <u>layout</u> of the <u>petition</u> must be <u>revised</u>, because it may need to be <u>fold</u> many times if we get a lot of
    　　　　A　　　　　　　B　　　　　　　　　C　　　　　　　　　　　　　　　　D
    signatures.
    _____

Reading Comprehension

Read the following passage and write the words in the blanks below.

assemble	courier	layout	proofed
beforehand	express	mention	register
complication	folding	petition	revision

In small offices, it is often the executive assistant who must manage all of the printed material that the firm produces. The job responsibilities include typing and printing out the correspondence. These letters and memos must all be carefully (11.) _____ to make sure they are error-free. If not, the errors should be corrected. If the meaning is not clear, the correspondence should be revised. This (12.) _____ should be done (13.) _____, not when the letter is ready to be sent.

Before putting correspondence into an envelope, the executive assistant must (14.) _____ all the various attachments and other documents to be enclosed with the letter. When (15.) _____ the correspondence, the assistant should make sure that when opening the envelope, the recipient sees the letterhead first.

Once prepared, the correspondence must be sent appropriately. Local, urgent mail could be hand-delivered by a (16.) _____ service. Long-distance, urgent mail could be sent overnight or by (17.) _____ mail. If a record is required, mail can be (18.) _____ and receipts are given.

In addition to transmitting and receiving faxes, the executive assistant must work closely with company officials. When the company executives have to make a presentation, the executive assistant often becomes a graphic designer charged with the (19.) _____, or the look of, the graphics and text for the printed materials used during the presentations. Did I (20.) _____ that these duties generally involve learning extremely (21.) _____ design software? It's a wonder that more executive assistants don't (22.) _____ their bosses for a raise.

LISTENING COMPREHENSION

Listen to Track 10 of the Compact Disc to hear the statements for Lesson 10

Part I Picture

Look at the picture and listen to the sentences.
Choose the sentence that best describes the picture.

23. Ⓐ Ⓑ Ⓒ Ⓓ

Part II Question—Response

Listen to the question and the three responses. Choose the response that best answers the question.

24. Ⓐ Ⓑ Ⓒ   25. Ⓐ Ⓑ Ⓒ

Part III Short Conversations

Listen to the short dialogs. Then read the question and choose the best response.

26. Why won't the woman assemble the documents now?
    (A) She's in a meeting.
    (B) She hurt her hand.
    (C) She's too busy.
    (D) She needs to revise them first.

27. What should they do to the pamphlet?
    (A) Assemble it.
    (B) Revise it.
    (C) Send it by registered mail.
    (D) Mention it to a friend.

Part IV Short Talks

Listen to the short talk. Then read the questions and choose the best answer.

28. Where would you hear this talk?
    (A) A post office.
    (B) A grocery store.
    (C) A restaurant.
    (D) An assembly line.

29. What is the purpose of this talk?
    (A) To sell merchandise.
    (B) To inform customers of a new service.
    (C) To warn workers.
    (D) To recognize a new employee.

Word Review #2   Lessons 6–10 Office Issues

Choose the word that best completes the sentence

1. Who is _____ hiring?
    (A) in charge by
    (B) in charge on
    (C) in charge of
    (D) in charge for

2. Most office furniture is bought more on the basis of _____ than comfort.
    (A) afford
    (B) affording
    (C) afforded
    (D) affordability

3. The office _____ samples of its products.
    (A) display
    (B) displayed
    (C) displaying
    (D) displayable

4. The staff expressed their _____ for the leadership of their boss.
    (A) appreciate
    (B) appreciated
    (C) appreciating
    (D) appreciation

5. Ms. Ming was pleased that the new employee showed such _____ .
    (A) initiate
    (B) initiative
    (C) initiated
    (D) initiating

6. Before you send the letter, you should _____ it to make sure there are no errors.
    (A) proof
    (B) fold
    (C) petition
    (D) assemble

7. The secretary sent a copy of the revised contract by _____ mail.
    (A) register
    (B) registered
    (C) registering
    (D) registration

8. Many office supply businesses specialize in furniture that is as _____ as it is affordable.
    (A) duration
    (B) durable
    (C) durability
    (D) durableness

9. The office manager finally _____ why the new software wasn't working properly.
    (A) figured in
    (B) figured for
    (C) figured out
    (D) figured about

10. The letter from our accountant _____ that our petty cash spending was almost equal to budgeted items.
    (A) mention
    (B) mentioned
    (C) mentioning
    (D) mentionable

Choose the underlined word or phrase that should be rewritten and rewrite it.

11. The <u>technology</u> expert in charge of the office computers must <u>stay on top of</u> recent <u>software</u> applications and
        A   **B**   **C**
    order them as <u>needy</u>.
                  D

    _____

12. Although <u>affordable</u> is important, computer buyers need to be sure that the machines are <u>durable</u> and have
              A   **B**
    sufficient RAM <u>capacity</u> for file <u>storage</u>.
                      C   **D**

    _____

13. Writing letters on a computer makes <u>layout</u> and revision simple, allows the writer to <u>store</u> addresses
                                       A   **B**
    <u>beforehand</u>, and lets the writer <u>displayable</u> previous correspondence to the same client.
         C   **D**

    _____

14. The company has just <u>brought on</u> a junior executive who seems to <u>appreciate</u> being exposed to <u>complicated</u>
                                 A   B   C
     business <u>practical</u>.
              D

———————————————

15. The <u>courier</u> insisted that I sign the document as <u>prove</u> that he had delivered the <u>software</u> from our <u>provider</u>.
        A   B   C   D

———————————————

16. The office manager doesn't want anyone to <u>mention</u> things like a product that is <u>out of</u> stock, programs that
                                          A   B
     are <u>outdated</u>, or computers that have <u>shut up</u>.
            C   D

———————————————

17. The office has a <u>recur</u> problem with an <u>outdated</u> <u>network</u> system that does not have the <u>capacity</u> to accommo-
                   A   B   C   D
     date all of our new employees.

———————————————

18. For most business presentations, computers have <u>complicated</u> tables that can be <u>assembling</u> <u>beforehand</u> and
                                                      A   B   C
     inserted in the <u>layout</u> where needed.
                     D

———————————————

19. The new <u>software</u> was the beginning of a <u>revolutionary</u> that would modernize <u>outdated</u> processes and
               A   B   C
     <u>practices</u>.
      D

———————————————

20. Our new copier will <u>duplicate</u>, <u>assemble</u>, <u>reduction</u>, and <u>fold</u> documents for mailing.
                        A   B   C   D

———————————————

Job Advertising and Recruiting

Words to learn

abundant
accomplishment
bring together
candidate
come up with
commensurate
match
profile
qualifications
recruit
submit
time-consuming

1. **abundant** adj., plentiful, in large quantities
   a. The computer analyst was glad to have chosen a field in which jobs were abundant.
   b. The recruiter was surprised by the abundant number of qualified applicants.
2. **accomplishment** n., an achievement, a success
   a. The success of the company was based on its early accomplishments.
   b. In honor of her accomplishments, the manager was promoted.
3. **bring together** v., to join, to gather
   a. Every year, the firm brings together its top lawyers and its newest recruits for a training session.
   b. Our goal this year is to bring together the most creative group we can find.
4. **candidate** n., one being considered for a position, office, or award
   a. The recruiter will interview all candidates for the position.
   b. The president of our company is a candidate for the Outstanding Business Award.
5. **come up with** v., to plan, to invent, to think of
   a. In order for that small business to succeed, it needs to come up with a new strategy.
   b. How was the new employee able to come up with that cost-cutting idea after only one week on the job?
6. **commensurate** adj., in proportion to, corresponding, equal to
   a. Generally the first year's salary is commensurate with experience and education level.
   b. As mentioned in your packets, the number of new recruits will be commensurate with the number of vacancies at the company.
7. **match** n., a fit, a similarity; v., to put together, to fit
   a. It is difficult to make a decision when both candidates seem to be a perfect match.
   b. A headhunter matches qualified candidates to suitable positions.
8. **profile** n., a group of characteristics or traits
   a. The recruiter told him that, unfortunately, he did not fit the job profile.
   b. As jobs change, so does the company's profile for the job candidate.
9. **qualifications** n., requirements, qualities, or abilities needed for something
   a. The job seeker had done extensive volunteer work and was able to add this experience to his list of qualifications.
   b. The applicant had so many qualifications that the company created a new position for her.
10. **recruit** v., to attract people to join an organization or a cause; n., a person who is recruited
    a. When the consulting firm recruited her, they offered to pay her relocation expenses.
    b. The new recruits spent the entire day in training.
11. **submit** v., to present for consideration
    a. Submit your résumé to the human resources department.
    b. The applicant submitted all her paperwork in a professional and timely manner.
12. **time-consuming** adj., taking up a lot of time, lengthy
    a. Even though it was time-consuming, all of the participants felt that the open house was very worthwhile.
    b. Five interviews later, Ms. Lopez had the job, but it was the most time-consuming process she had ever gone through.

Word Families

verb	accomplish	You can accomplish anything if you put your mind to it.
noun	accomplishment	The company is proud of our team's accomplishments.
adjective	accomplished	The accomplished artist had his paintings in all the major galleries.

noun	match	The former marketing director is a good match for this position in public relations.
verb	match	We need to match both job experience and personality for this position.
adjective	matching	The matching cushions look better on the chair.

noun	profile	His customer profile shows that he always pays on time.
verb	profile	Through telephone surveys, we try to profile our clientele in order to understand who is using our services.
adjective	profiled	The profiled candidate only met half of the job requirements.

verb	qualify	In order to qualify, you must have two years of work experience.
noun	qualifications	The manager made a list of qualifications for the vacant job position.
adjective	qualified	He found himself overqualified for the entry-level position.

verb	recruit	Large accounting firms recruit on college campuses every spring.
noun	recruitment	The company's recruitment resulted in ten highly qualified new employees.
noun	recruiter	As a recruiter, he traveled around the country speaking to recent college graduates.

verb	submit	Anyone who is interested in the position should submit a résumé and writing samples.
noun	submission	I'm very sorry, the submission date was last week. We can't take any more applications.
noun	submittal	The submittal of his resignation prompted his colleagues to apply for his job.

Incomplete Sentences

Choose the word that best completes the sentence.

1. Your résumé shows you have _____ a great deal in your last position.
   (A) accomplish
   (B) accomplishment
   (C) accomplished
   (D) accomplishing

2. This program is used to scan résumés and search for key words that _____.
   (A) match
   (B) matched
   (C) matching
   (D) will match

3. It is illegal to _____ candidates based on gender or ethnicity.
   (A) profile
   (B) profiling
   (C) profiled
   (D) will profile

4. The applicants who _____ will be flown to the corporate office and interviewed there.
   (A) qualification
   (B) qualify
   (C) qualifying
   (D) qualifies

5. The company hired a professional _____ to fill the vacant positions.
   (A) recruited
   (B) recruiting
   (C) recruitment
   (D) recruiter

6. After _____ all his materials, he had no option but to sit back and wait for some response.
   (A) submitting
   (B) submitted
   (C) submission
   (D) submit

Error Recognition

Choose the underlined word or phrase that should be rewritten and rewrite it.

7. When jobs are <u>abundant,</u> <u>recruit</u> are more flexible and often try to <u>match</u> job seekers with minimal
        A   B   C

   <u>qualifications</u> with any job.
      D

   _____

8. Employers <u>recruit</u> <u>candidacies</u> whose academic <u>accomplishments</u> are <u>commensurate</u> with the nature and
         A   B   C   D

   demands of a job.

   _____

9. The human resources manager <u>came up with</u> such a specific <u>profile</u> for the entry-level job that it was
                                   A   B

   impossible to find <u>qualify</u> <u>candidates</u>.
             C   D

   _____

10. If we could <u>bring together</u> the skills of these two <u>candidates</u>, we would have a perfect <u>matching</u> and this
              A   B   C

    <u>time-consuming</u> process would come to an end.
       D

    _____

Reading Comprehension

Read the following passage and write the words in the blanks below.

abundant	candidates	match	recruit
accomplishments	coming up with	profile	submit
bring together	commensurate	qualifications	time-consuming

Recruiting employees is a (11.) _____ and costly process. Therefore, employers want to (12.) _____ the right person with the right job the first time around. There are many ways to (13.) _____ good employees: advertising in newspapers and professional journals, recruiting on college campuses or at conferences, or getting referrals from headhunters.

Recruiting is a time for a company to brag about its (14.) _____ and excite people about its future. Each company is trying to (15.) _____ the best and the brightest, but they are not alone. Their competition is trying to do the same thing. When jobs are (16.) _____ and there is low unemployment, employers may face higher demands from job seekers. Conversely, when the economy is slowing down and jobs are few, employers are in a better position for attracting the best (17.) _____.

Employers look for certain characteristics and (18.) _____ in their employees. (19.) _____ a very specific (20.) _____ that fits the company culture and the specific job requirements is a difficult job. Employers want to see a well-rounded candidate and someone who has related work experience. They are willing to offer a salary that is (21.) _____ with that experience. Employers will make hiring and salary determinations based on the information candidates (22.) _____ throughout the application and interview process.

LISTENING COMPREHENSION

Listen to Track 11 of the Compact Disc to hear the statements for Lesson 11

Part I Picture

Look at the picture and listen to the sentences.
Choose the sentence that best describes the picture.

23. (A) (B) (C) (D)

Part II Question—Response

Listen to the question and the three responses. Choose the response that best answers the question.

24. (A) (B) (C)   25. (A) (B) (C)

Part III Short Conversations

Listen to the short dialogs. Then read the question and choose the best response.

26. What has the woman been doing lately?
    (A) Fixing her drain.
    (B) Earning money.
    (C) Looking for matches.
    (D) Searching for a job.

27. What worries the man?
    (A) There are too many applicants.
    (B) He's not a good match for the company.
    (C) The company looks like a bad place to work.

Part IV Short Talks

Listen to the short talk. Then read the questions and choose the best answer.

28. What should the résumé include?
    (A) Your major in college.
    (B) Your grade point average.
    (C) A current reference.
    (D) A list of concrete achievements.

29. What is the employer looking for?
    (A) Employees with long-term career plans.
    (B) People to fill positions immediately.
    (C) Aggressive marketers.
    (D) People willing to accept minimum wage.

Lesson 12

Applying and Interviewing

1. **ability** n., a skill, a competence
   a. The designer's ability was obvious from her portfolio.
   b. The ability to work with others is a key requirement.

2. **apply** v., to look for; to submit an application
   a. The college graduate applied for three jobs and received three offers.
   b. Everyone who is interested should apply in person at any branch office.

3. **background** n., a person's experience, education, and family history
   a. Your background in the publishing industry is a definite asset for this job.
   b. The employer did a complete background check before offering him the job.

4. **be ready for** v., to be prepared
   a. Thanks to her careful research, the applicant felt that she was ready for the interview with the director of the program.
   b. The employer wasn't ready for the applicant's questions.

5. **call in** v., to ask to come; to beckon
   a. The young woman was so excited when she was called in for an interview that she told everyone she knew.
   b. The human resources manager called in all the qualified applicants for a second interview.

6. **confidence** n., a belief in one's abilities, self-esteem
   a. Good applicants show confidence during an interview.
   b. He had too much confidence and thought that the job was his.

7. **constantly** adj., on a continual basis, happening all the time
   a. The company is constantly looking for highly trained employees.
   b. Martin constantly checked his messages to see if anyone had called for an interview.

8. **expert** n., a specialist
   a. Our department head is an expert in financing.
   b. The candidate demonstrated that he was an expert in marketing.

9. **follow up** v., to take additional steps, to continue; n., the continuation of a previous action
   a. Always follow up an interview with a thank-you note.
   b. As a follow up, the candidate sent the company a list of references.

10. **hesitant** adj., reluctant; with reservation
    a. Marla was hesitant about negotiating a higher salary.
    b. The recent college graduate was hesitant about accepting his first offer.

11. **present** v., to introduce; to show; to offer for consideration
    a. The human resources director presents each candidate's résumé to the department supervisor for review.
    b. The candidate presented her qualifications so well that the employer offered her a job on the spot.

12. **weakly** adv., without strength; poorly
    a. Her hands trembled and she spoke weakly at the interview.
    b. She wrote so weakly we couldn't read it.

Word Families

verb	apply	Your chances are better if you apply for a job in the spring.
noun	applicant	The manager selected him from all the applicants.
noun	application	The department can't process your application until all documents have been received.

noun	confidence	It's refreshing to see a manager with so much confidence in her employees.
adjective	confident	Don't be too confident until you actually have an offer.
adverb	confidently	The applicant confidently walked into the interview, sat down, and began to talk about himself.

noun	expert	Don't portray yourself as an expert if you aren't.
noun	expertise	The worker gained expertise over the years and was promoted to a higher position.
adjective	expert	As an expert negotiator, she should have no problems getting what the company wants.

adjective	hesitant	The applicant was hesitant to explain his reason for leaving his last job.
noun	hesitation	Her hesitation about accepting the job made the department wonder if she was really interested.
verb	hesitate	Don't hesitate to call if you have any questions concerning the job.

verb	present	I'd like to present my résumé for your consideration.
noun	presentation	The applicant's presentation made a favorable impression.
adjective	presentable	The applicant was well dressed and presentable.

adverb	weakly	The applicant shook hands weakly, making me question her strength of character.
adjective	weak	She gave a weak description of her computer skills.
noun	weakness	Interviewers often ask candidates about their strengths and weaknesses.

Incomplete Sentences

Choose the word that best completes the sentence.

1. So many well-qualified people _____ for the position that we won't be able to make a decision for several weeks.
   (A) apply   (C) applicant
   (B) application   (D) applied

2. As the interview continued, the applicant's _____ began to decline.
   (A) confidently   (C) confidence
   (B) confident   (D) confidential

3. The applicant's unique _____ enabled her to have almost any job that she wanted.
   (A) expertise   (C) expertly
   (B) experts   (D) expert

4. She spoke without _____, expressing self-confidence and projecting that she had a firm handle on the information.
   (A) hesitant   (C) hesitatingly
   (B) hesitate   (D) hesitation

5. During an interview, it is important to _____ your weaknesses in a way that shows you are working to improve them.
   (A) presentation   (C) presentable
   (B) present   (D) presenting

6. Her handshake had always felt like a dead fish and it was taken as a sign of a _____ character.
   (A) weak   (C) weakness
   (B) weakly   (D) weakening

Error Recognition

Choose the underlined word or phrase that should be rewritten and rewrite it.

7. The <u>application's</u> <u>hesitation</u> at answering questions about her <u>ability</u> led the employer to believe that she
      A   B   C
   wasn't <u>ready</u> for the position.
        D

   _____

8. Even though the applicant is an <u>expert</u> in the field, he didn't seem to <u>be ready by</u> the interview and wasn't
                                    A   B
   very skilled at <u>presenting</u> his achievements or <u>background</u>.
            C   D

   _____

9. Because the job hunter had evaluated his <u>abilities</u>, he was <u>confidence</u> that he would be <u>called in</u> to <u>present</u>
                                   A   B   C   D
   his credentials.

   _____

10. My <u>expert</u> advice is, after you have submitted your <u>application</u>, <u>follow up</u> <u>constant</u> to see if there are
       A   B   C   D
    any openings.

    _____

Reading Comprehension

Read the following passage and write the words in the blanks below.

abilities	backgrounds	constantly	hesitant
apply	called in	experts	present
are ready for	confidence	follow up	weaknesses

How many times in your life will you search for a new job? The (11.) _____ say probably more times than you think! Some people find the job search time-consuming and hard on their self- (12.) _____. The best job hunters are those who never stop looking and don't dwell on their (13.) _____. They network (14.) _____: at meetings, at social gatherings, and with people they meet on the street. They (15.) _____ periodically with contacts and acquaintances to keep up with new developments.

Good job hunters assess their (16.) _____ all the time. Before they even (17) _____ for a position, they have researched the field and the specific companies they are interested in. They know where they could fit into the company and they tailor their résumés for each position. They try to show how their (18.) _____ match the job opening. Therefore, when they are (19.) _____ for an interview, they're prepared. They (20.) _____ anything!

At the interview, these job hunters know that they must (21.) _____ themselves in the best way possible. This is their opportunity to shine. It is also their opportunity to see if this is truly the job that they want. If either party is (22.) _____ at the interview, it may be a sign that it isn't a good fit.

LISTENING COMPREHENSION

Listen to Track 12 of the Compact Disc to hear the statements for Lesson 12

Part I Picture

Look at the picture and listen to the sentences. Choose the sentence that best describes the picture.

23. Ⓐ Ⓑ Ⓒ Ⓓ

Part II   Question—Response

Listen to the question and the three responses. Choose the response that best answers the question.

24. Ⓐ Ⓑ Ⓒ   25. Ⓐ Ⓑ Ⓒ

Part III Short Conversations

Listen to the short dialogs. Then read the question and choose the best answer.

26. What do people think about the woman?
     (A) She has no confidence.
     (B) She is an expert.
     (C) She is a beginner at networking.
     (D) Her computer skills are weak.

27. What decision are the speakers facing?
     (A) How to present themselves.
     (B) Whether to apply for a job.
     (C) When to explain their abilities.
     (D) Which applicant to hire.

Part IV Short Talks

Listen to the short talk. Then read the questions and choose the best answer.

28. Who would call in to this hotline?
     (A) An expert in Salvo's product line.
     (B) An employer.
     (C) A human resources presenter.
     (D) A job seeker.

29. What is the purpose of this recording?
     (A) To inform callers about Salvo.
     (B) To explain to callers what they can do.
     (C) To present the company's philosophy.
     (D) To give background information about a
          product problem.

Hiring and Training

1. **conduct** n., one's behavior; v., to hold, to take place, to behave
   a. The trainees' conduct during training was unacceptable.
   b. Interviews were conducted over a period of three weeks.
2. **generate** v., to create, to produce
   a. The new training program generated a lot of interest among employees.
   b. The job fair at the college campus should generate interest in our company.
3. **hire** n., an employee; v., to employ, to offer a job or position
   a. The new hire has integrated well with his colleagues.
   b. She was hired after her third interview.
4. **keep up with** v., to stay equal with
   a. The workers were told that they must keep up with the changes or they would find themselves without jobs.
   b. Employees are encouraged to take courses in order to keep up with new developments.
5. **look up to** v., to admire, to think highly of
   a. Staff members looked up to the director because he had earned their respect over the years.
   b. There are few people in this world that I look up to as much as I look up to you.
6. **mentor** n., a person who guides and instructs, a resource
   a. The mentor helped her make some decisions about combining career and family.
   b. One problem with many programs is that the mentors don't feel invested in the progress of the employees with whom they are working.
7. **on track** adj., on schedule; focused
   a. If we stay on track, the meeting should be finished at 9:30.
   b. You have a lot of work; if you can't stay on track, let me know immediately.
8. **reject** n., something that has been turned down; v., to turn down; to say no, to not accept
   a. We put the rejects in this box.
   b. Even though Mr. Lukin rejected their offer, they remained in contact.
9. **set up** adj., established, arranged; v., to establish, to arrange
   a. Check with your supervisor to make sure that your office is all set up before you begin work.
   b. Set up a time and place for the meeting and then inform everyone who is involved.
10. **success** n., an accomplishment; reaching a goal
    a. The director's success came after years of hiring the right people at the right time.
    b. When the manager won an award, he attributed his success to his colleagues.
11. **training** n., the preparation or education for a specific job
    a. The new hire received such good training that, within a week, she was as productive as the other workers.
    b. The training is designed to prepare all workers, new and old, for the changes that the company will face.
12. **update** v., to make current; n., the latest information
    a. The personnel officer updated the employees on the latest personnel changes.
    b. Our latest update shows that business is down 15 percent.

Word Families

noun	conduct	Your conduct during the meeting reflected poorly on the company.
verb	conduct	If you conduct yourself with professionalism, you will always impress your coworkers.
noun	conductor	The conductor gathered tickets before the first stop.

verb	generate	The purpose of the demonstration is to generate interest in the new product.
noun	generator	The generator goes on automatically when the electricity goes off.
adjective	generated	The sales that were generated by the giveaway surprised even the sales department.

verb	hire	The personnel director needed to hire 15 people within a week.
noun	hire	The new hire quickly gained a reputation for excellent work.
gerund	hiring	The hiring took the company much longer than expected.

verb	reject	The candidate rejected the offer the first time, but the second time she accepted it.
noun	rejection	Rejections are difficult, but you can learn something from them.
gerund	rejecting	Rejecting a job offer before you have it is not a smart thing to do.

verb	succeed	In order to succeed in this business, you must be persistent.
noun	success	Don't let success go to your head!
adjective	successful	The trainers were very successful with this last group of new hires.

verb	train	Even though you were trained on a Macintosh, you'll have to learn how to use a PC.
noun	trainer	The trainer stayed after the meeting to answer any questions.
noun	trainee	Each new employee spends six weeks as a trainee.

Incomplete Sentences

Choose the word that best completes the sentence.

1. The presentation was _____ seamlessly, giving an impressive image of the team.
    (A) conduct   (C) conducting
    (B) conducted   (D) conductor

2. You need to consider how many new sales you _____ in comparison to how many standing clients put in orders.
    (A) generator   (C) generating
    (B) generated   (D) generation

3. After he was _____, he continued to take classes to upgrade his skills.
    (A) hiring   (C) hired
    (B) hires   (D) hire

4. Unfortunately, not all candidates can be offered a job; some have to be _____.
    (A) rejected   (C) rejection
    (B) rejecting   (D) reject

5. The _____ of the program depends on the active participation of everyone.
    (A) successfully (C) successful
    (B) succeed   (D) success

6. In all my years of _____, I have never seen such a motivated group of new hires.
    (A) trainee   (C) trains
    (B) training   (D) trainer

Error Recognition

Choose the underlined word or phrase that should be rewritten and rewrite it.

7. The <u>training</u> session will be <u>conduct</u> by someone the participants can <u>look up to</u> and who will <u>generate</u>
       A   B   C   D
    interest.

    _____

8. The new <u>hired</u> felt <u>rejected</u> when his <u>mentor</u> didn't respond to his request for <u>training</u>.
            A   B   C   D

    _____

9. In order to stay <u>on track</u> and to <u>keep up with</u> the latest changes, he asked his newly <u>hired</u> secretary to send
               A   B   C
    him <u>updating</u> on the hour.
       D

    _____

10. They <u>set up</u> the program so that the employees could <u>conduct</u> research and <u>generate</u> materials and feel very
       A   B   C
    <u>succeeded</u> when they were finished.
      D

    _____

Reading Comprehension

Read the following passage and write the words in the blanks below.

conducted	keep up with	on track	successfully
generate	look up to	rejected	training
hires	mentor	set up	update

After the ads have been placed, and the interviews have been (11.) _____, decisions have to be made. Who should the company bring onboard? Job offers are extended and they are either accepted or (12.) _____. For those who accept the offer, the job search has been completed (13.) _____. But for both the employer and the new hire, the job has just begun.

Companies want new employees to (14.) _____ new business and new ideas as soon as possible. Before they can do that, the new (15.) _____ need some (16.) _____. All companies have unique expectations and methods of operating. Company trainers conduct workshops and seminars for both experienced and new workers. All employees must prepare for the future and continuously (17.) _____ themselves in their field. Nowadays, workers are expected to (18.) _____ the latest trends and information. Otherwise, they fall behind.

Many companies (19.) _____ a mentoring program for new employees. The (20.) _____ is usually an experienced manager or employee and should be someone whom the new employee can (21.) _____. Mentors often review goals and objectives with their mentorees and help them to stay (22.) _____.

LISTENING COMPREHENSION

Listen to Track 13 of the Compact Disc to hear the statements for Lesson 13

Part I Picture

Look at the picture and listen to the sentences. Choose the sentence that best describes the picture.

23. Ⓐ Ⓑ Ⓒ Ⓓ

Part II Question—Response

Listen to the question and the three responses. Choose the response that best answers the question.

24. Ⓐ Ⓑ Ⓒ   25. Ⓐ Ⓑ Ⓒ

Part III Short Conversations

Listen to the short dialogs. Then read the question and choose the best response.

26. What is the response to the training program?
    (A) Boredom.
    (B) Confusion.
    (C) Chaos.
    (D) Enthusiasm.

27. How would the new hires be described?
    (A) Sluggish.
    (B) Demanding.
    (C) Difficult to reach.
    (D) Energetic.

Part IV Short Talks

Listen to the short talk. Then read the questions and choose the best answer.

28. Who is listening to this talk?
    (A) New workers.
    (B) Annual trainers.
    (C) Patients.
    (D) New mentors.

29. What will they do first?
    (A) Select participants for the program.
    (B) Think of traits of good teachers.
    (C) Generate a list of rules.
    (D) Hear an update on sales figures.

Lesson 14

Salaries and Benefits

Words to learn

basis
be aware of
benefit
compensate
delicately
eligible
flexibly
negotiate
raise
retire
vested
wage

1. **basis** n., the main reason for something; a base or foundation
   a. The manager didn't have any basis for firing the employee.
   b. On the basis of my ten years of loyalty to this company, I feel that I deserve three weeks vacation.

2. **be aware of** v., to be conscious of; to be knowledgeable about
   a. The new staff member wasn't aware of the company's position on working a second job.
   b. Are you aware of the new employee's past work history?

3. **benefit** n., an advantage provided to an employee in addition to salary; v., to take advantage of
   a. Although the analyst earned a better salary at his new job, his benefits were better at his previous job.
   b. We all benefit from the company's policy of semiannual reviews.

4. **compensate** v., to pay; to make up for
   a. The company compensates employees for overtime by paying double for extra hours.
   b. The company will compensate employees for any travel expenses.

5. **delicately** adv., with sensitivity
   a. Senior management is handling these contract negotiations delicately.
   b. The manager delicately asked about the health of his client.

6. **eligible** adj., able to participate in something; qualified
   a. Some employees may be eligible for the tuition reimbursement plan.
   b. I don't understand why I'm not eligible if I have been with the company for over a year.

7. **flexibly** adv., with the ability to change; loosely
   a. My manager thinks flexibly, enabling herself to solve many sticky problems.
   b. We need to respond flexibly if we want to keep customers in this competitive market.

8. **negotiate** v., to talk for the purpose of reaching an agreement, especially on prices or contracts
   a. You must know what you want and what you can accept when you negotiate a salary.
   b. The associate looked forward to the day that she would be able to negotiate her own contracts.

9. **raise** n., an increase in salary; v., to move up
   a. With his raise, Mr. Drvoshanov was able to afford to buy a new car.
   b. We need to raise the standard for timeliness.

10. **retire** v., to stop working; to withdraw from a business or profession
    a. She retired at the age of 64 but continued to be very active with volunteer work.
    b. Many people would like to win the lottery and retire.

11. **vested** adj., guaranteed as a right, involved
    a. The day that Ms. Weng became fully vested in the retirement plan, she gave her two weeks' notice.
    b. The company has a vested interest in the happiness of its employees.

12. **wage** n., the money paid for work done, usually hourly
    a. Hourly wages have increased by 20 percent over the last two years.
    b. The intern spends more than half of her wages on rent.

Word Families

noun	basis	Your raise will be determined on the basis of performance alone.
verb	base	We base promotions on seniority.
adjective	based	Based on the assumption that you will earn more in your new position, you can afford the car you've been wanting.

verb	benefit	In order to benefit from the plan, you must fill out the paperwork and submit it to the personnel office.
noun	benefits	The new employee's benefits went into effect three months after his start date.
adjective	beneficial	The service that the insurance has provided has been very beneficial.

verb	compensate	The company compensates its full-time employees well.
noun	compensation	Compensation will be based on your work performance over the past six months.
adjective	compensatory	Compensatory time is given in lieu of overtime pay.

adverb	flexibly	She approaches problems flexibly, looking at the situation from every different angle.
adjective	flexible	Younger workers tend to be more flexible with their work schedules.
noun	flexibility	His flexibility on benefits was one of the main reasons we were able to hire him at this time.

verb	negotiate	The employee prepared a list of her accomplishments to share with her supervisor so that she could negotiate a higher salary.
noun	negotiation	The director was very pleased that the negotiations brought about the end of the strike.
noun	negotiator	I should take lessons from Mr. Tarsa; he is such a skilled negotiator.

verb	retire	Many people don't know what to do with all their time when they retire from work.
noun	retirement	The administrator added more money to the fund for her retirement.
adjective	retired	The retired worker came back to the office from time to time to see his friends.

Incomplete Sentences

Choose the word that best completes the sentence.

1. All temporary workers are paid on an hourly
   _____ and receive no benefits.
   (A) base   (C) basis
   (B) based   (D) basic

2. What is the company's policy on _____ for
   part-time workers?
   (A) benefited   (C) benefits
   (B) beneficial   (D) benefit

3. The tired employee hoped that she would be
   _____ for all the long hours she kept and weekends she worked.
   (A) compensation (C) compensated
   (B) compensates   (D) compensate

4. Sometimes the manager is too _____ and his
   workers take advantage of him.
   (A) flex   (C) flexibly
   (B) flexible   (D) flexibility

5. If the _____ continue into the evening, we will
   break for dinner at six.
   (A) negotiator   (C) negotiate
   (B) negotiations (D) negotiated

6. No one is sure what will happen to the company
   when the president finally _____.
   (A) retires   (C) retired
   (B) retirement   (D) retiree

Error Recognition

Choose the underlined word or phrase that should be rewritten and rewrite it.

7. He was not <u>aware of</u> the changes to the <u>benefits</u> plan, which placed a limit on the contributions he could make
         A   B

   to his <u>retirement</u> account; they had previously been very <u>flexibility</u>.
          C   D

   _____

8. The employees waited until they were fully <u>vest</u> and then <u>delicately</u> made their boss <u>aware of</u> their plans for
                                A   B   C

   <u>retirement</u>.
     D

   _____

9. Salary <u>negotiation</u> is a <u>delicately</u> matter, but necessary if you want to be <u>compensated</u> well and get the <u>raises</u>
         A   B   C   D

   you deserve.

   _____

10. Only employees who are paid on the <u>basis</u> of an hourly <u>wage</u> are <u>eligibility</u> for the <u>raise</u>.
                                     A   B   C   D

    _____

Reading Compehension

Read the following passage and write the words in the blanks below.

basis	compensated	flexibility	retirement
be aware of	delicate	negotiated	vested
benefits	eligible	raise	wage

An important part of the job search often comes after an offer has been made. Papers should not be signed until you have successfully (11.) _____ your salary and (12.) _____. You want to make sure you will be adequately (13.) _____ for your skills, work, and time. This is a (14.) _____ and difficult area. You should (15.) _____ what the salary ranges are at the company and in the field.

Some workers are not on a salary; rather they work for an hourly (16.) _____. In some cases, workers who earn an hourly wage have more (17.) _____ with the hours they work. The trade-off is that the worker may not receive any benefits. For those workers on a salary, the base salary that is negotiated is critical, because most subsequent pay raises come in small incremental amounts. Most companies have a review process either on an annual or semiannual (18.) _____. As a result of the review, an employee may receive a (19.) _____.

Each employee has a unique situation. Health insurance coverage and (20.) _____ plans may be essential to some employees, whereas they are not important to others. Many companies will offer benefits in such a way that it is to the employee's advantage to stay with the company for a longer period of time. Employees may not be (21.) _____ to sign up for a retirement plan until they have been with the company for one year and employees are not fully (22.) _____ in these plans until they have five years of service under their belts. Some bonus plans are paid out over a period of years. Vacation time increases after more years of service.

LISTENING COMPREHENSION

Listen to Track 14 of the Compact Disc to hear the statements for Lesson 14

Part I Picture

Look at the picture and listen to the sentences. Choose the sentence that best describes the picture.

23. Ⓐ Ⓑ Ⓒ Ⓓ

Part II Question—Response

Listen to the question and the three responses. Choose the response that best answers the question.

24. Ⓐ Ⓑ Ⓒ   25. Ⓐ Ⓑ Ⓒ

Part III Short Conversations

Listen to the short dialogs. Then read the question and choose the best response.

26. What is the topic of the conversation?
    (A) Travel.
    (B) The supervisor.
    (C) Vacation policy.
    (D) Communication.

27. Why is the man disappointed?
    (A) His health coverage is poor.
    (B) He asked for too much compensation.
    (C) He doesn't know how to negotiate.
    (D) He doesn't earn enough money.

Part IV Short Talks

Listen to the short talk. Then read the questions and choose the best answer.

28. How often are raises given?
    (A) Once a year.
    (B) Twice a year.
    (C) At an employee's request.
    (D) Whenever an employee is eligible for a raise.

29. Where should employees go to learn more about wage increases?
    (A) The Employee Handbook.
    (B) Their paycheck stubs.
    (C) Their contract.
    (D) Their supervisor.

Promotions, Pensions, and Awards

Words to learn

achievement
contribute
dedication
look forward to
look to
loyal
merit
obviously
productive
promote
recognition
value

1. **achievement** n., an accomplishment, a completed act
   a. Your main achievements will be listed in your personnel file.
   b. Joseph's achievements in R&D will go down in company history.
2. **contribute** v., to add to; to donate, to give
   a. Make sure your boss is aware of the work you contributed to the project.
   b. All employees are asked to contribute a few minutes of their spare time to clean up the office.
3. **dedication** n., a commitment to something
   a. The director's dedication to a high-quality product has motivated many of his employees.
   b. We would never be where we are today if it weren't for many long hours and so much dedication.
4. **look forward to** v., to anticipate, to be eager for something to happen
   a. The regional director was looking forward to the new, larger offices.
   b. We look forward to seeing you at the next meeting.
5. **look to** v., to depend on, to rely on
   a. The workers always looked to him to settle their disagreements.
   b. The staff is looking to their supervisor for guidance and direction.
6. **loyal** adj., faithful, believing in someone or something
   a. You have been such a loyal advisor for so many years, I'm not sure what I'll do without you.
   b. Even though your assistant is loyal, you have to question his job performance.
7. **merit** n., excellence, high quality
   a. Employees are evaluated on their merit and not on seniority.
   b. Your work has improved tremendously and is of great merit.
8. **obviously** adv., clearly, evidently
   a. Her tardiness was obviously resented by her coworkers.
   b. This is obviously not the first time that the customer has had problems with this particular model of sander.
9. **productive** adj., useful, getting a lot done
   a. The researcher wasn't as productive when he first started working here.
   b. The managers had a very productive meeting and were able to solve many of the problems.
10. **promote** v., to give someone a better job; to support, to make known
    a. Even though the sales associate had a good year, it wasn't possible to promote him.
    b. The assistant director promoted the idea that the director was incompetent.
11. **recognition** n., credit, praise for doing something well
    a. The president's personal assistant was finally given the recognition that she has deserved for many years.
    b. Recognition of excellent work should be routine for every manager.
12. **value** v., to state the worth
    a. Employees value their colleagues' opinions.
    b. The expert valued the text at $7,000.

Word Families

noun	achievement	His achievements were noticed by the vice president and he was sent to the London office.
verb	achieve	Making a list of your objectives will help you achieve them.
noun	achiever	Mr. Vadji always considered himself a high achiever.

verb	contribute	All employees were urged to contribute something useful at the staff meetings.
noun	contribution	Each of you has made a significant contribution to our team's success.
noun	contributor	As contributors to the company's outstanding year, all employees will receive an additional holiday bonus.

verb	dedicate	The manager dedicates too much time to reports and not enough time to the customer.
noun	dedication	Margo's dedication to the company was rewarded with a two-week trip to Hawaii.
adjective	dedicated	Before the change in management, he used to be a more dedicated worker.

adjective	loyal	He has been both a loyal coworker and a loyal friend.
noun	loyalty	Her loyalty to the company impressed even the owners.
adverb	loyally	The security officer loyally guarded the company's vault.

adjective	productive	The most productive team in the department will win a two-day vacation in the Bahamas.
noun	product	The new product will be released in the early spring.
verb	produce	The film was produced in Manila.

verb	promote	In order to move ahead in the company, you must promote yourself.
noun	promotion	Promotions are given to those who prove their worth.
noun	promoter	As the main promoter of the product, Ms. Ross was responsible for the marketing campaign.

Incomplete Sentences

Choose the word that best completes the sentence.

1. When he thought about his long career, he realized that his biggest _____ was in developing the new leaders of the company.
   (A) achiever
   (B) achieved
   (C) achievement
   (D) achieves

2. She has _____ so much time and energy to the project that her name should appear on the award.
   (A) contributes
   (B) contribution
   (C) contributed
   (D) contributor

3. Hard work and _____ will help you move up the corporate ladder.
   (A) dedicated
   (B) dedicates
   (C) dedication
   (D) dedicated

4. There is no reason to question her _____ to our company.
   (A) loyal
   (B) loyally
   (C) loyalty
   (D) laurels

5. These microchips are _____ faster and more cheaply in Asia.
   (A) produce
   (B) produced
   (C) product
   (D) production

6. Because you are a valued and dedicated employee, we are _____ you to director of the department.
   (A) promoting
   (B) promote
   (C) promotion
   (D) promoter

Error Recognition

Choose the underlined word or phrase that should be rewritten and rewrite it.

7. The assistant looked forward to the time when she would finally be recognized for her hard work and
   A   B
   dedicated and be promoted to director.
   C   D
   _____

8. The worker made value contributions to the project and he looked forward to receiving a promotion.
   A   B   C   D
   _____

9. The merit of his work was never recognized by all but the obviously lack of loyalty led to his dismissal.
   A   B   C   D
   _____

10. It is obvious that we must look to our customers for ideas in order for us to become more production and
    A   B   C
    achieve greater results.
    D
    _____

Reading Comprehension

Read the following passage and write the words in the blanks below.

achievements	look forward	merits	promotions
contributions	look to	obvious	recognizes
dedicate	loyalty	productivity	value

Congratulations. You have been chosen by your colleagues to receive the Keeler Award of Excellence. This prestigious award (11.) _____ employees who have made extraordinary (12.) _____ to the corporation over the years.

Your coworkers gave several reasons for selecting you. First, they mentioned your (13.) _____ in the marketing department. In the past four years, you have had four (14.) _____ in this department, all based on the many (15.) _____ of your work in developing our image in new markets. In addition, your (16.) _____ to the department is (17.) _____ to all. Many of your coworkers mention that they (18.) _____ you for advice. Your supervisor praised your high (19.) _____.

The Keeler Award acknowledges an employee's (20.) _____ with a $1,000 bonus. We (21.) _____ to the opportunity to (22.) _____ a rosebush in the company garden in each recipient's name.

The awards ceremony will be held on August 7 on the front lawn at 10:30 A.M. Again, congratulations.

LISTENING COMPREHENSION

Listen to Track 15 of the Compact Disc to hear the statements for Lesson 15

Part I Picture

Look at the picture and listen to the sentences. Choose the sentence that best describes the picture.

23. Ⓐ Ⓑ Ⓒ Ⓓ

Part II Question—Response

Listen to the question and the three responses. Choose the response that best answers the question.

24. Ⓐ Ⓑ Ⓒ   25. Ⓐ Ⓑ Ⓒ

Part III Short Conversations

Listen to the short dialogs. Then read the question and choose the best response.

26. Why are they holding a ceremony?
    (A) To honor Darrell.
    (B) To boast about production figures.
    (C) To celebrate the opening of the new office.
    (D) To give awards.

27. What is the woman's complaint?
    (A) Her assistant is often late.
    (B) She doesn't value merit.
    (C) She thinks there's too much paperwork.
    (D) She can't please anybody.

Part IV Short Talks

Listen to the short talk. Then read the questions and choose the best answer.

28. Who is talking?
    (A) Two employees.
    (B) An award presenter.
    (C) Community volunteers.
    (D) A professor.

29. Who is the audience?
    (A) Students.
    (B) Customers.
    (C) Employees.
    (D) Citizens.

Word Review #3   Lessons 11–15 Personnel

Choose the word that best completes the sentence.

1. _____ with a good ad is time-consuming.
   (A) Coming up
   (B) Coming to
   (C) Coming by
   (D) Coming on

2. To _____ the best and the brightest, companies have to be willing to pay well.
   (A) recruit
   (B) recruits
   (C) recruiting
   (D) recruitment

3. A qualified candidate usually exudes _____.
   (A) confident
   (B) confidence
   (C) confidential
   (D) confidentially

4. Any applicant is wise to _____ an interview with a note or a phone call.
   (A) follow after
   (B) follow behind
   (C) follow up
   (D) follow with

5. Workers are promoted on their _____ and merits.
   (A) achieve
   (B) achieved
   (C) achiever
   (D) achievements

6. The benefits package is an important aspect of contract _____.
   (A) negotiate
   (B) negotiable
   (C) negotiations
   (D) negotiated

7. Some employees have to wait years before they are fully _____ in the company pension plan.
   (A) vest
   (B) vested
   (C) vesting
   (D) vests

8. Health _____ are very important for an employee who develops a serious medical problem.
   (A) benefit
   (B) benefits
   (C) beneficial
   (D) beneficiary

9. A _____ and hard-working employee can look forward to rapid promotions.
   (A) dedicate
   (B) dedication
   (C) dedicating
   (D) dedicated

10. A company that recognizes _____ merit will receive employee loyalty in return.
    (A) obvious
    (B) obviously
    (C) oblivious
    (D) obliviously

Choose the underlined word or phrase that should be rewritten and rewrite it.

11. Candidates with backgrounds that match the company's profile should be success in getting a job.
       A   B   C   D

    _____

12. The manager conducts train sessions to help employees to keep up with changes in health benefits.
                    A   B   C   D

    _____

13. The employees had achieved recognizing for their valued contributions to the project.
                          A   B   C   D

    _____

14. The manager immediately recruitment the young woman who demonstrated the kind of confidence,
                              A   B
    background, and ability he had been looking for.
        C   D

    _____

15. The new employee looked forward to rapid promoted through dedication and high productivity.
                        A   B   C   D

    _____

16. You should <u>be aware that</u> employers don't always <u>compensation</u> their employees with wages <u>commensurate</u>
    A   B   C
    with their <u>merit</u>.
    D
    _____

17. <u>Negotiate</u> for a <u>raise</u> in <u>wages</u> can be a <u>delicate</u> process.
    A   B   C   D
    _____

18. <u>Loyal</u> workers should <u>be ready</u> to work overtime without <u>compensation</u> in exchange for <u>flexibility</u> schedules.
    A   B   C   D
    _____

19. If you are lucky, you can find an <u>expert</u> in your field who will be your <u>mentor</u>, keeping you <u>on tracks</u>
    A   B   C
    and helping you to overcome your <u>weaknesses</u>.
    D
    _____

20. Consultants were <u>called in</u> to <u>set by</u> new procedures for doing <u>background</u> checks and processing job
    A   B   C
    <u>applications</u>.
    D
    _____

Lesson 16

Shopping

Words to learn

- bargain
- bear
- behavior
- checkout
- comfort
- expand
- explore
- item
- mandatory
- merchandise
- strictly
- trend

1. **bargain** v., to negotiate; n., an advantageous purchase
   a. She bargained for over an hour, finally reducing the price by half.
   b. Lois compared the sweaters carefully to determine which was a better bargain.

2. **bear** v., to have tolerance for; to endure
   a. Moya doesn't like crowds so she cannot bear to shop during the holiday rush.
   b. If you can bear with me, I'd like to stop in one more store.

3. **behavior** n., the manner of one's actions
   a. Annu is conducting a survey on whether consumer behavior differs between men and women.
   b. Suspicious behavior in a department store will draw the attention of the security guards.

4. **checkout** n., the act, time, or place of checking out, as at a hotel, library, or supermarket
   a. The line at this checkout is too long, so let's look for another.
   b. Get in the checkout line now and I'll join you with the last items.

5. **comfort** v., to calm somebody; n., a condition or feeling of pleasurable ease, well-being, and contentment
   a. Comfort yourself with a down quilt this winter.
   b. I like to dress for comfort if I'm spending the day shopping.

6. **expand** v., to increase the size, volume, quantity, or scope of; to enlarge
   a. The new manager has significantly expanded the store's inventory.
   b. The shoe store is out of room and is thinking about expanding into the adjacent vacant building.

7. **explore** v., to investigate systematically
   a. The collector likes to explore antique shops looking for bargains.
   b. While his mother shopped for clothes, Michael wandered off to explore the toy section.

8. **item** n., a single article or unit
   a. The grocery store has a special checkout line for people who are purchasing fewer than ten items.
   b. Do you think I can get all these items into one bag?

9. **mandatory** adj., required or commanded; obligatory
   a. The jewelry store has a mandatory policy of showing customers only one item at a time.
   b. There is a mandatory limit of nine items for use of this checkout line.

10. **merchandise** n., items available in stores
    a. I am very impressed with the selection of merchandise at this store.
    b. Helen wanted to make sure that the store had a wide variety of merchandise before she committed to buying a gift certificate.

11. **strictly** adv., rigidly, without flexibility
    a. Our store strictly enforces its return policy.
    b. Their high turnover rate is no surprise, considering how strictly the manager deals with them.

12. **trend** n., the current style; vogue
    a. The clothing store tries to stay on top of all the new trends.
    b. Mioshi followed market trends closely before she bought a clothing franchise.

81

Word Families

noun	comfort	This car is designed with plush seats for your comfort and air bags for your safety.
adjective	comfortable	I prefer this sweater because it's more comfortable.
adverb	comfortably	I'd suggest buying the larger table, which comfortably seats six.

verb	expand	The music store expanded its selection by offering more classical music on compact discs.
noun	expansion	The expansion of our sales territory into a new region will mean more stock will have to be ordered.
adjective	expanded	The expanded inventory is great, but it's hard to find room to store it.

verb	explore	Ms. Marce explored the bins of hardware, looking for the right size nails.
noun	exploration	The store designer's exploration of the art of different cultures gave the store an exotic look.
adjective	exploratory	The oil company's exploratory drill led to a new supply of petroleum.

adjective	mandatory	Ankle-high boots are mandatory with that skirt.
noun	mandate	One of the company mandates is to treat the customer with the greatest respect.
verb	mandate	The handbook mandates that all keys be turned in to the night shift supervisor by 9:00.

noun	merchandise	The store's buyer is aggressive about finding unique, high-quality merchandise.
verb	merchandise	The home superstore merchandises hardware and other goods for do-it-yourself home improvements.
noun	merchant	The Downtown Merchants Association is offering free gift wrapping this year.

noun	strictness	Ms. Judd was appalled by the strictness of the store's policy not to renew her gift certificate after it had expired.
adjective	strict	Our store has a strict policy of no returns.
adverb	strictly	The no-food-or-drinks rule is strictly enforced in the bookstore.

Incomplete Sentences

Choose the word that best completes the sentence.

1. It's hard to tell if these shoes will be _____ because the leather is so stiff.
   (A) comfort
   (B) comfortably
   (C) comfortable
   (D) comforting

2. Due to the store's success, the owners began to plan an _____ into a larger location.
   (A) expansion
   (B) expand
   (C) expanse
   (D) expanded

3. I'd like to ____ this issue with you, but I don't have time today.
   (A) exploratory
   (B) exploration
   (C) explorer
   (D) explore

4. Our company policy used to _____ that male employees keep their hair short, but that policy was considered sexist.
   (A) mandate
   (B) mandates
   (C) mandated
   (D) mandatory

5. When you select _____ for the display windows, be sure to include seasonal gifts and clothing.
   (A) merchant
   (B) merchants
   (C) merchandise
   (D) merchandising

6. We _____ adhere to the store's policy of only specially ordering products that have been paid for in advance.
   (A) strictness
   (B) strict
   (C) strictly
   (D) strictest

Error Recognition

Choose the underlined word or phrase that should be rewritten and rewrite it.

7. The growing <u>trend</u> toward shopping by mail is based in part on changing patterns of <u>behave</u>, such as the
        A   B
   perceived lack of time, <u>expanded</u> activity schedules, and increased desire for <u>comfort</u>.
                      C   D

   _____

8. Radica couldn't <u>bearable</u> the thought of wasting money, so she <u>strictly</u> adhered to a budget that allowed her to
                   A   B
   look only for <u>merchandise</u> available at a <u>bargain</u>.
                    C   D

   _____

9. By <u>exploring</u> secondhand shops along the canal, Jorge found a number of <u>trendy</u> fashions that allowed him to
       A   B
   <u>expansion</u> his wardrobe at a <u>bargain</u> rate.
       C   D

   _____

10. The sign above the supermarket <u>checkout</u> made it clear that the line was for customers with 15 <u>itemize</u> or
                                   A   B
    fewer; Ivy quickly counted her <u>merchandise</u> to determine if she complied with the <u>mandatory</u> limit.
                                       C   D

    _____

Reading Comprehension

Read the following passage and write the words in the blanks below.

bargains	checkout	exploring	merchandise
bear	comforting	items	strictly
behavior	expand	mandatory	trend

Some people love to shop. Others can't (11.) _____ shopping and only go when their clothes are completely worn-out. No one can get away from shopping—unless you can do without eating! Consumption and consumer (12.) _____ affects everything we do.

Some purchases are absolutely (13.) _____. Everyone needs to eat, wear clothing, and sit on furniture. Other purchases are (14.) _____ for luxury (15.) _____. The vast majority of what most of us buy is somewhere in between essential items and frivolous items.

Most people shop by visiting stores on the weekend. It's fun to (16.) _____ the number of places you shop in by (17.) _____ new stores—even if you don't make a purchase. It's also (18.) _____ to return to stores you know well, where you know what the (19.) _____ selection is likely to be.

Most shoppers are looking for (20.) _____. Some people even check out all the aisles looking to see if the items they normally use have been marked down. Everyone loves finding that their favorite items are discounted to a lower price. A sale makes going to the (21.) _____ counter a happier event.

A steadily growing (22.) _____ is shopping from the comfort of home. Many people like to shop by catalogs and over the Internet. You can get almost everything, from books to apparel, by mail, without having to leave your home.

LISTENING COMPREHENSION

Listen to Track 16 of the Compact Disc to hear the statements for Lesson 16

Part I Picture

Look at the picture and listen to the sentences.
Choose the sentence that best describes the picture.

23. Ⓐ Ⓑ Ⓒ Ⓓ

Part II Question—Response

Listen to the question and the three responses. Choose the response that best answers the question.

24. Ⓐ Ⓑ Ⓒ   25. Ⓐ Ⓑ Ⓒ

Part III Short Conversations

Listen to the short dialogs. Then read the question and choose the best response.

26. What policy rules the aisle?
    (A) How many items you buy.
    (B) How you pay.
    (C) Whether you have returns or exchanges.
    (D) Whether you are handicapped.

27. What has the man learned about consumers'
    shopping habits?
    (A) They hunt for bargains.
    (B) They buy more during sales.
    (C) Color is a key motivator in clothing selections.
    (D) They feel comfortable with brands they know.

Part IV Short Talks

Listen to the short talk. Then read the questions and choose the best answer.

28. What items are reduced in price?
    (A) Scarves.
    (B) Boots.
    (C) Hats.
    (D) Coats.

29. What kind of merchandise does the store carry?
    (A) Sport vehicles.
    (B) Electronics.
    (C) Clothing.
    (D) Office supplies.

Ordering Supplies

1. **diversify** v., to broaden, to make more varied
   a. The stationery department plans to diversify its offering of paper products.
   b. The consultant that we hired recommends that we don't diversify at this time.

2. **enterprise** n., a business; a large project
   a. The new enterprise quickly established an account with the office supply store.
   b. This enterprise has become unmanageable and is beginning to lose money.

3. **essentially** adv., necessarily, basically, finally
   a. Essentially, she wants to win the contract and put the competition out of business.
   b. After distributing all of the cartridges that were ordered, we were essentially left with none.

4. **everyday** adj., routine, common, ordinary
   a. Though they are more expensive, these folders will withstand everyday wear and tear.
   b. This everyday routine of having to check inventory is boring.

5. **function** v., to perform tasks; n., a purpose
   a. She functioned as the director while Mr. Gibbs was away.
   b. What is the function of this device?

6. **maintain** v., to continue; to support, to sustain
   a. I've been maintaining a list of office supplies that are in greatest demand.
   b. Trying to maintain two different stockrooms is too much work.

7. **obtain** v., to acquire
   a. I've been trying to obtain a list of supplies from the administrator for three weeks now.
   b. The employee obtained the report from her supervisor.

8. **prerequisite** n., something that is required or necessary as a prior condition
   a. One of the prerequisites for this job is competence in bookkeeping.
   b. Here are the prerequisites that you need to purchase before coming to class.

9. **quality** n., a distinguishing characteristic; a degree of excellence
   a. The most important qualities we look for in a supplier are reliability and quick response.
   b. The quality of their clothes has fallen ever since they started using cheaper fabrics to make them.

10. **smooth** adj., without difficulties; deliberately polite and agreeable in order to win favor
    a. Thanks to our smooth transition to the new supplier, there was no interruption in shipments.
    b. Her smooth manner won her the appreciation of the manager but not her colleagues.

11. **source** n., the origin
    a. I can't tell you the source of this information.
    b. The source of this rare pottery that we are selling in our shop is a small village in India.

12. **stationery** n., writing paper and envelopes
    a. We do not have enough stationery, so please order some more.
    b. The new stationery featured the company's logo in blue ink at the top of the page.

Word Families

verb	diversify	We are going to diversify our product line and start selling software as well as computers.
noun	diversity	The diversity of services that your company offers amazes me.
adjective	diverse	The wholesaler offered a more diverse range of computer accessories than I expected.

noun	enterprise	When she began this enterprise, she had no idea of the time it would require.
adjective	enterprising	The program gives enterprising young people a chance to test their entrepreneurial skills.
noun	enterpriser	Many enterprisers find themselves in daring and exciting ventures that lack the structure for long-term success.

adverb	essentially	Essentially, you will be sitting in a bath of mud for two hours.
adjective	essential	Having Ann on this team is essential if we are to win the contract.
noun	essence	The essence of the problem lies in Jeff's relationship with his manager.

verb	function	He is still functioning as administrator until they find a replacement.
noun	function	The function was attended by all the leading scientists.
adjective	functional	This machine is not functional; we need to purchase a new one.

verb	maintain	Don't worry, I'll maintain the good relationships that you've established with our clients.
noun	maintainability	The maintainability of our second office is called into question by next year's budget cutbacks.
adjective	maintainable	This level of performance will not be maintainable without increasing salaries.

verb	smooth out	In order to smooth out the process of ordering supplies, we're going to use this new software to keep track of purchases and deliveries.
adverb	smoothly	The meeting went smoothly, and the contract was signed without any disagreements.
adjective	smooth	The vendor was so smooth on the phone that he had no difficulty in obtaining an appointment with the busy executive.

Incomplete Sentences

Choose the word that best completes the sentence.

1. Many customers find that product _____ is confusing and deceptive.
    (A) diversify   (C) diversity
    (B) diverse   (D) diversified

2. For the _____ designer, this job is full of rewards and opportunities.
    (A) enterprise   (C) enterprising
    (B) enterpriser   (D) enterpriseless

3. Your full participation is _____ to our timely completion of this project.
    (A) essence   (C) essential
    (B) essences   (D) essentially

4. We need to have a spare copier since the only one that is _____ is on its last leg.
    (A) functioned   (C) functional
    (B) functions   (D) function

5. In order to _____ our lead in the market, we'll have to find a cheaper source of industrial supplies.
    (A) maintainable   (C) maintaining
    (B) maintain   (D) maintainability

6. She _____ changed the topic of conversation, thus preventing a disagreement between her colleagues from turning into an argument.
    (A) smoothly   (C) smooth
    (B) smooth out   (D) smoothed

Error Recognition

Choose the underlined word or phrase that should be rewritten and rewrite it.

7. <u>Maintain</u> excellent relationships with clients is an <u>essential</u> component of the <u>quality</u> service that our
       A   B   C
    <u>enterprise</u> offers.
      D

    _____

8. Our <u>everyday</u> supplier of <u>stationery</u> has gone out of business, so finding another <u>source</u> to replace him is
        A   B   C
    <u>essentially</u>.
      D

    _____

9. A <u>prerequisite</u> for the <u>everyday</u> functioning of this international <u>enterprise</u> is an understanding of <u>diverse</u>.
        A   B   C   D

    _____

10. In order to ensure that operations continue to run <u>smooth</u> while the office administrator is on leave, you need
                                                  A
    to <u>obtain</u> a list of suppliers who can provide us with <u>essential</u> items, such as <u>stationery</u>, on short notice.
       B   C   D

    _____

Reading Comprehension

Read the following passage and write the words in the blanks below.

diverse	everyday	obtained	smooth
enterprise	functioning	prerequisite	source
essential	maintaining	quality	stationery

All businesses, large and small, must maintain an inventory of supplies. In most business offices, there are several essential (11.) _____ items, including (12.) _____, pens, staples, and folders. These are easily (13.) _____ from office supply stores that provide the most commonly used items under one roof. Some of these stores will even take orders by telephone with free delivery.

However, some businesses require a more (14.) _____ range of supplies. For example, businesses that ship their products usually need cartons, Styrofoam peanuts, mailing tape, and shipping labels on hand at all times. Though these items may be available from general office supply stores, there are other specialty stores that only sell packing and shipping supplies.

No matter what the type of business, the office administrator is in charge of ordering supplies and (15.) _____ an inventory. Having the (16.) _____ supplies on hand at all times is a (17.) _____ for the (18.) _____ and efficient (19.) _____ of the (20.) _____. The administrator should try to locate the cheapest (21.) _____ of the supplies required, but also pay attention to the (22.) _____ of the goods.

LISTENING COMPREHENSION

Listen to Track 17 of the Compact Disc to hear the statements for Lesson 17

Part I Picture

Look at the picture and listen to the sentences. Choose the sentence that best describes the picture.

23. Ⓐ Ⓑ Ⓒ Ⓓ

Part II Question—Response

Listen to the question and the three responses. Choose the response that best answers the question.

24. Ⓐ Ⓑ Ⓒ   25. Ⓐ Ⓑ Ⓒ

Part III Short Conversations

Listen to the short dialogs. Then read the question and choose the best response.

26. What is the man looking for?
    (A) A glass of water.
    (B) A warehouse.
    (C) A glassware merchant.
    (D) A diverse range of applicants.

27. What does the woman want to do?
    (A) Dress formally.
    (B) Take inventory.
    (C) Establish her priorities.
    (D) Dress casually.

Part IV Short Talks

Listen to the short talk. Then read the questions and choose the best answer.

28. Who is listening to this talk?
    (A) Upper management at a stationery supplier.
    (B) Employees at a stationery supplier.
    (C) Upper management at Margatel.
    (D) Employees at Margatel.

29. What is the problem?
    (A) There was an order with a mistake.
    (B) The company lost a $50,000 client.
    (C) Employees got locked out of the office.
    (D) A worker slipped and fell.

Shipping

1   **accurately** adv., correctly; without errors
   a.   To gauge these figures accurately, we first need to get some facts from the shipping department.
   b.   The container company must balance the load accurately or there could be a disaster at sea.

2.   **carrier** n., a person or business that transports passengers or goods
   a.   Lou, our favorite carrier, takes extra care of our boxes marked "fragile."
   b.   Mr. Lau switched carriers in order to get a price savings on deliveries out of state.

3.   **catalog** n., a list or itemized display; v., to make an itemized list of
   a.   The upcoming fall catalog shows a number of items from Laos that Mr. Lau has never before been able to offer.
   b.   Ellen cataloged the complaints according to severity.

4.   **fulfill** v., to finish completely
   a.   The engineers fulfilled a client's request for larger display screens.
   b.   Her expectations were so high, we knew they would be hard to fulfill.

5.   **integral** adj., necessary for completion
   a.   Good customer relations is an integral component of any business.
   b.   A dependable stream of inventory is integral to reliable shipping of orders.

6.   **inventory** n., goods in stock; an itemized record of these goods
   a.   The store closes one day a year so that the staff can take inventory of the stockroom.
   b.   Their inventory has not changed much over the years.

7.   **minimize** v., to reduce; to give less importance to
   a.   The shipping staff minimized customer complaints by working overtime to deliver the packages quickly.
   b.   To keep the customers happy and to minimize the effect of the carrier strike, we shipped orders directly to them.

8.   **on hand** adj., available
   a.   We had too much stock on hand, so we had a summer sale.
   b.   The new employee will be on hand if we need more help with shipping orders.

9.   **remember** v., to think of again; to retain in the memory
   a.   I remembered the delivery clerk's name as soon as I got off the phone.
   b.   I will remember the combination to the safe without writing it down.

10.   **ship** v., to transport; to send
   a.   Eva shipped the package carefully, since she knew the contents were made of glass.
   b.   Very few customers think about how their packages will be shipped, and are seldom home when the packages arrive.

11.   **sufficiently** adv., enough
   a.   The boxcar was sufficiently damaged that it could not be loaded on the truck.
   b.   We are sufficiently organized to begin transferring the palettes tomorrow.

12.   **supply** n., stock; v., to make available for use; to provide
   a.   By making better use of our supplies, we can avoid ordering until next month.
   b.   Gerald supplied the shipping staff with enough labels to last a year.

Word Families

noun	accuracy	His firm was well known for its accuracy in predicting how long shipping would take.
adjective	accurate	Don't forget to keep accurate records; you will need them when you have your annual inventory.
adverb	accurately	The in-depth shipping records made it possible for Max to accurately estimate when the mixing bowls would arrive in the store.

verb	fulfill	We take pride in fulfilling customers' unusual requests.
gerund	fulfilling	Fulfilling the requirement of the contract will necessitate hiring extra staff.
noun	fulfillment	Fulfillment of duties can be tedious, but job satisfaction demands attention to detail.

adjective	integral	This paperwork is integral to our ability to track packages.
verb	integrate	The new foreman is unable to integrate information about shipping perishables.
noun	integration	His full integration into the team could take weeks.

verb	minimize	To minimize any potential risk of injury, all workers must wear closed-toed shoes in the stockroom.
adjective	minimal	Luckily, the leak from the roof did only minimal damage to the inventory in the stockroom.
noun	minimum	The minimum is $50; orders of less will be assessed a shipping charge.

verb	ship	We ship all orders within 24 hours of your phone call.
noun	shipper	We can rely on our shipper to pack large, fragile items carefully.
noun	shipment	The shipment from the supplier was short a number of items, so we complained.

adverb	sufficiently	If you are sufficiently certain that the crate is in this room, I will check them one by one.
adjective	sufficient	The postage on that box is not sufficient to get it to its destination.
verb	suffice	Will this much Styrofoam suffice?

Incomplete Sentences

Choose the word that best completes the sentence.

1. To assure that your order is _____ filled, it will be checked by a two-person team.
   (A) accurately   (C) accurate
   (B) accurateness   (D) accuracy

2. The suppliers have _____ the terms of our agreement and are now our supplier of choice.
   (A) fulfilling   (C) fulfilled
   (B) fulfillment   (D) fulfill

3. Scanning the shipment number is an _____ part of tracking these containers.
   (A) integral   (C) integrating
   (B) integrate   (D) integration

4. Keeping customer complaints to a _____ is the job of everyone who works in the store.
   (A) minimum   (C) minimize
   (B) minimal   (D) minimally

5. To keep distribution costs low, we have selected only two _____ firms for the region.
   (A) ship   (C) shipping
   (B) shipment   (D) shipper

6. Based on their credit check, it seems likely that they have _____ funds to cover this order.
   (A) suffice   (C) sufficiently
   (B) sufficient   (D) sufficed

Error Recognition

Choose the underlined word or phrase that should be rewritten and rewrite it.

7. Keeping an <u>accurately</u> record of <u>inventory</u> and the names of <u>carriers</u> used for <u>shipping</u> is crucial in business.
             A   B   C   D
   _____

8. The ability to <u>fulfillment</u> customer requests <u>accurately</u> and quickly is <u>integral</u> to running a <u>catalog</u> business.
           A   B   C   D
   _____

9. Keeping a <u>sufficient</u> <u>supply</u> of packing materials <u>on hand</u> can <u>minimal</u> problems in getting products in the mail.
         A   B   C   D
   _____

10. Edwin did not <u>remembrance</u> to include a <u>catalog</u> in the package until after the request was <u>fulfilled</u> and the
            A   B   C
    <u>carrier</u> had arrived.
      D
    _____

Reading Comprehension

Read the following passage and write the words in the blanks below.

accurate	fulfill	minimize	shipping
carrier	integral	on hand	sufficient
catalog	inventory	remember	supplies

For Mr. Park's Asian housewares store, shipping is an (11.) _____ part of the business. Many customers need to send their purchases to friends or relatives who live far away. Other customers, who do not live near one of his stores, shop by (12.) _____ and need their orders sent by mail.

(13.) _____ is, of course, the process of getting goods delivered to a customer, but it is more than just getting a box in the mail. Goods must be packaged carefully to (14.) _____ breakage and ensure that they arrive safely. Staff members must keep (15.) _____ records of the inventory shipped, so Mr. Park knows at all times the answers to these questions: When did a box leave the store? Who was the (16.) _____ who delivered it? When did it arrive at its destination? Customers will have confidence in Mr. Park's business when he can give quick and accurate answers.

The shipping process must be tied to the store's (17.) _____. When orders are taken, the shipping staff must know that there is (18.) _____ inventory of the product on hand to (19.) _____ the request. If a product is on order, the sales staff should advise the customer to expect a delay. When orders are shipped out, they must be deleted from the inventory records so Mr. Park knows exactly how many items are (20.) _____ in his warehouse. It takes a good computer program to keep track of the additions and deletions to the inventory.

Sales staff must (21.) _____ to charge for shipping and appropriate taxes. Mr. Park must keep good records on the cost of the shipping and packing materials and other (22.) _____, the cost of the carriers, and staff time to assess whether he is billing enough to cover his shipping expenses.

LISTENING COMPREHENSION

Listen to Track 18 of the Compact Disc to hear the statements for Lesson 18

Part I Picture

Look at the picture and listen to the sentences. Choose the sentence that best describes the picture.

23. Ⓐ Ⓑ Ⓒ Ⓓ

Part II Question—Response

Listen to the question and the three responses. Choose the response that best answers the question.

24. Ⓐ Ⓑ Ⓒ   25. Ⓐ Ⓑ Ⓒ

Part III Short Conversations

Listen to the short dialogs. Then read the question and choose the best response.

26. What's the problem?
(A) The catalog price is inaccurate.
(B) The salesperson forgot the information.
(C) The shipment was sent to the wrong address.
(D) The customer feels edgy.

27. Who is responsible for the mistake?
(A) The woman.
(B) The man.
(C) The packers.
(D) The supplier.

Part IV Short Talks

Listen to the short talk. Then read the questions and choose the best answer.

28. What is the topic of the talk?
    (A) Company mottos.
    (B) High prices.
    (C) Customer loyalty.
    (D) A weak point in the catalog.

29. What is the company's basic philosophy?
    (A) Unsurpassed customer service.
    (B) A good catalog can sell anything.
    (C) Outperform the competition.
    (D) High quality at low cost.

Invoices

1. **charge** v., to demand payment; n., an expense or a cost
   a. The customer service representative was responsible for telling all existing customers that higher prices would be charged next month.
   b. The extra charge for gift wrapping your purchase will appear on your invoice.

2. **compile** v., to gather together from several sources
   a. I have compiled a list of the most popular items in our sales catalog
   b. The clerk is responsible for compiling the orders at the end of the day.

3. **customer** n., one who purchases a commodity or service
   a. Let's make sure all invoices sent to customers are kept in alphabetical order.
   b. As part of our customer satisfaction plan, let's offer a discount to customers who pay their invoices within a week.

4. **discount** n., a reduction in price; v., to reduce in price
   a. We are offering a 10 percent discount to all new customers.
   b. They discounted the price on the merchandise damaged in shipment.

5. **efficient** adj., acting or producing effectively with a minimum of waste or unnecessary effort
   a. The accountant was so efficient in processing the customer receipts that she had the job done before lunch.
   b. Electronic invoicing has helped us to be efficient.

6. **estimate** v., to approximate the amount or value of something; to form an opinion about something; n., an approximation
   a. We estimated our losses this year at about five thousand dollars.
   b. In the owner's estimation, the high level of customer satisfaction was an adequate measure of how well the company was doing.

7. **impose** v., to establish or apply as compulsory; to force upon others
   a. The company will impose a surcharge for any items returned.
   b. We should not impose upon our staff by requiring them to work on weekends.

8. **mistake** n., an error or a fault
   a. I made a mistake in adding up your bill and we overcharged you twenty dollars.
   b. It was a mistake thinking that my boss would be reasonable when I explained my situation to him.

9. **order** n., a request made to purchase something; v., to command or direct
   a. The customer placed an order for ten new chairs.
   b. We were ordered to take inventory immediately, so we could account for the missing items.

10 **promptly** adv., on time, punctually
   a. We always reply promptly to customers' letters.
   b. The new sales agent promptly offered a full refund for the damaged goods.

11. **rectify** v., to set right or correct
   a. He rectified the problem by giving the customer credit for the unused items that she returned.
   b. Embarrassed at his behavior, he rectified the situation by writing a letter of apology.

12. **terms** n., conditions
   a. The terms of payment were clearly listed at the bottom of the invoice.
   b. The terms of the agreement required that items be fully paid for before they would be shipped.

Word Families

verb	compile	Once the data is compiled, we will know more about sales of the R500 model.
noun	compilation	A compilation of factors led us to believe that employee theft had led to the missing inventory.
adjective	compiled	According to the numbers we've compiled, sales remained flat in the second quarter.

adjective	efficient	Counting by twos or threes is much more efficient than counting by one.
adverb	efficiently	If we work efficiently, we may be done by midnight.
noun	efficiency	His efficiency makes him one of the finest operators in the company.

verb	estimate	We need to estimate the number of work hours spent on this project.
noun	estimation	Clients prefer itemization to estimation on their invoices.
gerund	estimating	Estimating an order for office supplies is difficult because of the increased size of the staff.

verb	impose	The state intends to impose an additional tax on certain office equipment.
noun	imposition	Clients complained when they discovered the contractor's imposition of charges that should have been included under the terms of the contract.
adjective	imposing	The new clients found the company's reputation imposing.

verb	mistaken	The receptionist dialed the wrong number because she had mistaken a "7" for a "4" in the phone number she wrote down.
noun	mistake	The manager called the supplier as soon as he saw the mistake on his invoice.
adjective	mistaken	The director admitted that he was mistaken about the amount of the discount for payment received in 30 days.

verb	prompt	The computer cursor prompted the temporary employee about where to insert information on the billing form.
noun	promptness	Employers appreciate promptness in their employees.
adjective	prompt	I am happy to receive statements that thank me for prompt payment.

Incomplete Sentences

Choose the word that best completes the sentence.

1. After we have _____ all of the necessary documents, we will begin our analysis of the data.
   (A) compile
   (B) compiled
   (C) compiling
   (D) compilation

2. Though he worked very _____ with machines and figures, he was slow and awkward with customers and coworkers.
   (A) efficient
   (B) efficiently
   (C) efficiency
   (D) efficacy

3. Although _____ expenses works well when applying for a contract, clients appreciate itemization on their invoices.
   (A) estimate
   (B) estimator
   (C) estimated
   (D) estimation

4. The customers usually pay their invoices promptly in order to avoid the _____ of late charges.
   (A) imposed
   (B) imposingly
   (C) impose
   (D) imposition

5. The customer was angry at the _____ on her invoice.
   (A) mistakes
   (B) mistaken
   (C) mistakable
   (D) mistaking

6. The client would appreciate it if the invoice could be sent _____ so he can pay it before the end of the fiscal year.
   (A) promptly
   (B) promptness
   (C) prompted
   (D) prompt

Error Recognition

Choose the underlined word or phrase that should be rewritten and rewrite it.

7. I found a <u>mistake</u> in the <u>estimated</u> shipping costs that will have to be <u>rectify</u> before we process this <u>order</u>.
   A   B   C   D

   _____

8. We have <u>imposing</u> additional <u>charges</u> on the customer because she did not pay her bill <u>promptly</u> upon
   A   B   C

   receiving her <u>order</u>.
                 D

   _____

9. The <u>terms</u> of the agreement we <u>imposed</u> on them gave us a <u>discounting</u> if we paid all <u>charges</u> within 15 days.
   A   B   C   D

   _____

10. The customer service representative was very <u>efficiently</u>; she <u>promptly</u> dealt with any <u>mistakes</u> so as not to
    A   B   C

    upset the company's <u>customers</u>.
                        D

    _____

Reading Comprehension

Read the following passage and write the words in the blanks below.

charges   discount   imposed   promptly
compiled   efficient   mistake   rectified
customer   estimated   order   terms

Mail-order companies need to have an (11.) _____ process for invoicing and billing customers. When a customer places an (12.) _____, a list of items must be (13.) _____ and an invoice generated. The invoice will list the items purchased, along with the cost of each item, and the quantity desired. (14.) _____ that will be incurred in shipping the items to the (15.) _____ are also added to the invoice. Sometimes shipping charges are simply (16.) _____ based on the weight or value of the items ordered.

The invoice also shows the (17.) _____ of payment. Payment is usually due within 30 days. Extra charges are often (18.) _____ on overdue accounts. Many companies also offer a small (19.) _____ if invoices are paid promptly.

Sometimes items get damaged or lost in transit, or customers discover that the wrong items have been shipped by (20.) _____. They will usually call the company to have the problem (21.) _____. Such complaints should be dealt with (22.) _____. If an item is missing, a replacement will be sent, usually at no additional charge to the customer.

LISTENING COMPREHENSION

Listen to Track 19 of the Compact Disc to hear the statements for Lesson 19

Part 1 Picture

Look at the picture and listen to the sentences.
Choose the sentence that best describes the picture.

23. Ⓐ Ⓑ Ⓒ Ⓓ

Part II Question—Response

Listen to the question and the three responses. Choose the response that best answers the question.

24. Ⓐ Ⓑ Ⓒ   25. Ⓐ Ⓑ Ⓒ

Part III Short Conversations

Listen to the short dialogs. Then read the question and choose the best response.

26. What do they need to order?
    (A) Computers.
    (B) Temporary workers.
    (C) Order forms.
    (D) Office supplies.

27. How can they save money on the installation?
    (A) Pay at the time of service.
    (B) Pay in U.S. dollars.
    (C) Pay in cash.
    (D) Pay without demanding a receipt.

Part IV Short Talks

Listen to the short talk. Then read the questions and choose the best answer.

28. What is the topic of the talk?
    (A) Late payments.
    (B) Billing customers.
    (C) Immediate payment.
    (D) Discounts.

29. How does immediate payment benefit the company?
    (A) The company doesn't have to use collections agencies.
    (B) The company doesn't have to charge late fees.
    (C) The company gains customers.
    (D) The company doesn't have to send a bill to the customer.

Inventory

1. **adjustment** n., a change in order to match
   a. With these adjustments to the numbers of screws and nuts, we are close to having an accurate count.
   b. An adjustment to the number of damaged items would help us align our figures.

2. **automatically** adv., independently, without outside prompting
   a. The program automatically sends an e-mail response to all messages while she's out of town.
   b. The door opens automatically.

3. **crucial** adj., extremely significant or important
   a. Knowing how many products we have in stock is crucial to our shipping procedures.
   b. Inventory is a crucial process and must be taken seriously by all staff.

4. **discrepancy** n., a divergence or disagreement
   a. We easily explained the discrepancy between the two counts.
   b. Unless you catch the error immediately, the discrepancy gets entered into the computer and becomes very difficult to correct.

5. **disturb** v., to interfere with; to interrupt
   a. Let's see how many products we can count in advance of inventory so we disturb fewer customers.
   b. I hope I'm not disturbing you, but I need to ask you to move so I can record the products behind you.

6. **liability** n., an obligation; a responsibility
   a. The store's insured liability protects against theft and damaged inventory.
   b. The slippery steps were a terrible liability for the store.

7. **reflection** n., a likeness, an image
   a. She saw her reflection in the mirror.
   b. The reflection in the glass made it hard for her to distinguish how many were on the shelf.

8. **run** v., to operate
   a. As long as the computer is running, you can keep adding new data.
   b. We'll be running inventory next weekend, so don't make any other plans.

9. **scan** v., to look over quickly
   a. The computer's optical disk scanned in the price and ordering information.
   b. Jasmine quickly scanned the list to see if any information was missing.

10. **subtract** v., to take away; to deduct
    a. Once you ring up an item, the computer automatically subtracts it from the inventory log.
    b. Whoever did the inventory forgot to subtract the items that arrived damaged and were never put into the stockroom.

11. **tedious** adj., tiresome by reason of length, slowness, or dullness; boring
    a. This may be tedious work but you will be glad the inventory is accurate when you hit the busy holiday sales season.
    b. Counting merchandise all weekend is the most tedious job I can imagine.

12. **verify** v., to prove the truth of
    a. I can't verify the accuracy of these numbers, since I was not present for inventory weekend.
    b. The inventory process verifies that you have accounted for all the items that are supposed to be in the store.

Word Families

verb	adjust	After you've verified the quantities in the stockroom, I'll adjust the numbers in the computer.
noun	adjustment	While the adjustments are being made to the computer inventory, the computer will be off-line and unavailable for use.
adjective	adjustable	The height of the shelves is adjustable, which makes it easier to reach and count the merchandise.

noun	automation	Computers have brought a heightened level of automation into the retail industry.
adjective	automatic	The automatic updating of the inventory is convenient, but always a day behind.
adverb	automatically	After every cash register transaction, the computer automatically updates the inventory record.

verb	disturb	Count as many of the items on the salesroom floor as you can without disturbing the customers.
noun	disturbance	After considering all the options, Ellen decided that closing the store a day to do the annual inventory would cause the least amount of disturbance for customers.
adverb	disturbingly	The computer count and the physical count were disturbingly incongruous, which distressed the store manager.

verb	reflect	The numbers in the computer log should accurately reflect the actual numbers available on the shelf or in the warehouse.
noun	reflection	Upon reflection, the supply clerk decided that there was an error in the inventory.
noun	reflector	Reflectors were attached to the corners of the shelves to alert the clerks that the shelf edges were sharp.

verb	scan	Scan the aisles and see if you find the missing carton.
noun	scanner	We will install a scanner at two of the computer terminals.
adjective	scanned	These scanned documents need to be returned to their original owners.

verb	subtract	Subtract 50 from the total—I just found an unusable box.
noun	subtraction	If you feel confident doing basic addition and subtraction in your head, you don't have to carry the calculator with you.
adjective	subtracted	These subtracted figures don't add up to the total that was supposed to be subtracted.

Incomplete Sentences

Choose the word that best completes the sentence.

1. The computer's inventory figures will be considered inaccurate until the store manager enters the data from the physical count and _____ the figures.
   (A) adjustment
   (B) adjusts
   (C) adjustable
   (D) adjusted

2. Inventory control cannot be performed _____, but must be done by physically counting the merchandise.
   (A) automatically
   (B) automatic
   (C) automation
   (D) automated

3. Do not _____ the staff when they are counting the items; they need to concentrate.
   (A) disturb
   (B) disturbance
   (C) disturbing
   (D) disturbingly

4. Having an accurate inventory count is a good _____ on a competent store manager.
   (A) reflectively
   (B) reflective
   (C) reflect
   (D) reflection

5. In order to scan the bar code, you need to sweep the bar code directly in front of the _____.
   (A) scan
   (B) scanned
   (C) scanning
   (D) scanner

6. If we _____ the damaged merchandise from the inventory, our figures will accurately reflect what we have on hand.
   (A) subtract
   (B) subtracting
   (C) subtracted
   (D) subtraction

Error Recognition

Choose the underlined word or phrase that should be rewritten and rewrite it.

7. In order to <u>verification</u> our inventory records without <u>disturbing</u> our customers, we will attempt to resolve any
         A   B
   known <u>discrepancies</u> in the records and make <u>adjustments</u> while the store is still open.
             C   D

   _____

8. It is <u>crucial</u> to keep an accurate <u>run</u> total of items sold or damaged to avoid <u>adjusting</u> for any <u>discrepancies</u>
         A   B   C   D
   during a physical count.

   _____

9. Once you <u>scan</u> the bar code, the computer <u>automatically</u> <u>subtraction</u> the sold product from the inventory,
             A   B   C
   unless, of course, it is a return, in which case the <u>adjustment</u> is an addition.
                                             D

   _____

10. Doing a physical count of the inventory is a <u>tedious</u> job, but it is <u>crucial</u> to make sure the computer records
                                                A   B
    accurately <u>reflection</u> our holdings; this prevents any <u>discrepancies</u> from popping up later.
               C   D

    _____

Reading Comprehension

Read the following passage and write the words in the blanks below.

adjusted	discrepancies	reflect	subtracts
automatically	disturbances	running	tedious
crucial	liability	scanning	verifies

In a retail business, inventory has multiple meanings. Inventory means all the goods that a company has on hand or available to it in a warehouse. Inventory also means the process by which the business (11.) _____ the number of goods. An accurate account of the inventory available is (12.) _____. The amount of stock is a (13.) _____ because it is already owned by the business.

Taking an inventory is a physical count of the inventory holdings. Today, almost every business keeps a (14.) _____ inventory count by having its sales records tied by computer to its inventory. When a customer makes a purchase, the computer system tied to the register (15.) _____ the purchase from the inventory records. If a customer makes a return or an exchange, the inventory numbers will be (16.) _____ by the computer (17.) _____. That's often why (18.) _____ the bar code is so important in stores. If merchandise is broken or damaged in the stockroom or on the sales floor, the manager will ask the sales and stock help to change the stock holdings to (19.) _____ the loss.

As good as the computer records may be, they are just an estimate. At least once a year, most businesses do an actual physical count of the inventory. This process can be (20.) _____ but it is necessary as there are always (21.) _____ between what the computer says you own and what your physical count says. Often stores close for a day, or at least close early, so that staff can perform the inventory without (22.) _____.

LISTENING COMPREHENSION

Listen to Track 20 of the Compact Disc to hear the statements for Lesson 20

Part I Picture

Look at the picture and listen to the sentences.
Choose the sentence that best describes the picture.

23. Ⓐ Ⓑ Ⓒ Ⓓ

Part II Question—Response

Listen to the question and the three responses. Choose the response that best answers the question.

24. Ⓐ Ⓑ Ⓒ   25. Ⓐ Ⓑ Ⓒ

Part III Short Conversations

Listen to the short dialogs. Then read the question and choose the best response.

26. What is the problem with the platter?
    (A) It doesn't have a price tag.
    (B) It's cracked.
    (C) It won't fit on the bar.
    (D) It wasn't counted in the inventory.

27. What information does the man want to verify?
    (A) The size of the bedspreads.
    (B) The number of bedspreads on hand.
    (C) Why there is a discrepancy.
    (D) How many bedspreads the lady needs.

Part IV Short Talks

Listen to the short talk. Then read the questions and choose the best answer.

28. What happens every year in January?
    (A) They adjust the file drawers.
    (B) They record the audio portion.
    (C) They delete unnecessary computer files.
    (D) They do a physical count.

29. What is one problem with their work?
    (A) It consumes too much time.
    (B) Nobody appreciates it.
    (C) The hourly rate is low.
    (D) It's boring.

Word Review #4   Lessons 16–20 Purchasing

Choose the word that best completes the sentence.

1. Most merchants are happy to find any way to _____ their customer base.
   (A) expand
   (B) expanding
   (C) expansion
   (D) expanded

2. All fashion _____ have a limited life span.
   (A) trend
   (B) trends
   (C) trendy
   (D) trending

3. It is a poorly run office that does not _____ adequate office supplies.
   (A) maintain
   (B) maintained
   (C) maintaining
   (D) maintenance

4. Sometimes office policy doesn't allow the company to _____ less expensive supplies when they are available from someone other than a preferred provider.
   (A) obtain
   (B) obtained
   (C) obtaining
   (D) obtainable

5. A supplier who has chronic trouble _____ his obligations to a customer will quickly lose customers.
   (A) fulfill
   (B) fulfills
   (C) fulfilling
   (D) fulfillment

6. To _____ disruption, buyers should order well ahead of need.
   (A) minimum
   (B) minimal
   (C) minimize
   (D) minimally

7. It is wise to begin by _____ an inventory of equipment on hand.
   (A) compile
   (B) compiling
   (C) compiler
   (D) compilation

8. If the provider does not meet his client's demand, he should _____ the problem as soon as possible.
   (A) rectify
   (B) rectifier
   (C) rectifiable
   (D) rectification

9. If some supplies show a steady rise in consumption, the office manager should make an appropriate _____ in his standard order.
   (A) adjust
   (B) adjuster
   (C) adjusting
   (D) adjustment

10. The office manager should also ascertain whether the inventory of supplies properly _____ the volume of use in the office.
    (A) reflect
    (B) reflects
    (C) reflecting
    (D) reflection

Choose the underlined word or phrase that should be rewritten and rewrite it.

11. A wise <u>customer</u> will <u>efficiency</u> <u>catalog</u> all ordered <u>items</u> as they are received.
          A   **B**   **C**   **D**

    _____

12. Some <u>bargaining</u> hunters demonstrate unusual <u>behavior</u> as they <u>explore</u> the range of <u>merchandise</u>.
          A   **B**   **C**   **D**

    _____

13. The first priority should be to find a <u>source</u> for <u>essentially</u> <u>everyday</u> supplies such as <u>stationery</u>.
                       A   **B**   **C**   **D**

    _____

14. <u>Remember</u> to check the <u>accurate</u> of the <u>supply</u> invoice enclosed with each <u>shipment</u>.
      A   **B**   **C**   **D**

    _____

15. An <u>efficient</u> office will have someone check each invoice for such <u>mistakes</u> as whether the appropriate
    A   B
    <u>discounting</u> has been applied to the <u>charges</u>.
    C   D
    _____

16. However <u>tediously</u>, a <u>crucial</u> factor in maintaining inventory is to keep a <u>running</u> total of supplies used and to
    A   B   C
    <u>verify</u> that they are being used in the office.
    D
    _____

17. One should also <u>scan</u> the invoices for <u>discrepancies</u>, and be sure that overcharges are <u>prompt</u> <u>subtracted</u>.
    A   B   C   D
    _____

18. The <u>diversity</u> of supplies ordered demands an <u>efficient</u> and <u>functioning</u> system of <u>qualities</u> control.
    A   B   C   D
    _____

19. A <u>mandatory</u> checking system, <u>strict</u> enforced, will ensure that the <u>inventory</u> <u>on hand</u> is adequate for efficiently
    A   B   C   D
    running the office.
    _____

20. Other aspects of ordering supplies include <u>estimating</u> whether the use of specific items should increase or
    A
    decrease, or whether furniture is <u>comfortable</u> enough not to be a <u>liability</u> by <u>disturb</u> smooth operation of the
    B   C   D
    office.
    _____

Banking

1. **accept** v., to receive; to respond favorably
    a. The receptionist accepted the package from the courier.
    b. Without hesitating, she accepted the job of teller.

2. **balance** n., the remainder; v. to compute the difference between credits and debits of an account
    a. His healthy bank balance showed a long habit of savings.
    b. It took him over an hour to balance his checkbook.

3. **borrow** v., to use temporarily
    a. Do you want to borrow a pen?
    b. The couple borrowed money from the bank to buy a home.

4. **cautiously** adv., carefully, warily
    a. The bank manager spoke cautiously when giving out information to people she did not know.
    b. Act cautiously when signing contracts and read them thoroughly first.

5. **deduct** v., to take away from a total; to subtract
    a. Before computing his taxes, Christophe remembered to deduct allowable home improvement expenses.
    b. By deducting the monthly fee from her checking account, Yi was able to make her account balance.

6. **dividend** n., a share in a distribution
    a. The stockholders were outraged when their quarterly dividends were so small.
    b. The dividend was calculated and distributed to the group.

7. **down payment** n., an initial partial payment
    a. By making a large down payment, the couple saved a great deal in mortgage interest.
    b. Karl was disappointed when the real estate agent told him he needed a larger down payment on the house.

8. **mortgage** n., the amount due on a property; v., to borrow money with your house as collateral
    a. Due to low interest rates, Sheila moved quickly to find a good deal on a mortgage.
    b. Hiram mortgaged his home to get extra money to invest in his business.

9. **restricted** adj., limited
    a. The number of free withdrawals a customer can make from his or her account each month is restricted to five.
    b. Access to the safe deposit box vault is restricted to key holders.

10. **signature** n., the name of a person written by the person
    a. Once we have your signature, the contract will be complete.
    b. The customer's signature was kept on file for identification purposes.

11. **take out** v., withdraw; remove
    a. My checking account allows me to take out money at any bank branch without a fee.
    b. They took out the chairs in the bank lobby so now there is no place to sit.

12. **transaction** n., a business deal
    a. Banking transactions will appear on your monthly statement.
    b. The most common transactions can be made from your personal computer.

Word Families

verb	accept	The bank will not accept a student ID as a valid form of identification.
noun	acceptance	The bank's acceptance of checks allows extra time for out-of-state checks to clear before they are credited to your account.
adjective	acceptable	Shorter banking hours would not be acceptable to many customers, who might close their accounts as a result.

verb	caution	Our friends cautioned us against putting our money into an account that pays such a low interest rate.
adjective	cautious	The bank officer was cautious about approving Chen's loan because of his unfavorable credit history.
adverb	cautiously	We spent our money cautiously because we were not sure we would be able to borrow more.

verb	deduct	Remember to deduct the monthly bank fee from your statement.
noun	deductible	Taxes and health insurance payments are called deductibles because they are deducted from your paycheck.
noun	deduction	Deductions are made electronically every month and will appear on your statement.

verb	restrict	The bank's policies restrict the number of deductions you can make from your account without a penalty.
noun	restriction	The restrictions on who was eligible for a mortgage made it impossible for many low-income families to borrow money.
adjective	restricted	Information about your account is confidential and its use without your permission is restricted.

verb	sign	Once you have signed the mortgage contract, the bank will make a check payable to you.
noun	sign	The sign in the bank's lobby announces their rates for savings accounts and for loans.
noun	signature	Your signature can be electronically recorded to be verified later.

verb	transact	Our company transacts all its financial business at this bank.
noun	transaction	All parties concerned were pleased with the results of the business transactions.

Incomplete Sentences

Choose the word that best completes the sentence.

1. I'm going to call the bank manager ahead of time to make certain that she will _____ a personal check to start a new account.
   (A) accept
   (B) accepted
   (C) acceptance
   (D) acceptable

2. We felt _____ about applying for such a large loan.
   (A) cautiously
   (B) caution
   (C) cautioning
   (D) cautious

3. Every month my automatic car loan payment shows up as a _____ on my monthly statement.
   (A) deduct
   (B) deduction
   (C) deducting
   (D) deducted

4. The number of withdrawals at no charge from your savings account is _____ to three.
   (A) restricting
   (B) restricted
   (C) restrict
   (D) restriction

5. There is a counter in the bank lobby where customers can _____ their documents.
   (A) signing
   (B) signed
   (C) sign
   (D) signature

6. These _____ must be completed before the close of business today.
   (A) transacts
   (B) transacting
   (C) transacted
   (D) transactions

Error Recognition

Choose the underlined word or phrase that should be rewritten and rewrite it.

7. The cautious bank teller reluctantly accepting Charles's company ID card as valid identification, and he was
        A   **B**
   able to take out half of the balance of his savings account.
        C   **D**

   _____

8. Certain investment accounts are now earning higher dividends than before with fewer restrictive on the length
                   A   **B**
   of deposit, number of transactions, or amount of balance in the account.
            C   **D**

   _____

9. The mortgage application clearly states that monthly payments will be directly deduction from the balance of
        A   **B**   **C**   **D**
   your in-house checking account.

   _____

10. The restrictions on mortgages available at low interest rates made Chen more caution about taking out his
         A   **B**   **C**
    savings before they grew into a sizable down payment.
             D

    _____

Reading Comprehension

Read the following passage and write the words in the blanks below.

accept	cautious	down payment	signature
balance	deductions	mortgages	take out
borrow	dividends	restrict	transact

Banks are not only places in which to save money or to (11.) _____ your financial business, but also institutions from which people can (12.) _____ money. Every day, people look to banks for loans, such as (13.) _____ for new homes. A loan is essentially a contract that binds the lender to a schedule of payments, so both parties should be (14.) _____ and not enter into the arrangement without thinking. Banks will look at such factors as how much people have saved towards a (15.) _____ in determining whether to make a loan.

Banks have different kinds of accounts. Some pay high quarterly (16.) _____. Some accounts even severely (17.) _____ the number of times, if any, that you can access your account, or the amount of cash you can (18.) _____.

Today, electronic banking can be used to check the (19.) _____ on an account, or to see if automatic (20.) _____ have been made. This can all be done from your home or office computer. When you go to the bank, be sure to bring identification. Usually a bank will only (21.) _____ a photo ID; a (22.) _____ is not a valid ID.

LISTENING COMPREHENSION

Listen to Track 21 of the Compact Disc to hear the statements for Lesson 21

Part I Picture

Look at the picture and listen to the sentences.
Choose the sentence that best describes the picture.

23. Ⓐ Ⓑ Ⓒ Ⓓ

Part II Question—Response

Listen to the question and the three responses. Choose the response that best answers the question.

24. Ⓐ Ⓑ Ⓒ   25. Ⓐ Ⓑ Ⓒ

Part III Short Conversations

Listen to the short dialogs. Then read the question and choose the best answer.

26. What does the man want to do?
    (A) Open a bank account.
    (B) Get a new driver's license.
    (C) Put his signature on file.
    (D) Cash a check.

27. What are they discussing?
    (A) A contract for a loan.
    (B) A balance statement.
    (C) A check.
    (D) A tax deduction.

Part IV Short Talks

Listen to the short talk. Then read the questions and choose the best answer.

28. Who is this talk for?
    (A) People who are looking for a job.
    (B) People who want to borrow money.
    (C) People who work in a bank.
    (D) People who want to open a bank account.

29. How big a down payment is required?
    (A) Ten percent.
    (B) Three percent.
    (C) One percent.
    (D) Four percent.

Accounting

1. **accounting** n., the recording and gathering of financial information for a company
   a. Good accounting is needed in all businesses.
   b. Accounting for expenses is time-consuming.
2. **accumulate** v., to gather; to collect
   a. They have accumulated more than enough information.
   b. The bills started to accumulate after the secretary quit.
3. **asset** n., something of value
   a. The company's assets are worth millions of dollars.
   b. A sophisticated accounting system is an asset to a company.
4. **audit** n., a formal examination of financial records; v., to examine the financial records of a company
   a. No one looks forward to an audit by the government.
   b. The independent accountants audited the company's books.
5. **budget** n., a list of probable expenses and income for a given period; v., to plan for expenses
   a. The department head was pleased that she received a 10 percent increase in her budget.
   b. The company will have to budget more money for this department next year.
6. **build up** v., to increase over time
   a. The firm has built up a solid reputation for itself.
   b. Be careful, your inventory of parts is building up.
7. **client** n., a customer
   a. We must provide excellent services for our clients, otherwise we will lose them to our competition.
   b. Maintaining close contact with clients keeps the account managers aware of changing needs.
8. **debt** n., something owed, as in money or goods
   a. The company has been very careful and is slowly digging itself out of debt.
   b. The banks are worried about your increasing debt.
9. **outstanding** adj., still due; not paid or settled
   a. That client still has several outstanding bills.
   b. Clients with outstanding bills will not receive further service until the bills are paid.
10. **profitably** adv., advantageously
    a. The company used its accountant's advice profitably.
    b. We invested in the stock market profitably.
11. **reconcile** v., to make consistent
    a. The client uses his bank statements to reconcile his accounts.
    b. The accountant found the error when she reconciled the account.
12. **turnover** n., the number of times a product is sold and replaced or an employee leaves and another employee is hired
    a. We have to add another production shift to keep up with the high turnover rate.
    b. The overseas branch has much lower employee turnover than does domestic operations.

Word Families

noun	accountant	The accountant was precise and hardworking.
noun	accounting	Accounting is a popular field of study.
noun	account	The client closed his bank account and withdrew all of his money.

verb	accumulate	The owner's goal was to accumulate as much wealth as possible.
noun	accumulation	The accumulation of goods may lead to an inventory problem.
adjective	accumulated	The sum of all the accumulated resources equals your total assets.

verb	audit	Some bookkeeping inconsistencies showed up when our records were audited.
noun	audit	If you keep your financial records carefully, you will always be ready for audit.
noun	auditor	The tax auditor will ask to see records from the past several years.

verb	budget	There was no travel expense budgeted for the editorial department.
noun	budget	The boss asked for input on next year's budget.
adjective	budgetary	Due to budgetary constraints, we cannot hire additional staff at this time.

verb	build up	Over the years, our office has built up a solid list of clients.
noun	buildup	A buildup of debt will weaken the company's finances.

verb	profit	The engineer will profit from the successful introduction of the new product.
noun	profit	The profits exceeded all expectations.
adjective	profitable	Marketing is the most profitable department this year.

Incomplete Sentences

Choose the word that best completes the sentence.

1. The firm's _____ studied finance and business administration.
   (A) account
   (B) accounting
   (C) accounted
   (D) accountant

2. The account manager has _____ a tremendous amount of wealth in a very short time.
   (A) accumulated
   (B) accumulation
   (C) accumulating
   (D) accumulates

3. We went over our records carefully in order to prepare for the meeting with the _____.
   (A) audit
   (B) auditor
   (C) auditing
   (D) audited

4. At the end of next week, all the division heads will meet to present one consolidated _____.
   (A) budgeting
   (B) budget
   (C) budgeted
   (D) budgets

5. I _____ some savings in my bank account before I made any investments in business.
   (A) building up
   (B) buildup
   (C) built up
   (D) build

6. All the employees will benefit if the company's _____ continue to increase.
   (A) profited
   (B) profitable
   (C) profits
   (D) profitably

Error Recognition

Choose the underlined word or phrase that should be rewritten and rewrite it.

7. <u>Accountants</u> audit and <u>reconciliation</u> their <u>clients'</u> <u>accounts</u> at the end of each quarter.
       A   B   C   D

   _____

8. The <u>accumulated</u> of <u>debt</u> may be the result of a <u>buildup</u> of <u>outstanding</u> payments.
           A   B   C   D

   _____

9. The <u>auditors</u> have analyzed the company's <u>budget</u> and have come up with a list of questions concerning the
       A   B

   <u>assets</u>, revenue, and <u>profitable</u>.
     C   D

   _____

10. Because of slow <u>turnover</u> and <u>outstanding</u> payments, the projected <u>budgetary</u> was inaccurate and the <u>profit</u>
                A   B   C   D
    margin less than expected.

    _____

Reading Comprehension

Read the following passage and write the words in the blanks below.

accounting	audited	clients	profitable
accumulated	budget	debt	reconcile
assets	building up	outstanding	turnover

Accounting information is pulled together or (11.) _____ to help someone make decisions. A manager must come up with a (12.) _____ to help control expenses. A retail store owner realizes that her (13.) _____ have (14.) _____ bills. A restaurant owner wants to know if it is (15.) _____ to serve lunch. A nonprofit organization is being (16.) _____ by the government. All of these people and organizations could use the services of an accountant.

Accountants and (17.) _____ systems help a company stay on track. They raise flags when expenses are (18.) _____ and keep an eye on the (19.) _____ of inventory. They (20.) _____ their clients' accounts to ensure that their clients' records are correct. Good accounting systems allow managers to come up with ways to improve their business.

The accountant prepares information for both internal and external use. Financial statements provide a quick look into the life of a business. They show how much (21.) _____ the company is carrying and how much its (22.) _____ are worth. The outside world uses this information to judge the health of the company.

LISTENING COMPREHENSION

Listen to Track 22 of the Compact Disc to hear the statements for Lesson 22

Part I Picture

Look at the picture and listen to the sentences. Choose the sentence that best describes the picture.

23. Ⓐ Ⓑ Ⓒ Ⓓ

Part II Question—Response

Listen to the question and the three responses. Choose the response that best answers the question.

24. Ⓐ Ⓑ Ⓒ   25. Ⓐ Ⓑ Ⓒ

Part III Short Conversations

Listen to the short dialogs. Then read the question and choose the best answer.

26. What are they discussing?
    (A) The budget.
    (B) A meeting.
    (C) Their goals.
    (D) The company's assets.

27. What is the client's problem?
    (A) He doesn't understand his accountant.
    (B) He won't be in his office at 4:30.
    (C) He has a lot of debt.
    (D) He has accumulated a lot of savings.

Part IV Short Talks

Listen to the short talk. Then read the questions and choose the best answer.

28. What is the topic of this talk?
    (A) How to start an accounting firm.
    (B) How to avoid client turnover.
    (C) How to have a profitable accounting firm.
    (D) How to get clients.

29. How can an accounting firm make more money?
    (A) By charging higher fees.
    (B) By getting recommendations from their clients.
    (C) By hiring new accountants.
    (D) By making a new list of clients.

Lesson 23

Investments

Words to learn

agressively
attitude
commit
conservative
fund
invest
long-term
portfolio
pull out
resource
return
wisely

1. **aggressively** adv., competitively, assertively
   a. Some people are risk takers and prefer to invest aggressively.
   b. His ideas were not well received because he spoke so aggressively.
2. **attitude** n., a feeling about something or someone
   a. The new fund manager's attitude changed quickly after the first big downturn in the market.
   b. Each investor should assess his or her own attitude toward investment.
3. **commit** v., to consign for future use, to promise
   a. It is a good idea to commit a certain percentage of your income to investments.
   b. The stockbroker committed herself to finding the best investments for each client.
4. **conservative** adj., cautious, restrained
   a. Her conservative strategy paid off over the years.
   b. Generally, older people should be more conservative in their investing than younger people.
5. **fund** n., an amount of money for something specific; v., to provide money for
   a. He will have access to his trust fund when he is 21 years old.
   b. The company will fund the trip to the conference.
6. **invest** v., to put money into a business or activity with the hope of making more money; to put effort into something
   a. The chief financial officer invested in the stock at a very good time.
   b. Don't invest all of your time in just one project.
7. **long-term** adj., involving or extending over a long period
   a. The CEO's long-term goal was to increase the return on investment.
   b. Over the long term, unemployment is expected to remain steady.
8. **portfolio** n., a list of investments
   a. Investors are advised to have diverse portfolios.
   b. The investor's portfolio consisted of blue chip company stocks and government bonds.
9. **pull out** v., to withdraw, to stop participating; n., a withdrawal, removal
   a. His advisor suggested that she pull out her investments in the troubled country.
   b. The pull out of the bank has left the company without financing.
10. **resource** n., assets; valuable things
    a. If you don't invest in petroleum resources now, you will find that the stock prices will get away from you.
    b. The company's most valuable resource was its staff.
11. **return** n., the amount of money gained as profit
    a. The 44 percent return on the new stock was far more than the stockbroker had anticipated.
    b. Some investors are satisfied with a 15 percent return, while others want to see a much larger return.
12. **wisely** adj., knowledgeably, smartly
    a. If you invest wisely, you will be able to retire early.
    b. Mary wisely followed her stockbroker's advice and took her money out of some bad investments.

Word Families

noun	aggression	The act of aggression against our country caused a fear of war and had a negative effect on the stock market.
adjective	aggressive	The director's aggressive position on investing was frowned upon by the Board of Directors.
adverb	aggressively	I chose this stockbroker because he invests my money aggressively.

verb	commit	I'm committed to keeping the money in my pension fund until I retire.
noun	commitment	The employee's commitment to working hard and saving her money was commendable.
adjective	noncommittal	I had hoped that the discussion would yield a definite answer from them, but they were noncommittal.

verb	conserve	Conserve your money now so you will be able to invest when the stock market gets better.
adjective	conservative	Some people are conservative investors and take few risks with their money.
adverb	conservatively	If you invest too conservatively, you may lose some chances for making money.

verb	invest	The company has been successful because it has invested wisely in its resources.
noun	investment	The CFO is responsible for corporate investment.
noun	investor	The fall in the stock market shook up the investors.

verb	return	I wish I could return to the days where investing was simple.
noun	returns	Our returns on our investments exceeded expectations.
adjective	returnable	The merchandise is returnable as long as you have your receipt.

noun	wisdom	Common wisdom is to place your money in a variety of investments.
adjective	wise	The wise investor does her homework before parting with her money.
adverb	wisely	She planned her retirement wisely and was able to retire to her summer house.

Incomplete Sentences

Choose the word that best completes the sentence.

1. The stockbroker recommended investing some money more _____.
   (A) aggressive
   (B) aggression
   (C) aggressively
   (D) aggressor

2. All employees are encouraged to _____ a percentage of their earnings to the retirement fund.
   (A) committed
   (B) commit
   (C) commitment
   (D) committing

3. Because he had made such _____ investments, he lost very little money when the stock market went down.
   (A) conservative
   (B) conserved
   (C) conservatively
   (D) conserve

4. After months of study and research, the _____ decided to put his money into new facilities and materials.
   (A) investor
   (B) investment
   (C) investing
   (D) invested

5. A good financial analyst will advise investors on strategies that will generate higher _____.
   (A) returned
   (B) returning
   (C) returns
   (D) returnable

6. Is it _____ to consider funding a new project when we haven't even seen the returns from the last one?
   (A) wisdom
   (B) wisest
   (C) wisely
   (D) wise

Error Recognition

Choose the underlined word or phrase that should be rewritten and rewrite it.

7. The business woman decided to <u>invest</u> in <u>markets</u> that had a history of excellent <u>returning</u> in the <u>long term</u>.
                    A   **B**   **C**   **D**

   _____

8. The investor credited her stockbroker for changing her <u>attitude</u> and renewing her <u>committed</u> to her less than <u>conservative</u> <u>portfolio</u>.
         A   **B**
      C   **D**

   _____

9. The computer company, known for its <u>aggression</u> behavior, took a rather <u>conservative</u> position toward <u>investing</u> in new <u>resources</u>.
         A   **B**
      C   **D**

   _____

10. The <u>wise</u> <u>investor</u> knows when to <u>pulling</u> out and when to increase contributions to a <u>fund</u>.
        A   **B**   **C**   **D**

    _____

Reading Comprehension

Read the following passage and write the words in the blanks below.

aggressive	committed	long-term	resources
attitude	fund	portfolio	return
conservative	invest	pull out	wise

Investment is a common, everyday occurrence. Companies (11.) _____ time and money in finding and training their employees. Employees invest in their own training and education. Financial investment takes place at a corporate level and at an individual level. Whether an individual or a company, a decision must be made on the percentage of (12.) _____ to have invested and the percentage to have in cash.

To avoid making stupid decisions, many people use financial advisors. Financial advisors help individuals and corporations make (13.) _____ investment decisions. What kind of portfolio should be maintained? What should be in this (14.) _____. At what point should an investor pull back or (15.) _____ of the market? What kind of (16.) _____ should the investor realistically expect? How much risk can an investor take (both emotionally and financially)? Investors who are (17.) _____ for the (18.) _____ can more easily weather the ups and downs of a market. As one analyst commented, "If you're staying awake at night thinking about the stock market, you probably have too much invested."

Many employees have retirement plans at work. They decide what level of contribution to make to a certain (19.) _____. These decisions and large company decisions depend to a large degree on (20.) _____. Is the decision maker (21.) _____ or (22.) _____? That attitude often depends on the age of the investor or on the stage and the needs of the business.

LISTENING COMPREHENSION

Listen to Track 23 of the Compact Disc to hear the statements for Lesson 23

Part I Picture

Look at the picture and listen to the sentences.
Choose the sentence that best describes the picture.

23. Ⓐ Ⓑ Ⓒ Ⓓ

Part II Question—Response

Listen to the question and the three responses. Choose the response that best answers the question.

24. Ⓐ Ⓑ Ⓒ   25. Ⓐ Ⓑ Ⓒ

Part III Short Conversations

Listen to the short dialogs. Then read the question and choose the best answer.

26. What does the man recommend?
    (A) Investing mainly in natural resources.
    (B) Investing in various industries.
    (C) Investing aggressively.
    (D) Investing in the basket industry.

27. What kind of investments did the man make?
    (A) Wise.
    (B) Aggressive.
    (C) Conservative.
    (D) Long-term.

Part IV Short Talks

Listen to the short talk. Then read the questions and choose the best answer.

28. What is this talk about?
    (A) How to invest in the stock market.
    (B) How to choose a good college.
    (C) How to choose investments.
    (D) How to save money for college.

29. When should parents start saving money for college?
    (A) Two or three years from now.
    (B) When their children are small.
    (C) After they have had two or three children.
    (D) When their children are in high school.

Taxes

Words to learn

calculation
deadline
file
fill out
give up
joint
owe
penalty
preparation
refund
spouse
withhold

1. **calculation** n., computation; estimate
   a. It took my accountant some time to complete the calculations on my income tax.
   b. According to my calculations, I'll owe less money on my income taxes this year.

2. **deadline** n., a time by which something must be finished
   a. The deadline for paying this year's taxes is just two weeks away.
   b. My best work is done with strict deadlines.

3. **file** v., to enter into public record
   a. If you file your taxes late, you will have to pay a fine.
   b. If you believe the tax preparer gave you incorrect information, you should file a complaint with her boss.

4. **fill out** v., to complete
   a. I usually ask someone to help me fill out my tax form.
   b. Don't forget to sign the tax form after you have filled it out.

5. **give up** v., to quit; to stop
   a. Bruce gave up trying to prepare his tax return himself and now hires an accountant to do it.
   b. Ms. Gomez is so optimistic that she never gives up.

6. **joint** adj., together; shared
   a. We opened a joint bank account five years ago.
   b. The couple no longer files joint tax returns.

7. **owe** v., to have a debt; to be obligated to pay
   a. People are often surprised to discover that they owe more money in income taxes at the end of the year.
   b. As the business grew, the owner paid back loans and owed less money.

8. **penalty** n., a punishment; a consequence
   a. Anyone who pays less than they should in taxes will face a penalty.
   b. Penalties are imposed to discourage underpayment of taxes by adding a percentage to the taxes you already owe.

9. **preparation** n., the act of making something ready
   a. Income tax preparation can take a long time.
   b. It is important to do some preparation on your own before hiring an accountant to work on your tax form.

10. **refund** n., the amount paid back; v., to give back
    a. With the tax refund, we bought two plane tickets.
    b. The government will refund any money that you overpaid.

11. **spouse** n., a husband or wife
    a. You can claim your spouse as a dependent on your tax return if he or she doesn't earn an income.
    b. My spouse prepares the tax return for both of us.

12. **withhold** v., to keep from; to refrain from
    a. My employer withholds money from each paycheck to apply toward my income taxes.
    b. Do not withhold any information from your accountant or he will not be able to prepare your tax form correctly.

Word Families

verb	calculate	The young man tries to calculate his expenses every month.
noun	calculation	The calculation is no more difficult than high school math.
noun	calculator	In order to avoid making addition and subtraction errors, I suggest you use a calculator.

verb	file	Don't wait until the last minute to file your taxes.
noun	file	I keep all my tax information in one file.

adjective	joint	My husband and I filed a joint tax return.
adverb	jointly	Even though you are separated right now, you will save money if you and your wife file your taxes jointly.

verb	penalize	The government will penalize taxpayers who try to evade paying their fair share of taxes.
noun	penalty	For every dollar you owe in overdue taxes, a 10 percent penalty is imposed.
adjective	penal	Tax evasion is a penal offense.

verb	prepare	Most people wait until the last minute to prepare their tax returns.
noun	preparation	If you are organized, income tax preparation takes only a few hours.
adjective	preparatory	The preparatory work for doing my taxes is more time-consuming than filling out the forms.

verb	refund	The government should refund your overpaid taxes within a few weeks of filing your tax return.
noun	refund	If you have overpaid your income taxes, you will get a refund at the end of the year.
adjective	refundable	Sales tax that tourists pay in a foreign country may be refundable when they leave the country.

Incomplete Sentences

Choose the word that best completes the sentence.

1. According to my _____, we owe a lot of money in taxes this year.
   (A) calculations   (C) calculators
   (B) calculated   (D) calculate

2. Those _____ on my desk contain all the information we'll need for preparing our taxes.
   (A) filed   (C) file
   (B) files   (D) filing

3. It is usually advantageous for spouses to file their income taxes _____.
   (A) joints   (C) joint
   (B) jointly   (D) jointed

4. We didn't know we had to claim the interest from our savings account and were _____ for the error.
   (A) penalize   (C) penalty
   (B) penalizing   (D) penalized

5. The _____ of the forms took much less time than we expected.
   (A) preparatory   (C) prepared
   (B) preparation   (D) prepares

6. I didn't overpay my taxes this year so I didn't get a _____.
   (A) refunded   (C) refund
   (B) refundable   (D) refunds

Error Recognition

Choose the underlined word or phrase that should be rewritten and rewrite it.

7. The woman who <u>prepares</u> our taxes took such a long time to <u>fill out</u> our forms that we had to <u>filing</u> for an
             A   B   C
   extension of the <u>deadline</u>.
                   D

   _____

8. Monies <u>withheld</u> before the <u>deadline</u> to <u>file</u> taxes may be <u>refunding</u>.
          A   B   C   D

   _____

9. You can be <u>penalized</u> if you do not have enough of your earnings <u>withholding</u> from your salary, or if you leave
             A   B
   your <u>spouse's</u> income out of a joint <u>return</u>.
        C   D

   _____

10. Millions of Americans never <u>give up</u> the hope that, years after <u>filing</u> their tax forms, an error in <u>calculated</u> will
                                     A   B   C
    be found that results in a large <u>refund</u> from the government.
                                        D

   _____

Reading Comprehension

Read the following passage and write the words in the blanks below.

calculated	fill out	owe	refund
deadline	gave up	penalized	spouse
filed	joint	prepares	withhold

Every year, my wife gathers all of our pay stubs and expense reports and (11.) _____ to fill out our tax forms. She tries to finish them in March, well before the April 15th (12.) _____. It's a time-consuming process. There are receipts to find, records to organize, and forms to (13.) _____. When we first got married, we (14.) _____ separate returns. But now she marks me as her (15.) _____ and files the (16.) _____ return. It saves us money and saves me time!

My wife is very proud of her accuracy. The government has never sent the forms back with corrections. For several years now, we have received a (17.) _____. But this year, she (18.) _____ the numbers over and over again and found we had not paid enough taxes throughout the year. She didn't want to (19.) _____ any money. Finally, she (20.) _____ and sent in our check. Actually, it was my fault. I had changed jobs and didn't ask my employer to (21.) _____ enough money from my paychecks. I'm just glad we found and corrected the mistake before we got (22.) _____.

LISTENING COMPREHENSION

Listen to Track 24 of the Compact Disc to hear the statements for Lesson 24

Part I Picture

Look at the picture and listen to the sentences. Choose the sentence that best describes the picture.

23. Ⓐ Ⓑ Ⓒ Ⓓ

Part II Question—Response

Listen to the question and the three responses. Choose the response that best answers the question.

24. Ⓐ Ⓑ Ⓒ   25. Ⓐ Ⓑ Ⓒ

Part III Short Conversations

Listen to the short dialogs. Then read the question and choose the best answer.

26. When is the deadline for the project?
    (A) Tomorrow.
    (B) Next week.
    (C) This afternoon.
    (D) This morning.

27. Who prepares the taxes?
    (A) The husband.
    (B) The wife.
    (C) The husband and wife together.
    (D) An accountant.

Part IV Short Talks

Listen to the short talk. Then read the questions and choose the best answer.

28. Who is the speaker?
    (A) A tax preparer.
    (B) A government tax agent.
    (C) A tax filer.
    (D) An employer.

29. When can the refund check be expected?
    (A) In eighteen weeks.
    (B) Before six weeks.
    (C) In four weeks.
    (D) In ten weeks at the latest.

Financial Statements

1. **desire** v., to wish for
   a. We desire to have our own home.
   b. He desires to retire when he becomes forty.
2. **detail** v., to report or relate minutely or in particulars
   a. The office manager detailed each step of the inventory process at the staff meeting.
   b. Fabio created a financial statement that detailed every expected expenditure for the next quarter.
3. **forecast** n., a prediction of a future event; v., to estimate or calculate in advance
   a. The financial forecast indicates a deficit in the next quarter.
   b. Analysts forecast a strong economic outlook.
4. **level** n., a relative position or rank on a scale
   a. We have never had an accountant work at such a sophisticated level before.
   b. The meeting was only open to staff at the assistant director level or higher.
5. **overall** adj., regarded as a whole; general
   a. The company's overall expectations were out of proportion.
   b. Overall, our costs are running true to prediction.
6. **perspective** n., a mental view or outlook
   a. The budget statement will give the manager some perspective on where the costs of running the business are to be found.
   b. Joseph's accountant gave him some perspective as well as some data on how much he could expect to earn in his first year in business.
7. **project** v., to estimate or predict
   a. We need to project our earnings and expenses in order to plan next year's budget.
   b. The director projects that the company will need to hire ten new employees this year.
8. **realistic** adj., tending to or expressing an awareness of things as they really are
   a. Stefano found that an accurate accounting gave him a realistic idea of his business's financial direction.
   b. Realistic expectations are important when you review your financial statements.
9. **target** v., to establish as a goal; n., a goal
   a. We targeted March as the deadline for completing the financial statement.
   b. Most managers target desired income as the primary criterion for success.
10. **translation** n., the act or process of translating
    a. The translation of the statement from Japanese into English was very helpful.
    b. The accountant was able to provide a translation of the economic terms used in the meeting.
11. **typically** adv., acting in conformity to a type; characteristically
    a. Office expenses typically include such things as salaries, rent, and office supplies.
    b. The director typically dominates the staff meetings.
12. **yield** n., an amount produced; v., to produce a profit
    a. Henry's budget gave him the desired yield: a better indication of his expected profit.
    b. The company's investment yielded high returns.

Word Families

verb	desire	Our manager is trying to predict how many customers will desire our product over the next quarter.
noun	desire	Her desire for greater control of the business led her to discuss her need for more information with her accountant.
adjective	desirable	The category summary, while desirable, was time-consuming to prepare.

verb	detail	The job description details all the duties of this position.
noun	detail	The budget report needs to be accurate down to the last detail.
adjective	detailed	The director asked for a detailed description of our meeting.

verb	project	The budget summary helped us project our expenditures for the year.
noun	project	The financial project was time-consuming and challenging.
noun	projection	Maurice's projections for the upcoming fiscal year were not as helpful as we had hoped.

verb	realize	The plan helps her realize her dream of having the business turn a profit.
noun	reality	The financial statement reinforced the reality that our business is in deep trouble.
adjective	realistic	The accountant needs realistic numbers on which to base his plan.

verb	translate	The computer was able to translate data from the created spreadsheet into the spreadsheet program I prefer.
noun	translation	The translation of the document was provided at no charge.
adjective	translatable	The data was not translatable between programs and had to be entered by hand, which took hours.

noun	type	This type of business requires a lot of start-up money.
adjective	typical	Part of a category summary is defining the expenses that are typical of the business in question.
adverb	typically	Typically, we finished preparing the budget just in time to meet the deadline.

Incomplete Sentences

Choose the word that best completes the sentence.

1. Before we begin, I think we should all focus on the _____ outcome of this effort.
   (A) desirableness
   (B) desire
   (C) desired
   (D) desirability

2. The accountant can review all the _____ of the financial statement with you.
   (A) detailed
   (B) detailing
   (C) details
   (D) detail

3. The _____ figures for the next quarter will not be available until a week from tomorrow.
   (A) project
   (B) projected
   (C) projection
   (D) projects

4. The projected financial statement demonstrated to Susan that her business had a _____ chance of increasing its profit over the next two quarters.
   (A) realistic
   (B) realist
   (C) realistically
   (D) reality

5. To create our financial strategy, our consultant took the experiences of similar businesses and _____ relevant outcomes to our situation.
   (A) translatable
   (B) translation
   (C) translator
   (D) translated

6. Our business experienced a _____ fall in profits during the third quarter of the year.
   (A) typical
   (B) typically
   (C) type
   (D) typed

Error Recognition

Choose the underlined word or phrase that should be rewritten and rewrite it.

7. When the business did not <u>yield</u> the <u>desiring</u> profit <u>level</u>, the owner raised the daily sales <u>targets</u>.
   　　　　　　　　　　　　　　A　　　　　　B　　　　　　　　C　　　　　　　　　　　　　　　　　　　　　　　　　　D

   _____

8. The <u>projection</u> income statement <u>forecast</u> a <u>detailed</u> pathway for attaining the <u>desired</u> growth.
   　　　　　A　　　　　　　　　　　　　B　　　　C　　　　　　　　　　　　　　　　　　　D

   _____

9. A financial statement offers managers a <u>detailed</u> "snapshot" of what a <u>typical</u> day's sales must be in order to
   　　　　　　　　　　　　　　　　　　　　A　　　　　　　　　　　　　　　　B

   set a <u>reality</u> income <u>target</u>.
   　　　　C　　　　　　　　D

   _____

10. By posting the financial statement, the director gave the staff some <u>perspective</u> on how sales <u>targets</u>
   　　　　　　　　　　　　　　　　　　　　　　　　　　　　　　　　　　　　　A　　　　　　　　　　　　B

   <u>translation</u> into <u>desired</u> financial goals.
   　　　C　　　　　　　　D

   _____

Reading Comprehension

Read the following passage and write the words in the blanks below.

desired	level	projected	translate
detailed	overall	realistic	typical
forecasts	perspective	target	yield

A business budget focuses on future profits and future capital requirements. A budget can help the business owner determine the amount of profit the business is expected to make, the amount of sales it will take to reach a goal, and what (11.) _____ of expenses are attached to those sales. A business establishes a (12.) _____, a goal to work toward. A business (13.) _____ the sales that will be needed to reach this target.

Projecting or planning ahead is part of (14.) _____ business planning. When creating a (15.) _____ income statement, a business owner tries to determine how to reach the (16.) _____ target. The annual profit must be sufficient to (17.) _____ the owner a return for his or her time spent operating the business, plus a return on the investment. The owner's target income is the sum of a reasonable salary for the time spent running the business and a normal return on the amount invested in the firm.

After projecting the income needed, the business owner has to (18.) _____ the target profit into a net sales figure for the forecasted period. The owner has to determine whether this sales volume is (19.) _____. One useful technique is to break down the required annual sales into a daily sales figure to get a better (20.) _____ of the sales required to yield the annual profit.

At this stage in the financial plan, the owner should create a (21.) _____ picture of the firm's expected operating expenses. Many books and business organizations give (22.) _____ operating statistics data, based on a percentage of net sales. The business's accountant can help you assign dollar values to anticipated expenses.

Developing a projected income statement is an important part of any financial plan, as the process forces the business owner to examine the firm's future profitability.

LISTENING COMPREHENSION

Listen to Track 25 of the Compact Disc to hear the statements for Lesson 25

Part I Picture

Look at the picture and listen to the sentences. Choose the sentence that best describes the picture.

23. Ⓐ Ⓑ Ⓒ Ⓓ

Part II Question—Response

Listen to the question and the three responses. Choose the response that best answers the question.

24. Ⓐ Ⓑ Ⓒ   25. Ⓐ Ⓑ Ⓒ

Part III Short Conversations

Listen to the short dialogs. Then read the question and choose the best answer.

26. What is the speakers' opinion of the sales targets?
    (A) They are realistic.
    (B) They are too high.
    (C) They are easy to reach.
    (D) They are typical.

27. What is the woman doing?
    (A) Developing a project report.
    (B) Preparing a financial statement.
    (C) Making a weather forecast.
    (D) Writing an expense report.

Part IV Short Talks

Listen to the short talk. Then read the questions and choose the best answer.

28. Who is this talk directed at?
    (A) Large companies.
    (B) Financial advisors.
    (C) Small business owners.
    (D) Finance companies.

29. When does a business typically become profitable?
    (A) During the first five years.
    (B) During the first year.
    (C) After five years.
    (D) After two years.

Word Review #5   Lessons 21–25 Financing and Budgeting

Choose the word that best completes the sentence.

1. The Small Business Administration will help you to arrange to _____ money to start a business.
    (A) borrow
    (B) borrowed
    (C) borrowing
    (D) borrower

2. When we _____ a loan, we found very good terms.
    (A) take out
    (B) took out
    (C) taken out
    (D) taking out

3. Most people get nervous when someone is _____ their books.
    (A) audit
    (B) audits
    (C) audited
    (D) auditing

4. Sometimes it is difficult to _____ of bad investments.
    (A) pull up
    (B) pull out
    (C) pull at
    (D) pull to

5. I prefer _____ in social-conscience funds.
    (A) invest
    (B) investment
    (C) investing
    (D) investor

6. When the Dow is dropping, investors need to be _____.
    (A) resource
    (B) resources
    (C) resourceful
    (D) resourcefulness

7. Sometimes it is difficult to understand how the government _____ tax liability.
    (A) calculating
    (B) calculations
    (C) calculators
    (D) calculates

8. One decision with tax returns is whether to _____ itemizing in favor of the standard deduction.
    (A) give up
    (B) giving up
    (C) gave up
    (D) given up

9. The company's _____ earnings over the next six months were exciting.
    (A) project
    (B) projects
    (C) projection
    (D) projected

10. Some parts of the tax code are so confusing that they need _____.
    (A) translate
    (B) translates
    (C) translated
    (D) translation

Choose the underlined word or phrase that should be rewritten and rewrite it.

11. Banks are getting more demanding about minimum <u>down payments</u> they <u>accepting</u>, comparing <u>signatures</u> on
                                              A   **B**   **C**
    checks, and imposing <u>restrictions</u> on withdrawals.
                         D

    _____

12. When you are <u>aggressively</u> <u>building up</u> a <u>client</u> list, you need to <u>budgeted</u> extra funds for entertaining.
                               A   **B**   **C**   **D**

    _____

13. A <u>long-term</u> investment <u>portfolio</u> should include some <u>conservatively</u> funds with reinvested <u>dividends</u>.
        A   **B**   **C**   **D**

    _____

14. Financial statements should include <u>realistic</u> <u>targets</u> and a <u>detailing</u> <u>forecast</u>.
                                     A   **B**   **C**   **D**

    _____

15. Bank customers should use <u>cautious</u> about maintaining a <u>balance</u> so low that the bank <u>deducts</u> additional
        　　　　　　　　　　　　　A　　　　　　　　　　　　　　　　　B　　　　　　　　　　　　　　　　　C

    <u>penalties</u>.
    　D
    _____

16. Investing in a <u>conservative</u> fund requires a patient <u>attitude</u> and a <u>commitment</u> to not <u>pulled out</u> your
        　　　　　　　A　　　　　　　　　　　　　　　　　　B　　　　　　　C　　　　　　　　D

    investment.
    _____

17. <u>Filing</u> your tax <u>returning</u> after the <u>deadline</u> can cost you more in <u>penalties</u>.
    　A　　　　　　B　　　　　　　　　C　　　　　　　　　　　　　　　　D
    _____

18. To reach your <u>desired</u> goal, check the <u>overall</u> <u>yielding</u> of the <u>fund</u> you are considering.
    　　　　　　　　A　　　　　　　　　　　B　　　C　　　　　　D
    _____

19. Filing a <u>joint</u> <u>return</u> with your <u>spouse</u> could leave you <u>owe</u> more than filing individually.
    　　　　　A　　B　　　　　　　C　　　　　　　　　D
    _____

20. <u>Filling up</u> a <u>withholding</u> form <u>wisely</u> can cost you less in tax payments or increase the size of your <u>refund</u>.
    　A　　　　　B　　　　　　　C　　　　　　　　　　　　　　　　　　　　　　　　　　　　　　　　　　　D
    _____

Property and Departments

1. **adjacent** adj., next to
   a. My office is adjacent to the receptionist area on the third floor.
   b. The office manager found it very efficient to have the copier adjacent to the mail room.

2. **collaboration** n., the act of working with someone
   a. The manager had never seen such effective collaboration between two groups.
   b. We believe that it was our collaboration that enabled us to achieve such favorable results.

3. **concentrate** v., to focus; to think about
   a. In his quiet, corner office, the manager could finally concentrate and finish his work.
   b. We should concentrate our efforts on the last quarter of the year.

4. **conducive** adj., contributing to; leading to
   a. The new office arrangement is much more conducive to work than the dark, depressing space the company had before.
   b. Arranging chairs so that participants can see each other easily is conducive to open communication.

5. **disruption** n., interruption; disturbance
   a. If there are no disruptions, the office renovations will be finished this week.
   b. The strike caused a disruption in production at the factory.

6. **hamper** v., to impede or interfere
   a. When the weight of the freezing rain broke the telephone lines, the telemarketers' jobs were seriously hampered.
   b. The lack of supplies hampered our ability to finish on schedule.

7. **inconsiderately** adv., rudely; impolitely
   a. The manager inconsiderately scheduled the meeting for late Friday afternoon.
   b. Mr. Peterson inconsiderately disrupted the meeting by asking a lot of irrelevant questions.

8. **lobby** n., an anteroom, foyer, or waiting room
   a. The salesperson waited in the busy lobby for the buyer to see him.
   b. The reception area was moved from the lobby of the building to the third floor.

9. **move up** v., to advance, improve position
   a. As the employee moved up the corporate ladder, she never forgot where she started.
   b. In order to move up in the company, employees had to demonstrate their loyalty.

10. **open to** adj., receptive to; vulnerable
    a. What I valued most in my previous supervisor was that she was always open to ideas and suggestions.
    b. Since the junior executive was still on probation, he was open to much scrutiny and criticism.

11. **opt** v., to choose, to decide on
    a. The operations manager opted for the less expensive office design.
    b. If Mary opts to join that department, you will be working together.

12. **scrutiny** n., close, careful examination
    a. After a great deal of scrutiny, the manager decided that the employee's work had improved considerably.
    b. Jim left his old job because he found it difficult to work under the close scrutiny of his boss.

Word Families

verb	collaborate	If we collaborate on this project, you will be sure to receive credit.
noun	collaboration	Collaboration often brings about results that no one could have predicted.
adjective	collaborative	The new project is a collaborative effort among several departments.

verb	concentrate	Some people find it difficult to concentrate when there is a lot of noise and activity around them.
noun	concentration	The concentration of a large percentage of the company's funds in just a few areas left several departments underfunded.
adjective	concentrated	With some concentrated effort, we should be able to finish this work by the deadline.

verb	disrupt	Try not to disrupt the meeting being held in the sales department.
noun	disruption	I'm sorry for the disruption, but this phone call is very important.
adjective	disruptive	Having to temporarily move the offices proved to be very disruptive and sales decreased during that quarter.

noun	inconsiderateness	The inconsiderateness of many of the customers caused several employees to quit their jobs.
adjective	inconsiderate	Would it be inconsiderate to ask to use your office while you are away?
adverb	inconsiderately	John inconsiderately looked through his coworker's mail before putting it on his desk.

verb	opt	When we moved offices, I opted for the one without a window.
noun	option	Presented with several options, we chose the one that required the least amount of effort.
adjective	optional	Attendance at tomorrow's meeting is optional for the people working in this department.

verb	scrutinize	The auditor carefully scrutinized the financial records.
noun	scrutiny	Employees under constant scrutiny tend to perform worse than those employees who have more freedom.
adjective	inscrutable	You can never tell what she is thinking, since her facial expressions are inscrutable.

Incomplete Sentences

Choose the word that best completes the sentence.

1. The data entry clerk is so accustomed to working by herself that I really doubt if she is capable of _____ on this project.
   (A) collaborated
   (B) collaborating
   (C) collaborator
   (D) collaborates

2. Sue always _____ so hard on her work that she forgets where she is.
   (A) concentrated
   (B) concentrates
   (C) concentration
   (D) concentrating

3. The constant flow of traffic by the researcher's desk proved to be very _____.
   (A) disruptive
   (B) disrupts
   (C) disruption
   (D) disrupted

4. The employee lounge is for everyone's enjoyment so please don't use it _____.
   (A) inconsiderate
   (B) inconsiderateness
   (C) inconsiderately
   (D) inconsideration

5. Some people always _____ for the easy way out.
   (A) opt
   (B) option
   (C) optional
   (D) options

6. After close _____ of the options, the managers chose an advertising company to do all the publicity for the new campaign.
   (A) scrutinize
   (B) scrutinizing
   (C) scrutiny
   (D) scrutable

Error Recognition

Choose the underlined word or phrase that should be rewritten and rewrite it.

7. <u>Moving up</u> to another position will remove Ms. Sams from the <u>scrutinize</u> of her current boss and will allow her
      A   B
   to <u>concentrate</u> on other <u>options</u>.
      C   D

   _____

8. The new office <u>layout</u> is more <u>conducive</u> to <u>collaborated</u> between the different <u>departmental</u> teams.
             A   B   C   D

   _____

9. The manager was <u>open to</u> any ideas about how to lessen the <u>disrupted</u> from the construction in the <u>lobby</u>,
                  A   B   C
   which was <u>hampering</u> the staff's work.
                D

   _____

10. After much <u>scrutiny</u> of the layout designs, the president <u>opted</u> for an open work space, knowing that some
                 A   B
    employees might have difficulty <u>concentrating</u> and find the decision <u>inconsideration</u> of their needs.
                                            C   D

    _____

Reading Comprehension

Read the following passage and write the words in the blanks below.

adjacent	conducive	inconsiderate	open to
collaboration	disruptive	lobby	opting
concentrate	hampered	move up	scrutinized

The layout of any office has an important influence on the atmosphere and operations in the company. The shipping department most likely will not be located next to the customer service department. The noise would be too (11.) _____. Likewise, locating a kitchen (12.) _____ to the (13.) _____ would be (14.) _____ for office visitors and clients. The marketing department is often situated close to the sales department due to their necessary (15.) _____.

Employee productivity may be (16.) _____ or improved by the arrangement of workers and departments. Employees vie for corner offices as they (17.) _____ the corporate ladder. They want to be accessible to top management, but not so close that everything that they do is (18.) _____. At the same time, many companies are (19.) _____ for open work spaces versus traditional offices. Open spaces are more (20.) _____ to team projects, where employees interact freely. However, some employees feel that such an environment makes it difficult to (21.) _____. Employees know under which conditions they work the best. If employers are willing to listen and are (22.) _____ suggestions, they can take advantage of office space and help employees to realize their full potential.

LISTENING COMPREHENSION

Listen to Track 26 of the Compact Disc to hear the statements for Lesson 26

Part I Picture

Look at the picture and listen to the sentences. Choose the sentence that best describes the picture.

23. Ⓐ Ⓑ Ⓒ Ⓓ

Part II Question—Response

Listen to the question and the three responses. Choose the response that best answers the question.

24. Ⓐ Ⓑ Ⓒ   25. Ⓐ Ⓑ Ⓒ

Part III Short Conversations

Listen to the short dialogs. Then read the question and choose the best answer.

26. What does the man think of the current lobby?
    (A) People conduct a lot of conversations there.
    (B) It's quite pleasant.
    (C) More people should use it.
    (D) It's not a good place for conversations.

27. What did the director do?
    (A) She disrupted the meeting.
    (B) She invested in the stock market.
    (C) She went home in the middle of the afternoon.
    (D) She stopped the party.

Part IV Short Talks

Listen to the short talk. Then read the questions and choose the best answer.

28. What is this talk about?
    (A) How to encourage collaboration.
    (B) How to increase productivity.
    (C) How to concentrate.
    (D) How to design an office.

29. What is the problem with a large, open office?
    (A) It isn't conducive to collaboration.
    (B) It doesn't include options.
    (C) Work is easily disrupted.
    (D) It isn't adjacent to a lobby.

Words to learn

adhere to
agenda
bring up
conclude
go ahead
goal
lengthy
matter
periodically
priority
progress
waste

Board Meetings and Committees

1. **adhere to** v., to follow; to pay attention to
    a. The chairman never adhered to his own rules.
    b. The best committee members are those who adhere to the time limits and speak only when they have something important to add.

2. **agenda** n., a list of topics to be discussed
    a. The board was able to cover fifteen items on the agenda.
    b. The agenda was sent out three weeks ago so that everyone could prepare for the meeting.

3. **bring up** v., to introduce a topic
    a. Just as the meeting was about to finish, the manager brought up a controversial issue.
    b. No one brought up the resignation of the director.

4. **conclude** v., to stop; to come to a decision
    a. The committee members concluded the meeting early so that they could finish their budgets.
    b. After long discussions, the board has concluded that the project has to be canceled.

5. **go ahead** v., to proceed with; n., permission to do something
    a. Five of the six members felt that they should go ahead with the plan.
    b. The manager was just waiting for the go ahead from her boss before mailing the report.

6. **goal** n., objective, purpose
    a. Employees are expected to analyze and evaluate their annual goals.
    b. The director had to report to the committee that his department would not reach its goal of 35 percent growth.

7. **lengthy** adj., long in time, duration, or distance
    a. After lengthy discussions, the chairperson was reelected for another term.
    b. The report was so lengthy that members had to take it home and read it over the weekend.

8. **matter** n., an item, issue, topic of interest
    a. If there are no other matters to discuss, we will conclude the meeting.
    b. This is not the place to bring up personal matters.

9. **periodically** adv., from time to time
    a. The group tried to meet periodically.
    b. Periodically, new members were nominated to the committee.

10. **priority** n., something of importance, something that should be done before other things
    a. Since the remaining issues were not a priority, the group decided to move them to the next week's agenda.
    b. The manager was ineffective because she was unable to set priorities.

11. **progress** n., a movement forward; v., to move forward on something, especially work or a project
    a. The executive committee asked each group to present a report showing their progress for the year.
    b. Progress is being made on the annual report; we expect to see a finished product by next week.

12. **waste** v., not to use wisely; n., not worthwhile
    a. Without a leader, the group members wasted time and energy trying to organize themselves.
    b. The meeting wasn't a waste of time, but the members had hoped to accomplish more than they did.

Word Families

verb	adhere	The chairperson asked us to adhere to the items on the agenda.
noun	adherence	Your adherence to these guidelines would be appreciated.

verb	conclude	To conclude, we must all focus on the year ahead of us and the challenges that we will face.
noun	conclusion	Unfortunately, the conclusion of the meeting was that they needed to downsize their workforce.
adjective	conclusive	There is no conclusive evidence to back up the report.

verb	lengthen	Ms. Greene decided to lengthen the time allotted to the meeting to allow each person a chance to speak.
noun	length	Because of its length, we decided not to read the entire report at the meeting.
adjective	lengthy	A presentation that is too lengthy will only put the audience to sleep.

noun	period	The sales reports for the current period are excellent.
adjective	periodic	They received periodic updates from the overseas licensees.
adverb	periodically	The employee checked his messages periodically during the week-long seminar.

verb	prioritize	Once the team members learned to prioritize their work, they were much more productive.
noun	priority	The committee member has difficulties setting priorities for herself.
adjective	prior	The director did not give much attention to Ellen's proposal as he had several prior matters to attend to.

verb	progress	Everyone was surprised at how quickly the meeting had progressed.
noun	progression	The quick progression of events didn't surprise anyone.
adjective	progressive	The new president is very progressive and is always looking for ways to improve the business.

Incomplete Sentences

Choose the word that best completes the sentence.

1. When using these facilities, please _____ to the rules posted by the door.
   (A) adhere   (C) adherence
   (B) adhering   (D) adhered

2. As the chairman stood to give his _____, everyone in the room was listening.
   (A) conclusion   (C) conclusive
   (B) conclude   (D) concluding

3. George decided to _____ his business trip by a few days so he could do some sightseeing.
   (A) length   (C) lengthy
   (B) lengthen   (D) lengthened

4. The original members of the committee met _____ for lunch or dinner.
   (A) period   (C) periodically
   (B) periods   (D) periodic

5. As her first _____, the committee chairwoman wanted to attract new, energetic members to the group.
   (A) prior   (C) prioritize
   (B) priority   (D) prioritized

6. Even as they _____ through the hundreds of pages of supporting material, the committee was still not convinced that the project was justified.
   (A) progression   (C) progresses
   (B) progressed   (D) progressive

Error Recognition

Choose the underlined word or phrase that should be rewritten and rewrite it.

7. The chairman was incapable of <u>adhere</u> to the <u>agenda</u> and his meetings were typically <u>lengthy</u> and <u>inconclusive</u>.
                                    A   **B**   **C**   **D**

   _____

8. After they received the <u>go ahead</u>, the team drew up an <u>agenda</u> and met <u>periodically</u> to check on each
                                       A   **B**   **C**

   member's <u>progression</u>.
           D

   _____

9. Even after the <u>matter</u> was given <u>prioritize</u> status, the results proved to be <u>inconclusive</u> and the project a <u>waste</u>
                       A   **B**   **C**   **D**

   of money.

   _____

10. The most important new <u>matter</u> were <u>brought up</u> and integrated with the existing <u>priorities</u> and <u>goals</u>.
                                            A   **B**   **C**   **D**

    _____

Reading Comprehension

Read the following passage and write the words in the blanks below.

adhered to	concluded	lengthy	priority
agenda	go ahead	matters	progress
brought up	goals	periodically	waste

Committee meetings are a frequent and necessary event at almost every company. In order for meetings to be productive and not viewed as a (11.) _____ of time, they should be run efficiently. Critical to the success of any meeting is the (12.) _____. Everyone who attends the meeting should be aware of the agenda and be prepared to discuss the (13.) _____ at hand and the (14.) _____ to be accomplished. To avoid (15.) _____ discussions, time frames should be set and (16.) _____.

The meeting is called to order by the chairperson. Attendance is taken and agenda items are (17.) _____ one by one. In general, (18.) _____ topics should be at the beginning of the agenda, to make sure that the attendees are able to discuss them fully and make timely decisions. Once the (19.) _____ is given for a plan or project, a plan of action is developed. The committee must then (20.) _____ check up on the (21.) _____ of that plan. The meeting is (22.) _____ without any outstanding issues and a date for the next meeting is set.

LISTENING COMPREHENSION

Listen to Track 27 of the Compact Disc to hear the statements for Lesson 27

Part I Picture

Look at the picture and listen to the sentences. Choose the sentence that best describes the picture.

23. Ⓐ Ⓑ Ⓒ Ⓓ

Part II Question—Response

Listen to the question and the three responses. Choose the response that best answers the question.

24. Ⓐ Ⓑ Ⓒ   25. Ⓐ Ⓑ Ⓒ

Part III Short Conversations

Listen to the short dialogs. Then read the question and choose the best answer.

26. What do the speakers say about the meeting?
    (A) They had a good time.
    (B) A lot was accomplished.
    (C) Important matters were discussed.
    (D) It was too long.

27. What are the speakers discussing?
    (A) New goals.
    (B) An agenda.
    (C) Top priorities.
    (D) Plans for next year.

Part IV Short Talks

Listen to the short talk. Then read the questions and choose the best answer.

28. What is this talk about?
    (A) How to have a better staff meeting.
    (B) How to make speeches.
    (C) How to write an agenda.
    (D) How to develop guidelines.

29. What are the listeners asked to do?
    (A) Make long speeches.
    (B) Discuss personal matters.
    (C) Bring something to the meeting.
    (D) Follow the agenda.

Lesson 28

Quality Control

1. **brand** n., an identifying mark or label; a trademark
   a. Consumers often buy highly advertised brands of athletic shoes.
   b. All brands of aspirin are the same.
2. **conform** v., to match specifications or qualities
   a. The quality control manager insisted that every product that left the plant conform to the company's rigorous standards.
   b. Our safety standards conform to those established by the government.
3. **defect** n., an imperfection or flaw
   a. Because of a defect in stitching, the entire suit was thrown out.
   b. One way to sell a product with a defect is by labeling it as such and reducing the price.
4. **enhance** v., to make more attractive or valuable
   a. The reason behind quality control is to enhance the company's reputation for superior products.
   b. A stylish color enhances the appeal of a car.
5. **garment** n., an article of clothing
   a. Every garment must be carefully inspected for defects before it is shipped.
   b. The garment workers are accountable for production mistakes.
6. **inspect** v., to look at closely; to examine carefully or officially
   a. A quality control agent who does not inspect every product carefully can ruin his company's reputation.
   b. Children's car seats are thoroughly inspected and tested for safety before being put on the market.
7. **perceptive** adj., able to see or understand
   a. Dora always hires good workers because she is very perceptive about people's abilities.
   b. It takes a perceptive person to be a good manager.
8. **repel** v., to keep away; to fight against
   a. Umbrellas that do not repel water should never be passed through quality control.
   b. Faulty products repel repeat customers.
9. **take back** v., to return something; to withdraw or retract
   a. Good quality control significantly limits the number of products taken back for a refund.
   b. The quality inspector took the shoddy work back to the assembly line to confront the workers.
10. **throw out** v., to dispose of
    a. It is cheaper to throw out shoddy products than to lose customers.
    b. The factory decided to throw out hundreds of lightbulbs that might have been damaged, rather than lose customers.
11. **uniformly** adv., in the same way; consistently
    a. The products are checked to make sure they are uniformly packaged before they leave the factory.
    b. The food at chain restaurants is uniformly prepared so that customers will always find the same quality at each restaurant.
12. **wrinkle** n., a crease, ridge, or furrow, especially in skin or fabric
    a. A wrinkle that is ironed into a permanent-press product will annoy the consumer each time the garment is worn.
    b. A wrinkle in the finish can be repaired more economically before a sale than after.

Word Families

verb	defect	Disgusted by the poor quality of products at the factory, the employee defected to a plant that took pride in its work.
noun	defect	Even a small defect can cause a product to fail.
adjective	defective	Good quality control employees will notice defective machinery before a serious breakdown occurs.

verb	inspect	We must inspect every product before we sell it.
noun	inspection	Each employee must conduct a careful inspection.
noun	inspector	The inspector leaves his identification number on the product to ensure accountability.

verb	perceive	The worker perceived that the stitching on the seams could not withstand normal strain.
noun	perception	Customers' perception of quality is often based on their experience with a given store or brand.
adjective	perceptive	Perceptive workers are excellent quality control inspectors.

verb	repel	A quality raincoat can repel rain and keep you dry.
noun	repellent	Testing insect repellent is never a pleasant task.
adjective	repellent	Testing stain removers can be repellent to workers because of the toxic fumes.

noun	uniform	The employees at this company are required to wear uniforms.
adjective	uniform	A successful company will ensure the uniform quality of its products.
adverb	uniformly	All of our company's products must be uniformly labeled.

verb	wrinkle	Linen is not a practical fabric because it wrinkles easily.
noun	wrinkle	Inspect garments carefully and remove any wrinkles that you find.
adjective	wrinkled	Garments become wrinkled after they have been tried on several times at the store.

Incomplete Sentences

Choose the word that best completes the sentence.

1. _____ equipment on a new car is not only costly, but also dangerous.
   (A) Defect
   (B) Defector
   (C) Defective
   (D) Defection

2. Rebecca is known as _____ #321 among her quality control coworkers.
   (A) inspect
   (B) inspection
   (C) inspector
   (D) inspecting

3. An employee who _____ his job as important performs better than one who wants only a paycheck.
   (A) perceives
   (B) perceived
   (C) perceptive
   (D) perception

4. Agnes was _____ by the odor of the waterproofing.
   (A) repel
   (B) repellent
   (C) repelled
   (D) repelling

5. Standardized products are _____ in appearance.
   (A) uniforms
   (B) uniformly
   (C) uniform
   (D) unformed

6. Sarah wants to return her dress to the store because it _____ too easily.
   (A) wrinkles
   (B) wrinkly
   (C) wrinkle
   (D) wrinkling

Error Recognition

Choose the underlined word or phrase that should be rewritten and rewrite it.

7. Ms. Nell <u>inspected</u> every <u>brand</u> of jeans that her company manufactured and <u>threw out</u> any with <u>defective</u>.
         A   **B**   **C**   **D**

   _____

8. When the <u>inspect</u> checked the <u>garments</u>, he found a few with <u>wrinkles</u>, which he <u>took back</u> to the presser.
         A   **B**   **C**   **D**

   _____

9. The color of the <u>garment</u> <u>enhancing</u> its visual appeal, its <u>water-repellent</u> nature made
           A   **B**   **C**
   it practical, and its <u>brand</u> made it fashionable.
           D

   _____

10. When one of the <u>inspectors</u> found evidence of a leak in the most expensive <u>brand</u> of duplicating machines, he
            A   **B**
    was <u>repellent</u> by the idea of having to <u>throw out</u> the equipment.
        C   **D**

    _____

Reading Comprehension

Read the following passage and write the words in the blanks below.

brand	enhance	perceive	throws out
conform	garment	repel	uniform
defects	inspect	take back	wrinkle

Alex is excited about his new job with Parapluie Rain Wear. As quality control manager, his job is to make sure that his company's goods (11.) _____ to standardized quality criteria and are free from (12.) _____. Before any (13.) _____ leaves the factory, Alex must (14.) _____ it. He knows that if he (15.) _____ a damaged garment before a customer sees it, he will (16.) _____ his company's reputation and increase the demand for their products. Alex must ensure that all products meet certain criteria: A customer who buys a raincoat that does not (17.) _____ rain will probably (18) _____ the raincoat to the store and buy another (19.) _____. The same is true if the seams are not sewn tightly or the color is not (20.) _____. Alex knows that, in addition to keeping out rain, the product must be attractive to look at and to touch. It should not (21.) _____ easily, and it should last a long time. Alex knows that it is important for customers to (22.) _____ his company's goods as quality products so that his company will profit—and he can get a raise.

LISTENING COMPREHENSION

Listen to Track 28 of the Compact Disc to hear the statements for Lesson 28

Part I Picture

Look at the picture and listen to the sentences. Choose the sentence that best describes the picture.

23. Ⓐ Ⓑ Ⓒ Ⓓ

Part II Question—Response

Listen to the question and the three responses. Choose the response that best answers the question.

24. Ⓐ Ⓑ Ⓒ   25. Ⓐ Ⓑ Ⓒ

Part III Short Conversations

Listen to the short dialogs. Then read the question and choose the best answer.

26. What does the company do with garments that have defects?
    (A) It exchanges them for better products.
    (B) It throws them out.
    (C) It stores them at the factory.
    (D) It sells them at a discount.

27. What is inspected?
    (A) Only the best products.
    (B) Uniforms.
    (C) Every item.
    (D) Test products.

Part IV Short Talks

Listen to the short talk. Then read the questions and choose the best answer.

28. Who is this talk directed at?
    (A) Store employees.
    (B) Factory workers.
    (C) Product inspectors.
    (D) Customers.

29. When is a product inspected?
    (A) When it reaches the store.
    (B) Before it leaves the factory.
    (C) Before the customer takes it home.
    (D) When the customer returns it.

Product Development

Words to learn

anxious
ascertain
assume
decade
examine
experiment
logical
research
responsibility
solve
supervisor
sytematically

1. **anxious** adj., worried
    a. The developers were anxious about the sales forecast for the new product.
    b. The graphic designers tried to be calm during their presentation, but you could tell they were anxious it would not be well received.

2. **ascertain** v., to discover; to find out for certain
    a. A necessary part of product development is to ascertain whether the product is safe.
    b. A customer survey will help to ascertain whether there is a market for the product.

3. **assume** v., to take upon oneself; to believe to be true
    a. The young man felt ready to assume the new responsibilities of his promotion.
    b. A company should assume nothing about the market but instead pay close attention to research results.

4. **decade** n., a period of ten years
    a. After a decade of trying, the company finally developed a vastly superior product.
    b. Each decade seems to have its own fad products.

5. **examine** v., to interrogate; to scrutinize
    a. Before marketing a new product, researchers must carefully examine it from every aspect.
    b. Good researchers have to examine every possible option, including some that seem bizarre.

6. **experiment** v., to try out a new procedure or idea; n., a test or trial
    a. Product developers must conduct hundreds of experiments in their research.
    b. After designing a new product, researchers continue experimenting to determine whether it has other uses.

7. **logical** adj., formally valid; using orderly reasoning
    a. It is only logical for a research and development team to concentrate on one or two new products at a time.
    b. In addition to logical thinkers, a good research and development team should include a few dreamers.

8. **research** n., the act of collecting information about a particular subject.
    a. Part of the research the team does is to determine whether similar products are already on the market.
    b. For toy manufacturers, research can be pure fun.

9. **responsibility** n., a task
    a. The product development department has a huge responsibility to be sure that the product is safe, even if used improperly.
    b. Another responsibility of product development is to ensure that there will be a demand for the product.

10. **solve** v., to find a solution, explanation, or answer
    a. Researchers find that every time they solve one problem, two more result.
    b. One of the biggest problems to solve is why people would want to own the new product.

11. **supervisor** n., an administrator in charge
    a. The department supervisor has to balance his department's responsibilities in order to keep the president satisfied with its progress.
    b. A good supervisor gets his team to work with him, not just for him.

12. **systematically** adv., methodically; following a system
    a. Once the creative development is completed, the department works systematically toward making the idea a reality.
    b. While creative thinking is necessary, analyzing a problem systematically is indispensable.

Word Families

noun	anxiety	The level of anxiety was high when the experimental car underwent road tests.
adjective	anxious	If you feel anxious, sit down and try to relax.
adverb	anxiously	The stockholders anxiously awaited the release of the new drug that, if successful, would make their stocks more valuable.

verb	assume	Product developers should assume nothing that research does not support.
noun	assumption	Most consumers make the assumption that, unless they are warned otherwise, the products they buy are safe.
adjective	assumed	The assumed results should be kept confidential until the product is retested.

verb	experiment	The product developer had experimented with improving electronic equipment since she was in the sixth grade.
noun	experimentation	Hi-tech companies are constantly involved in experimentation with new products in order to stay ahead of their competitors.
adjective	experimental	The new computer was experimental, so you could try it at the store, but you couldn't buy one.

noun	logic	Most problems can be easily solved by the application of logic.
adjective	logical	It was logical to put Martha in charge of the project as she had spent so much time developing the idea.
adverb	logically	I thought Mr. Lee answered the question quite logically.

noun	responsibility	Although the ultimate responsibility falls on the supervisor, every employee shares it.
adjective	responsible	The researcher responsible for passing the defective product has joined the cafeteria workers' assembly line.
adverb	responsibly	Product designers must act responsibly when they consider how a product might be misused.

verb	supervise	It's important to carefully supervise the collection of research data to ensure its accuracy.
noun	supervisor	George hopes to be promoted to supervisor of his department.
noun	supervision	Many employees do better work when they are under less supervision.

Incomplete Sentences

Choose the word that best completes the sentence.

1. The product development team were _____ that the competition would produce a similar product and get it on the market before they did.
   (A) anxious   (C) anxiousness
   (B) anxiously   (D) anxiety

2. The designer made the _____ that people are attracted to boxes in primary colors.
   (A) assumption   (C) assuming
   (B) assumed   (D) assume

3. The _____ model of the new car drew attention wherever it was shown.
   (A) experiment   (C) experimental
   (B) experimentation   (D) experimenting

4. Our team came up with the most _____ solution to the problem.
   (A) logic   (C) logically
   (B) logical   (D) logician

5. The new employee accepted _____ for not discovering a trademarked toy exactly like his own company's.
   (A) responsible   (C) responsibly
   (B) responsibility (D) response

6. Mr. Oh did not give the project adequate _____ and the product never made it to market.
   (A) supervisor   (C) supervised
   (B) supervision   (D) supervise

Error Recognition

Choose the underlined word or phrase that should be rewritten and rewrite it.

7. For more than a <u>decade</u> the young woman had <u>systematically</u> <u>experimented</u> with ways to generate more
            A   B   C
   power from trash, <u>to solve</u> two problems at once.
                  D

   _____

8. When the new manager <u>assumed</u> his new <u>responsible</u>, he <u>anxiously</u> called in his employees to help him to
                      A   B   C
   <u>solve</u> some problems with safety issues on the recently developed toy line.
    D

   _____

9. <u>Research</u> is always based on <u>assumptions</u>, which are <u>examined</u> to <u>ascertaining</u> their validity.
    A   B   C   D

   _____

10. To <u>examination</u> whether his <u>supervisor's</u> ideas were on target, one of the team members developed a <u>systematic</u>
       A   B   C
    plan to <u>ascertain</u> whether a hidden defect existed.
         D

    _____

Reading Comprehension

Read the following passage and write the words in the blanks below.

anxious	decade	logical	solve
ascertain	examining	researched	supervisor
assume	experiments	responsible	systematic

Michael was worried about his promotion. He needn't have been (11.) _____ though. He had worked in the Product Development Division for nine and a half years, almost a (12.) _____. He knew the department inside out. Now, however, he would be the director. As a member of the department, he had only to do what his (13.) _____ told him. As the director, he would be the person (14.) _____ for the success of his department. Fears are not always (15.) _____; in fact, they are often illogical.

As his first task, he decided to conduct a (16.) _____ analysis of the steps required to develop new products, and to organize the tasks into a logical order. The first step in developing new products would be to (17.) _____ what kind of products the market needed and what problems existed with the products currently being used.

The second task would be to find out how best to examine these problems and determine what kind of research would be needed to (18.) _____ the problems. It would be better to say, reexamine these problems, since most of these unsolved problems had been thoroughly (19.) _____ over the years.

The third task would be to look at the quality and characteristics of the competition's products. By (20.) _____ the competition's products, he would know where he should improve. And the final task would be to decide how to gather the most substantial information from the fewest number of (21.) _____. Michael smiled and sat back to read over his list. Confident that he had a good team and a good plan, he felt ready to (22.) _____ his new job.

LISTENING COMPREHENSION

Listen to Track 29 of the Compact Disc to hear the statements for Lesson 29

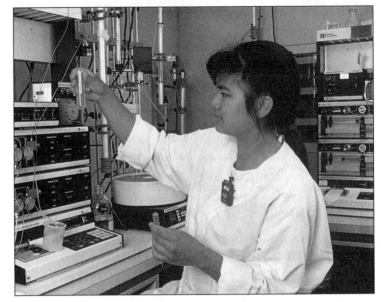

Part I Picture

Look at the picture and listen to the sentences. Choose the sentence that best describes the picture.

23. Ⓐ Ⓑ Ⓒ Ⓓ

Part II Question—Response

Listen to the question and the three responses. Choose the response that best answers the question.

24. Ⓐ Ⓑ Ⓒ   25. Ⓐ Ⓑ Ⓒ

Part III Short Conversations

Listen to the short dialogs. Then read the question and choose the best answer.

26. What do the speakers say about stuffed toys?
    (A) They last forever.
    (B) Children prefer them to storybooks.
    (C) They have been popular for several decades.
    (D) Children need more of them.

27. What does the woman want to do with the doll?
    (A) She wants to make it less expensive.
    (B) She wants to examine it.
    (C) She wants to change its color.
    (D) She wants to make it bigger.

Part IV Short Talks

Listen to the short talk. Then read the questions and choose the best answer.

28. Why is the product popular?
    (A) It has a low price.
    (B) People are familiar with it.
    (C) It is available everywhere.
    (D) Nobody is sure of the reason.

29. How long has the product been on the market?
    (A) Exactly two years.
    (B) Exactly twenty years.
    (C) More than twenty years.
    (D) About ten years.

Renting and Leasing

1. **apprehensive** adj., anxious about the future
   a. Most new home buyers are apprehensive about their decision.
   b. The mortgage lender was apprehensive about the company's ability to pay.

2. **circumstance** n., a condition; a situation
   a. Under the current economic circumstances, they will not be able to purchase the property.
   b. If the circumstances change in the near future and we have new properties, we will be sure to call you.

3. **condition** n., the state of something; a requirement
   a. Except for some minor repairs, the building is in very good condition.
   b. There are certain conditions that are unique to leasing a property.

4. **due to** prep., because of
   a. Due to the low interest rates, good office space is difficult to find.
   b. He didn't believe that the low prices were due only to the neighborhood.

5. **fluctuate** v., to go up and down; to change
   a. No one is very comfortable making a large investment while the currency values fluctuate almost daily.
   b. Prime business areas fluctuate with local economies, crime rates, and cost of living indices.

6. **get out of** v., to escape; to exit
   a. The agent wasn't sure if the executives could get out of their prior real estate arrangement.
   b. The company wanted to get out of the area before property values declined even further.

7. **indicator** n., a sign, a signal
   a. If the economy is an accurate indicator, rental prices will increase rapidly in the next six months.
   b. The results of the elections were seen as an important indicator of the stability in the area.

8. **lease** n., a contract to pay to use property for an amount of time; v., to make a contract to use property
   a. With the lease expiring next year, they need to start looking for a new location as soon as possible.
   b. They decided to lease the property rather than buy it.

9. **lock into** v., to commit; to be unable to change
   a. The company locked itself into a ten-year lease that they didn't want.
   b. Before you lock yourself into something, check all your options.

10. **occupy** v., to dwell or reside in
    a. Tenants are usually allowed to occupy their space beginning on the first day of the month.
    b. Our company has occupied this office for more than five years.

11. **option** n., a choice, an alternative
    a. You could arrange the lease with an option to buy after a certain amount of time.
    b. With the real estate market so tight right now, you don't have that many options.

12. **subject to** adj., under legal power; dependent
    a. This contract is subject to all the laws and regulations of the state.
    b. The go-ahead to buy is subject to the president's approval.

Word Families

verb	apprehend	A child can't apprehend the importance of saving for the future.
noun	apprehension	The air was thick with apprehension as the landlord met with the tenants.
adjective	apprehensive	The tenants were apprehensive about the conditions of their rental agreement.

adverb	circumstantially	The building owner circumstantially takes money out of the escrow account for emergency repairs.
noun	circumstance	Because of our circumstances, the rental agent kindly allowed us to get out of our lease early.
adjective	circumstantial	The judge's decision that the tenant was responsible for repairing the damage was based solely on circumstantial evidence.

verb	condition	The president conditioned her acceptance on two factors that were spelled out in the letter of agreement.
noun	condition	They decided to rent the space, under the condition that the price would not be raised for the next two years.
adjective	conditional	If you give a conditional go-ahead, we will start drawing up the plans.

verb	indicate	As was indicated in the terms of the lease, any changes to the property must be approved by the owners.
noun	indicator	The state of local schools is a good indicator of the health of the economy.
noun	indication	The management team had every indication that the tenants were planning to stay for the near future.

verb	fluctuate	As interest rates began to fluctuate, many investors became nervous and took their money out of the real estate market.
noun	fluctuation	Construction is sensitive to any fluctuations in the economy.
gerund	fluctuating	Any additional fluctuating on prices will not be accepted.

verb	occupy	The owner must make sure that the space is in good condition before the tenant occupies it.
noun	occupant	Most of the occupants of this building are doctors and lawyers.
noun	occupancy	The occupancy rate of the building has never fallen below 85 percent.

Incomplete Sentences

Choose the word that best completes the sentence.

1. The president was _____ about adding more space to the factory.
   (A) apprehend   (C) apprehension
   (B) apprehensive   (D) apprehended

2. The financial _____ of our business don't allow us to lease an office with such a high monthly rent.
   (A) circumstances (C) circumstantially
   (B) circumstantial (D) circumstanced

3. The real estate agent couldn't determine how to best work with a company that placed so many _____ on everything that they did.
   (A) conditional   (C) conditioned
   (B) condition   (D) conditions

4. The buyer _____ with a nod of his head that he was placing a bid on the property.
   (A) indicates   (C) indicated
   (B) indication   (D) indicator

5. _____ as it does, I don't understand how anyone can depend on that country's market to provide a safe investment.
   (A) Fluctuated   (C) Fluctuation
   (B) Fluctuating   (D) Fluctuate

6. The lawyers signed the papers and the company took _____ of the new building.
   (A) occupied   (C) occupancy
   (B) occupants   (D) occupying

Error Recognition

Choose the underlined word or phrase that should be rewritten and rewrite it.

7. Under the <u>conditions</u> of this <u>leased</u>, you have virtually no flexibility and are <u>locked into</u> <u>occupying</u> this space
        A   B   C   D
   for at least ten years.

   _____

8. The <u>circumstances</u> under which we committed to the <u>occupancy</u> made us <u>apprehension</u> about the <u>lease</u>.
        A   B   C   D

   _____

9. We are <u>subjected to</u> price <u>fluctuating</u> that are <u>due to</u> outside <u>conditions</u>.
          A   B   C   D

   _____

10. Because they had the <u>option</u> to buy in the contract, they were able to <u>get out on</u> an unfavorable leasing
                          A   B
    <u>arrangement</u> and were not <u>subject to</u> any penalties.
       C   D

    _____

Reading Comprehension

Read the following passage and write the words in the blanks below.

apprehensive	due to	indicator	occupancy
circumstances	fluctuations	lease	options
condition	get out of	lock into	subject to

Starting a new business is both an exciting and frightening undertaking. Most new business owners are (11.) _____ about their ability to make all the decisions that arise during the course of opening a business. One of the first issues that will arise is whether to buy or (12.) _____ property. In order to evaluate the options, business owners research the current real estate market. (13.) _____ rates are a good (14.) _____ of the overall business climate. Prices per square foot will increase as the occupancy rate increases.

Economic change is part of the business climate. There are often large (15.) _____ in prices within a given city. These fluctuations are (16.) _____ many factors like the (17.) _____ of the building, the surrounding neighborhood, access to public transportation, and business projections for the area.

Because there is so much uncertainty in starting a business, many owners do not want to (18.) _____ themselves _____ a long-term lease. Many negotiate clauses in their contracts to (19.) _____ a lease under certain (20.) _____. They want to insure the prices and conditions of a property before making a large commitment. Leases often provide more flexibility than buying a property. They like to leave their (21.) _____ open. They don't like to be (22.) _____ the whims of the marketplace.

LISTENING COMPREHENSION

Listen to Track 30 of the Compact Disc to hear the statements for Lesson 30

Part I Picture

Look at the picture and listen to the sentences. Choose the sentence that best describes the picture.

23. Ⓐ Ⓑ Ⓒ Ⓓ

Part II Question—Response

Listen to the question and the three responses. Choose the response that best answers the question.

24. Ⓐ Ⓑ Ⓒ   25. Ⓐ Ⓑ Ⓒ

Part III Short Conversations

Listen to the short dialogs. Then read the question and choose the best answer.

26. What does the man want to do?
    (A) Validate his signature.
    (B) Sign a contract.
    (C) Become a lawyer.
    (D) Get out of a lease.

27. Why is now a good time to buy?
    (A) All the indicators are good.
    (B) Interest rates are fluctuating.
    (C) There are some interested sellers.
    (D) Property is selling at a fast rate.

Part IV Short Talks

Listen to the short talk. Then read the questions and choose the best answer.

28. Who is the audience for this talk?
    (A) Customers and clients.
    (B) Landlords.
    (C) Lawyers.
    (D) Tenants.

29. What should a business owner do before signing a lease?
    (A) Make sure her business is successful.
    (B) Ask for a long-term lease.
    (C) Get more customers.
    (D) Look at the neighborhood.

Word Review #6   Lessons 26–30 Management Issues

Choose the word that best completes the sentence.

1. The owner of the new company personally
   _____ every expense.
   (A) scrutiny
   (B) scrutinize
   (C) scrutinized
   (D) scrutinizing

2. Several employees will _____ on
   designing the office for efficiency.
   (A) collaborate
   (B) collaborated
   (C) collaborating
   (D) collaboration

3. When there is a problem with company policy, it
   should be _____ before the board of
   directors.
   (A) bring up
   (B) bring in
   (C) brought up
   (D) brought in

4. The quality control department felt it was making
   good _____ when the number of
   defects declined.
   (A) progress
   (B) progressed
   (C) progressing
   (D) progressive

5. _____ goods can ruin the future of a
   new company.
   (A) Defect
   (B) Defects
   (C) Defective
   (D) Defection

6. The public's _____ of a company
   depends on how solidly the company stands
   behind its products.
   (A) perceive
   (B) perceptive
   (C) perceived
   (D) perception

7. The market research matched our
   _____.
   (A) assumes
   (B) assuming
   (C) assumed
   (D) assumptions

8. Determining the safeness of a particular appli-
   ance requires a _____ investigation of the
   electrical components.
   (A) system
   (B) systems
   (C) systematic
   (D) systematize

9. When _____ office space, it is wise to insist
   upon an option to renew.
   (A) lease
   (B) leasing
   (C) leased
   (D) lessor

10. _____ a lease might be expensive.
    (A) Getting in
    (B) Getting on
    (C) Getting off of
    (D) Getting out of

Choose the underlined word or phrase that should be rewritten and rewrite it.

11. Those who arrange the office should <u>concentrate</u> on creating a space that is <u>conducive</u> to work, free of
                                              A   B
    <u>disrupting</u>, and <u>unhampered</u> by nonessential foot traffic.
        C   D

    _____

12. Efficient managers <u>adherence to</u> the <u>agenda</u>, keep <u>goals</u> in focus, and avoid <u>lengthy</u> meetings.
                              A   B   C   D

    _____

13. The interior designer tried to <u>enhance</u> the appearance of the <u>lobby</u> by <u>throw out</u> the old furniture that
                                       A   B   C
    unfortunately belonged to the <u>lessor</u>.
                                      D

    _____

14. Sometimes <u>circumstantial</u> force a <u>supervisor</u> to become <u>locked into</u> a committment that is hard to <u>get out of</u>.
                   A   B   C   D

    _____

15. Product development <u>responsibilities</u> include <u>ascertain</u> what is needed, <u>examining</u> options, and <u>researching</u>
    A   **B**   **C**   **D**
    the competition.

    _____

16. A committee that does not <u>concentrate</u> on <u>priorities</u> often <u>wasting</u> time wallowing through an <u>agenda</u>.
    A   **B**   **C**   **D**

    _____

17. Although the board members meet <u>periodically</u> and could have finished <u>matters</u> at the next meeting, they
    A   **B**
    decided to <u>go ahead</u> and not <u>conclusion</u> until all issues were addressed.
    C   **D**

    _____

18. Before taking <u>occupancy</u> of a commercial site, check whether poor maintenance <u>conditions</u> are <u>due to</u> faulty
    A   **B**   **C**
    plumbing or electrical wiring that does not <u>conformation</u> to code.
    D

    _____

19. If you <u>opt</u> for <u>move up</u> the corporate ladder, be prepared for some <u>anxious</u> moments when you <u>assume</u> your
    A   **B**   **C**   **D**
    new responsibilities.

    _____

20. An effective quality control <u>supervisor</u> of a reputable <u>brand</u> will ensure that products <u>uniformity</u> <u>conform</u> to their
    A   **B**   **C**   **D**
    set standards.

    _____

Lesson 31

Selecting a Restaurant

1. **appeal** n., the ability to attract
    a. A restaurant with good food and reasonable prices has a lot of appeal.
    b. The pleasing decor and friendly waiters are what give that restaurant its appeal.

2. **arrive** v., to reach a destination
    a. By the time our meal arrived, it was cold.
    b. Frank arrived at the restaurant only minutes after Claudia left.

3. **compromise** n., a settlement of differences; v., to settle differences
    a. The couple made a compromise and ordered food to take out.
    b. John doesn't like sweet dishes so I compromised by adding just a small amount of sugar.

4. **daringly** adj., bravely
    a. We daringly ordered the raw squid.
    b. Bob daringly asked to see the menu in French.

5. **familiar** adj., often encountered or seen; common
    a. It's nice to see some familiar items on the menu.
    b. The chef blends the familiar tastes with the unusual.

6. **guide** n., one who leads, directs, or gives advice; a guidebook
    a. The guide led our tour group to a small restaurant only known to the locals.
    b. I don't know where to go, so why don't we consult the guide.

7. **majority** n., the greater number or part
    a. The majority of the group wanted to try the new Chinese restaurant.
    b. Claude was in the majority, so he was very pleased with the decision.

8. **mix** v., to combine or blend into one mass; n., a combination
    a. The daring chef mixed two uncommon ingredients.
    b. The mix of bright colors on the plate was very pleasing.

9. **rely** v., to have confidence in; to depend on
    a. I have always relied on the restaurant advice this guidebook gives.
    b. I seldom rely on the restaurant reviews in the paper when choosing a restaurant.

10. **secure** v., to get possession of; to obtain
    a. Despite the popularity of the restaurant, Max was able to secure reservations for this evening.
    b. The hostess secured us another chair, so we could eat together.

11. **subjective** adj., particular to a given person; highly personal; not objective
    a. Food preferences are subjective and not everyone agrees on what tastes good.
    b. The reviews in this guidebook are highly subjective, but fun to read.

12. **suggestion** n., a proposal; advice
    a. Can I make a suggestion about what to order?
    b. We followed the waiter's suggestion and ordered one of the specials.

Word Families

verb	appeal	On a beautiful spring day, a sidewalk café appeals to many people.
noun	appeal	That restaurant has been around for a long time but it hasn't lost its appeal.
adjective	appealing	An ice-cold drink seems very appealing on a hot day.

verb	dare	I prefer familiar things and don't usually dare to try new restaurants.
adjective	daring	Kobi had more daring tastes than the rest of his family.
adverb	daringly	Jane daringly refused a fork and attempted to eat her entire meal with chopsticks.

verb	guide	The hostess guided us to our table.
noun	guidance	Li asked the waiter for guidance in selecting the wine.
adjective	guidable	Finding the patrons to be very guidable, the waiter steered them to the most expensive items on the menu.

verb	mix	The chef was famous for mixing unfamiliar ingredients.
noun	mixture	The texture of the vegetable mixture was too lumpy for my taste.
adjective	mixable	Oil and water are not mixable.

verb	rely	We will rely on the hostess's recommendations.
noun	reliability	The reliability of deliveries became a problem for the manager.
adjective	reliable	Hiring a reliable staff is the first priority for every restaurant manager.

verb	suggest	Can I suggest a good wine to go with the entrée?
noun	suggestion	Clark asked his boss for a suggestion for a good place to eat.
adjective	suggestible	The patrons were in a suggestible mood, and were easily convinced to have dessert.

Incomplete Sentences

Choose the word that best completes the sentence.

1. The colorful vegetables made the dish look
    _____.
    (A) appealed   (C) appeals
    (B) appealing   (D) appealingly

2. Even though the restaurant looked expensive, Pat
    _____ to order her meal without asking about
    the prices.
    (A) daring   (C) dared
    (B) daringly   (D) dares

3. If you need some _____ on what to order, be
    sure to consult your server.
    (A) guide   (C) guided
    (B) guides   (D) guidance

4. Your father is in the kitchen _____ a batch of
    his famous chocolate chip cookies.
    (A) mixture   (C) mix
    (B) mixed   (D) mixing

5. This guidebook is several years old, so I would
    question its _____.
    (A) rely   (C) reliability
    (B) reliance   (D) relying

6. I have always found Lola's restaurant _____ to
    be very good, so I continue to seek her guidance.
    (A) suggestions   (C) suggestive
    (B) suggest   (D) suggestible

Error Recognition

Choose the underlined word or phrase that should be rewritten and rewrite it.

7. The <u>majority</u> of diners like to order <u>familiar</u> food from the menu, but the waiter will be happy to
       A   B
    <u>suggestion</u> specials for those with more <u>daring</u> tastes.
       C   D
    _____

8. Although different tastes <u>appeal</u> to different palates, it is still a good plan to <u>rely</u> on the <u>guidance</u> of friends
                               A   C   B
    who have recently eaten out, despite the <u>subjective</u> of their opinions.
                                                 D
    _____

9. Your guests may feel more <u>secure</u> if you take them to a restaurant with a menu that <u>mixture</u> <u>familiar</u> favorites
                               A   B   C
    and <u>daring</u> trendy dishes.
           D
    _____

10. Fabrice didn't like Mimi's <u>suggestion</u> for a restaurant and Mimi didn't like his, so they <u>relied</u> on a restaurant
                               A   B
    <u>guide</u> to come up with a <u>compromised</u>.
       C   D
    _____

Reading Comprehension

Read the following passage and write the words in the blanks below.

appeal	daring	majority	secure
arrive	familiar	mix	subjective
compromise	guidance	relies	suggestion

When Atul is trying to impress business contacts who are potential new clients, he takes them to the best restaurant in town. He hopes this will help (11.) _____ a new contract for his telecommunications business.

It's hard to determine which restaurants are best. Atul (12.) _____ on newspaper and magazine reviews. He also asks his friends and colleagues for (13.) _____. They are happy to make a (14.) _____.

Food tastes are (15.)_____. Although Atul likes to be (16.) _____ and take risks, he knows that the food should (17.) _____ to a variety of palates. He wants the (18.) _____ of his guests to be happy. He usually decides to (19.) _____ on a restaurant that offers a menu with a (20.) _____ of (21.) _____ standards and some exciting specials.

When he calls to book the table, he tells the person taking the reservation what time his party will (22.) _____ and the number of people he needs seating for.

LISTENING COMPREHENSION

Listen to Track 31 to the Compact Disc to hear the statements for Lesson 31

Part I Picture

Look at the picture and listen to the sentences. Choose the sentence that best describes the picture.

23. Ⓐ Ⓑ Ⓒ Ⓓ

Part II Question—Response

Listen to the question and the three responses. Choose the response that best answers the question.

24. Ⓐ Ⓑ Ⓒ   25. Ⓐ Ⓑ Ⓒ

Part III Short Conversations

Listen to the short dialogs. Then read the question and choose the best answer.

26. Who suggested the seafood restaurant?
    (A) The tour guide.
    (B) The people at the office.
    (C) The man.
    (D) The woman.

27. What is the speakers' opinion of restaurant reviews?
    (A) They are appealing.
    (B) They are usually helpful.
    (C) They are very subjective.
    (D) They are mean.

Part IV Short Talks

Listen to the short talk. Then read the questions and choose the best answer.

28. Where is the listener now?
    (A) At home.
    (B) In the bar.
    (C) At the restaurant.
    (D) In the parking lot.

29. What does the speaker suggest?
    (A) Driving to the restaurant.
    (B) Arriving early for drinks.
    (C) Making a reservation.
    (D) Bringing a big appetite.

Lesson 32

Eating Out

Words to learn

basic
complete
excite
flavor
forget
ingredient
judge
mix-up
patron
predict
randomly
remind

1. **basic** adj., serving as a starting point or basis; simple
   a. The new restaurant offers a very basic menu.
   b. The restaurant manager ordered enough basic supplies to get through the first month.

2. **complete** v., to finish or make whole
   a. We ordered some dessert to complete our meal.
   b. Some restaurants want to hear their customers' opinions and ask them to complete a short evaluation form.

3. **excite** v., to arouse an emotion
   a. Exotic flavors always excite me.
   b. The new Asian restaurant has excited the interest of many people.

4. **flavor** n., a distinctive taste
   a. Fusion cooking is distinguished by an interesting mix of flavors.
   b. The cook changed the flavor of the soup with a unique blend of herbs.

5. **forget** v., to be unable to remember
   a. The waiter forgot to bring the rolls, annoying the customer.
   b. Don't forget to tell your friends what a great meal you had tonight.

6. **ingredient** n., an element in a mixture
   a. The chef went to the farmer's market to select the freshest ingredients for tonight's menu.
   b. I was unfamiliar with some of the ingredients in the dish.

7. **judge** v., to form an opinion
   a. Hector was not familiar with Asian cooking, so he was unable to judge if the noodles were cooked correctly.
   b. The restaurant review harshly judged the quality of the service.

8. **mix-up** n., a confusion
   a. There was a mix-up in the kitchen so your order will be delayed.
   b. There was a mix-up about the ingredients and the dish was ruined.

9. **patron** n., a customer, especially a regular customer
   a. Once the word was out about the new chef, patrons lined up to get into the restaurant.
   b. This restaurant has many loyal patrons.

10. **predict** v., to state, tell about, or make known in advance
    a. I predicted this restaurant would become popular and I was right.
    b. Kona was unable to predict what time Andy, who is always late, would show up at the restaurant.

11. **randomly** adv., without any specific pattern
    a. We randomly made our selections from the menu.
    b. That chef chooses his spices randomly, but his dishes always taste great.

12. **remind** v., to cause to remember
    a. Ms. Smith was annoyed at having to remind the waitress to bring the check.
    b. I reminded the client that we are meeting for dinner tomorrow.

Word Families

verb	complete	The meal could not be completed without dessert.
noun	completion	The coffee was the last item ordered and brought the meal to completion.
adverb	completely	The chef forgot that the dessert was in the oven and completely ruined it.

verb	excite	The chef knows how to excite his patrons.
noun	excitement	You can feel the excitement in the air.
adjective	excited	I am really excited about trying out this new restaurant.

verb	flavor	I like a chef who uses exotic spices to flavor the food.
noun	flavor	Some people don't like Mexican food because the flavors are too spicy.
adjective	flavorful	The special ingredients made the dish very flavorful.

verb	forget	Don't forget to bring us the check.
adjective	forgetful	The forgetful waitress put a burden on the rest of the staff.
adjective	forgettable	The meal was bland and forgettable.

verb	mix up	An inexperienced waiter can easily mix up orders.
noun	mix-up	We had a big mix-up in our plans and I ended up waiting for my friends at the wrong restaurant.
adjective	mixed up	Bob always gets mixed up when he tries to order food at a foreign restaurant.

verb	predict	I predict that this restaurant will be a success.
noun	prediction	The manager's prediction came true, and the chef was named to the "Top 100" list.
adverb	predictably	Predictably, because the waiter neglected to write down the order, he forgot some necessary items.

Incomplete Sentences

Choose the word that best completes the sentence.

1. Would you like to _____ your meal with an after-dinner drink?
   (A) complete
   (B) completed
   (C) completely
   (D) completion

2. I've had enough _____ for the day.
   (A) excite
   (B) exciting
   (C) excitement
   (D) excites

3. I can't figure out which ingredients the chef used to _____ this dish.
   (A) flavored
   (B) flavorful
   (C) flavors
   (D) flavor

4. I've already _____ what the last table of guests ordered.
   (A) forget
   (B) forgetful
   (C) forgotten
   (D) forgetfulness

5. Unfortunately, on the day the restaurant opened there was a huge _____ in the kitchen.
   (A) mix-up
   (B) mixed up
   (C) mix up
   (D) mixing up

6. No one could have _____ how successful the restaurant would become.
   (A) predictive
   (B) predictably
   (C) predictable
   (D) predicted

Error Recognition

Choose the underlined word or phrase that should be rewritten and rewrite it.

7. The restaurant <u>patrons</u> orderedly <u>randomly</u> from the menu, so when the waiter <u>mix up</u> their orders, they had
         A   B   C
   <u>forgotten</u> what they ordered.
     D

   _____

8. The chef prepared a <u>basic</u> dish with daring <u>ingredients</u> that gave it an exotic <u>flavor</u> none of us could have
               A   B   C
   <u>prediction</u>.
     D

   _____

9. Before we <u>completed</u> our entrée, we had to <u>reminder</u> our waiter that we needed bread; we wondered how he
            A   B
   could <u>forget</u> such a <u>basic</u> component of the meal.
       C   D

   _____

10. Some of the most <u>exciting</u> and <u>flavor</u> dishes contain only <u>basic</u> <u>ingredients</u>.
                A   B   C   D

    _____

Reading Comprehension

Read the following passage and write the words in the blanks below.

basic	flavor	judged	predict
complete	forget	mix up	randomly
excite	ingredients	patrons	remind

The key to a happy meal is that everyone should enjoy eating what they ordered. Before the waiter takes your order, you can ask him for a recommendation or you can select (11.) _____ from the menu.

Good service is part of the overall enjoyment of the meal. The waiter should make the (12.) _____ feel welcome and comfortable. Good waiters can (13.) _____ what you need, like more water, without having to be asked for it. It's easy for a waiter to (14.) _____ something, but you should not have to (15.) _____ a waiter more than once to bring you something. Nor do you want the waiter to (16.) _____ the food orders. You should get what you ordered, and your order should be (17.) _____.

The quality of the food is the primary way restaurants are (18.) _____. The food should taste and look wonderful. Your plate of food should (19.) _____ all your senses and be fragrant and colorful. Even the most (20.) _____ or familiar dishes can taste different from restaurant to restaurant. A chef can bring out a distinct (21.) _____ in a dish, depending on the (22.) _____ he or she uses.

LISTENING COMPREHENSION

Listen to Track 32 of the Compact Disc to hear the statements for Lesson 32

Part I Picture

Look at the picture and listen to the sentences. Choose the sentence that best describes the picture.

23. Ⓐ Ⓑ Ⓒ Ⓓ

Part II Question—Response

Listen to the question and the three responses. Choose the response that best answers the question.

24. Ⓐ Ⓑ Ⓒ   25. Ⓐ Ⓑ Ⓒ

Part III Short Conversations

Listen to the short dialogs. Then read the question and choose the best answer.

26. What are the speakers discussing?
    (A) The flavor of the food.
    (B) Their last vacation.
    (C) The restaurant decor.
    (D) The serving dishes.

27. What did the waiter do?
    (A) He got excited.
    (B) He completed the order.
    (C) He forgot to serve water.
    (D) He came back several times.

Part IV Short Talks

Listen to the short talk. Then read the questions and choose the best answer.

28. Who is speaking?
    (A) The kitchen assistant.
    (B) The head chef.
    (C) A patron.
    (D) A waitress.

29. What does the speaker offer?
    (A) To cook the meal.
    (B) To take the order.
    (C) To bring some free food.
    (D) To serve water.

Ordering Lunch

1. **burden** n., a responsibility; something that is carried
   a. The secretary usually takes on the burden of ordering lunch for business meetings.
   b. The deliveryman's back ached from the heavy burden he carried.

2. **commonly** adv., usually, habitually
   a. The people who work in this building commonly order their lunch from the sandwich shop on the first floor.
   b. The restaurants in this area commonly serve office workers and are only open during the week.

3. **delivery** n., the act of conveying or delivering
   a. The caterer hired a courier to make the delivery.
   b. The restaurant is reluctant to make deliveries, but makes an exception for our office.

4. **elegance** n., refinement, beauty, grace
   a. The elegance of the restaurant made it a pleasant place to eat.
   b. A sandwich may lack elegance, but it makes a convenient and inexpensive lunch.

5. **fall to** v., to become one's responsibility
   a. The task of preparing the meal fell to the assistant chef when the chief chef was ill.
   b. The menu was in French, so ordering for us fell to Monique, who spoke French.

6. **impress** v., to affect strongly, often favorably
   a. I was impressed with how quickly they delivered our lunch.
   b. If you want to impress the new staff member, order her a nice lunch.

7. **individual** adj., by or for one person; special; particular
   a. We had the delivery man mark the contents of each individual order.
   b. The jaunty whistle of the delivery woman marked her individual style.

8. **list** n., a series of names, words, or other items
   a. The office manager compiled a list of everyone's order.
   b. We keep a list of all the restaurants in this area that deliver.

9. **multiple** adj., having, relating to, or consisting of more than one part
   a. The delivery person was not able to keep track of the multiple order, causing a food mix-up.
   b. It takes multiple steps to get into this building, which frustrates all our employees.

10. **narrow** v., to limit or restrict
    a. Etseko narrowed the restaurant possibilities down to three.
    b. This restaurant delivers only pizza and sandwiches, so that certainly narrows down the choices.

11. **pick up** v., to take on passengers or freight
    a. The delivery man picks up lunch orders on his motor scooter.
    b. If you ask me nicely, I will pick up the order on my way home.

12. **settle** v., to make compensation for, to pay; to choose
    a. We settled the bill with the cashier.
    b. After much debate, we finally settled on the bistro on the corner.

Word Families

verb	burden	The frequently complicated lunch orders unfairly burdened Jacques.
noun	burden	In addition to all her other responsibilities, Marie had the burden of picking up the daily lunch order.
adjective	burdensome	Keeping track of everybody's lunch orders can be a burdensome task.

noun	in common	The two secretaries keep a file of restaurant menus in common to facilitate placing an order.
adjective	common	It is a common practice for restaurants to deliver.
adverb	commonly	It was commonly known that the sandwich shop had slow deliverymen.

verb	deliver	That restaurant delivers food at no extra charge.
noun	delivery	We all got very hungry waiting for the delivery to arrive.

noun	elegance	The elegance of the surroundings was accentuated by the wonderful meal the caterers delivered.
adjective	elegant	Delores set an elegant table that was sure to impress.
adverb	elegantly	The tasty appetizers were elegantly served from silver platters.

verb	impress	I am favorably impressed by how quickly the pizza was delivered.
noun	impression	She gave the impression that the food would be delivered within the hour.
adjective	impressionable	I have an impressionable child, so I don't like him to see deliverymen running red traffic lights.

verb	individualize	The take-out shop does not allow you to individualize your order by asking for substitutions.
noun	individual	The portions are large enough to feed two individuals.
adverb	individually	The individually marked boxes made it easy for us to claim our orders.

Incomplete Sentences

Choose the word that best completes the sentence.

1. George no longer wants to be in charge of lunch orders because he finds that job too _____.
    (A) burdens
    (B) burdened
    (C) burden
    (D) burdensome

2. We _____ meet the delivery person in the lobby to pick up our orders.
    (A) common
    (B) in common
    (C) commonly
    (D) commonness

3. The _____ from that restaurant always arrive late.
    (A) delivers
    (B) deliveries
    (C) delivered
    (D) delivering

4. Despite being served in disposable containers, the meal had an _____ touch.
    (A) elegant
    (B) elegance
    (C) elegantly
    (D) elegancy

5. Our office manager was so _____ by the speed of the delivery, she decided to order from them again.
    (A) impressive
    (B) impressed
    (C) impression
    (D) impressionable

6. Let's order _____ so we can all get what we want for lunch.
    (A) individualize
    (B) individualist
    (C) individually
    (D) individual

Error Recognition

Choose the underlined word or phrase that should be rewritten and rewrite it.

7. At a lunch to win the new advertising account, we served each potential new client an <u>individual</u> specialty
    A

    dessert; this <u>elegant</u> touch <u>impressive</u> those attending and helped <u>settle</u> any questions about our staff's level
    <u> </u>B   C   D

    of creativity.

    _____

8. The <u>delivery</u> service is unique in that it will <u>pick up</u> various orders from <u>multiples</u> restaurants, making it
    A   B   C

    unnecessary for everyone to <u>narrow</u> their choice to one type of food.
    D

    _____

9. Ordering food for work lunches is a <u>burden</u> that <u>falls on</u> the office manager, so he sends us a <u>list</u> of the
    A   B   C

    choices and asks us to vote for our preference and then orders the most <u>commonly</u> response.
    D

    _____

10. I think it is easiest to <u>narrow</u> the choices to a small <u>list</u> of sandwiches, which will appeal to <u>individual</u> tastes
    A   B   C

    and can be <u>delivery</u> without becoming cold, like pizza.
    D

    _____

Reading Comprehension

Read the following passage and write the words in the blanks below.

burdensome	elegant	individual	narrow
common	falls to	list	pick up
delivered	impress	multiple	settled

As the office manager, it usually (11.) _____ Lucia to order the food for a working lunch or an office party. Lucia finds ordering food for a working lunch to be especially (12.) _____. First, in order to avoid placing (13.) _____ small orders from different food establishments, she must (14.) _____ down the choice to one kind of food. The most (15.) _____ choices are sandwiches and (16.) _____ pizzas.

Once she has (17.) _____ on a good choice, she calls a restaurant or other food service on her approved (18.) _____. Usually she needs the food (19.) _____ so she does not have to leave the office and (20.) _____ the order herself.

In case of a more formal lunch, where her boss is trying to (21.) _____ new clients, for example, Lucia will call a catering service that can provide a more (22.) _____ meal.

LISTENING COMPREHENSION

Listen to Track 33 of the Compact Disc to hear the statements for Lesson 33

Part I Picture

Look at the picture and listen to the sentences. Choose the sentence that best describes the picture.

23. Ⓐ Ⓑ Ⓒ Ⓓ

Part II Question—Response

Listen to the question and the three responses. Choose the response that best answers the question.

24. Ⓐ Ⓑ Ⓒ   25. Ⓐ Ⓑ Ⓒ

Part III Short Conversations

Listen to the short dialogs. Then read the question and choose the best answer.

26. Why does the man want to have lunch at the office?
    (A) It is burdensome to leave the office.
    (B) He has a bad impression of the restaurant.
    (C) The office is more elegant than the restaurant.
    (D) He wants to show slides during lunch.

27. What are the speakers doing?
    (A) Getting ready to deliver an order.
    (B) Looking for a restaurant that delivers.
    (C) Paying the check.
    (D) Selecting the items they want to eat.

Part IV Short Talks

Listen to the short talk. Then read the questions and choose the best answer.

28. What takes ten minutes?
    (A) Delivering the order.
    (B) Selecting a meal from the list.
    (C) Getting the food ready to be picked up.
    (D) Making a group order.

29. How much does a delivery cost?
    (A) 15 percent.
    (B) 50 cents.
    (C) It's free.
    (D) 50 percent.

Cooking as a Career

1. **accustom to** v., to become familiar with, to become used to
   a. Chefs must accustom themselves to working long hours.
   b. It can be hard to accustom oneself to eating new types of food.

2. **apprentice** n., a student worker in a chosen field
   a. Instead of attending cooking school, Raul chose to work as an apprentice with an experienced chef.
   b. The cooking school has an apprentice program that places students in restaurants to gain work experience.

3. **culinary** adj., relating to the kitchen or cooking
   a. The chef was widely known for his culinary artistry.
   b. His interest in culinary arts drew him to a commercial foods program.

4. **demand** v., to require
   a. Theodore was always exhausted because his new job at the restaurant demanded so much of him.
   b. This style of cooking demands many exotic ingredients and a lot of preparation time.

5. **draw** v., to cause to come by attracting
   a. We hope the new restaurant will draw other business to the area.
   b. Matthew was drawn to a career in cooking.

6. **incorporate** v., to unite one thing with something else already in existence
   a. Coca incorporated the patron's suggestions into her new menu.
   b. Here are the fresh greens for you to incorporate into a salad.

7. **influx** n., a flowing in
   a. An influx of new chefs is constantly needed to fill open jobs.
   b. Due to the rise in popularity of cooking as a career, cooking schools report an influx of applications.

8. **method** n., a procedure
   a. Gloria perfected a simple method for making croissants.
   b. Many chefs borrow cooking methods from a variety of cultures and incorporate them into their cooking style.

9. **outlet** n., a means of release or gratification, as for energies, drives, or desires
   a. Even before he became a professional baker, Jacob used baking as an outlet for frustration.
   b. Many people find cooking to be a hands-on outlet for their creativity.

10. **profession** n., an occupation requiring considerable training and specialized study
    a. Cooking is considered as much a profession as is law or medicine.
    b. Lulu took up cooking as her profession and is very happy with her decision.

11. **relinquish** v., to let go; to surrender
    a. People find it hard to relinquish their accustomed food preferences and try something new.
    b. After Claude married Kiki, he had to relinquish his exclusive hold on the kitchen and learn to share the joys of cooking.

12. **theme** n., an implicit or recurrent idea; a motif
    a. The caterers prepared food for a party with a tropical island theme.
    b. The restaurant's food and decor demonstrated its southwestern theme.

Word Families

verb	accustom to	Shirley could not accustom herself to the demands of her new job.
noun	custom	It is the custom at this restaurant to offer free meals to patrons on their birthdays.
adjective	accustomed to	Janet has become accustomed to eating spicy food.

verb	apprentice	Instead of attending cooking school, Michael decided to apprentice to a master chef.
noun	apprentice	The new group of apprentices will start working any day now.
noun	apprenticeship	The apprenticeship was a grueling period, but George learned a lot.

verb	demand	The head chef demands a lot from his assistants.
noun	demand	Pierre could not keep up with the many demands of the customers.
adjective	demanding	Working as a chef is a very demanding job.

verb	incorporate	Take these items and incorporate them into a stew.
noun	incorporation	The restaurant was the incorporation of every good idea the chef had thought of in his career.
gerund	incorporating	Chef Tao was famous for incorporating different cooking styles into one.

noun	method	The chef discovered a more efficient method of peeling boiled eggs.
noun	methodology	Even the order of adding ingredients is an unappreciated aspect of cooking methodology.
adjective	methodical	The head cook was not so artistic as methodical in preparing standard dishes.

noun	profession	The number of people choosing cooking as a profession has risen over the past decade.
adjective	professional	She was professional in her approach to dealing with the problem of late deliveries.
adverb	professionally	Although the customer was rude and loud, the waiter handled the situation very professionally.

Incomplete Sentences

Choose the word that best completes the sentence.

1. Susannah is having a hard time becoming
    _____ to the long hours of her job at the
    restaurant.
    (A) custom   (C) accustoms to
    (B) customs   (D) accustomed to

2. The student accepted a six-month _____ with a
    famous chef.
    (A) apprentice   (C) apprenticing
    (B) apprenticed   (D) apprenticeship

3. The patrons at this restaurant are often _____,
    but they usually tip well.
    (A) demands   (C) demanding
    (B) demanded   (D) demand

4. I love this chef's cooking style, which _____ so
    many different tastes.
    (A) incorporation   (C) incorporating
    (B) incorporates   (D) incorporator

5. The experienced chef was _____ about the way
    he prepared his award-winning dish.
    (A) method   (C) methodically
    (B) methodical   (D) methodology

6. The _____ attitude of the staff is one of the keys
    to a restaurant's success.
    (A) professional   (C) profession
    (B) professionalism (D) professionally

Error Recognition

Choose the underlined word or phrase that should be rewritten and rewrite it.

7. Regular patrons recognized the chef's unique <u>culinary</u> style, which <u>incorporated</u> both traditional and
    A B
    unconventional <u>methodological</u>, and were <u>drawn</u> to the innovative menu.
    C D

    _____

8. While he was still a young <u>apprentice</u>, the chef found that the cooking <u>professional</u> was a good <u>outlet</u> for his
    A B C
    <u>demand</u> for hands-on creativity.
    D

    _____

9. The <u>influx</u> of immigrants into this country over the centuries has meant that diners had to <u>relinquishing</u> menus
    A B
    to which they had grown <u>accustomed</u> in order to make room for different cooking <u>methods</u>.
    C D

    _____

10. Chefs draw from cultural <u>themes</u> and cooking <u>methods</u> of many national origins, which they <u>incorporation</u> into
    A B C
    meals that expand the tastes that one is <u>accustomed</u> to.
    D

    _____

Reading Comprehension

Read the following passage and write the words in the blanks below.

accustomed	demanding	influx	profession
apprenticeship	drawn	methods	relinquish
culinary	incorporate	outlet	themes

When people start thinking about careers, they may be looking for an (11.) _____ for their creativity. Many people are (12.) _____ to cooking as a career and see it as a (13.) _____, not merely a trade. The restaurant business is (14.) _____ and needs a constant (15.) _____ of new talent.

Chefs (16.) _____ ingredients and (17.) _____ of cooking from around the world into successful menus. Most chefs offer meals that are variations on standard (18.) _____. They will try to stretch their patrons' range of food tastes by taking food that is still recognized as traditional and infuse it with something new, like a rare spice or seasoning. People (19.) _____ to certain tastes and textures aren't going to (20.) _____ their preferences immediately.

Chefs attend (21.) _____ school or train in restaurants with experienced chefs, in an (22.) _____. For those of you who like hands-on creativity, being a chef might be a good choice.

LISTENING COMPREHENSION

Listen to Track 34 of the Compact Disc to hear the statements for Lesson 34

Part I Picture

Look at the picture and listen to the sentences. Choose the sentence that best describes the picture.

23. Ⓐ Ⓑ Ⓒ Ⓓ

Part II Question—Response

Listen to the question and the three responses. Choose the response that best answers the question.

24. Ⓐ Ⓑ Ⓒ   25. Ⓐ Ⓑ Ⓒ

Part III Short Conversations

Listen to the short dialogs. Then read the question and choose the best answer.

26. What has the woman become accustomed to?
    (A) Eating late.
    (B) Making different kinds of soup.
    (C) Discovering secrets.
    (D) Using a new herb.

27. According to the conversation, what do good chefs do?
    (A) Demand a lot from their assistants.
    (B) Manage their restaurants well.
    (C) Attract customers.
    (D) Influence new chefs.

Part IV Short Talks

Listen to the short talk. Then read the questions and choose the best answer.

28. Who is this talk for?
    (A) Cooking instructors.
    (B) People who work in the culinary arts.
    (C) People looking for a profession.
    (D) Career counselors.

29. What kind of people are attracted to the cooking profession?
    (A) Bored.
    (B) Demanding.
    (C) Exciting.
    (D) Creative.

Events

1. **assist** v., to give help or support to
   a. Bonnie hired a secretary to assist her with the many details of the event.
   b. The hotel manager was able to assist us with some last-minute advice.

2. **coordinate** v., to adjust or arrange parts to work together
   a. Benet tried to coordinate all departments to make sure the event ran smoothly.
   b. The colors of the flowers were ordered to coordinate with the colors in the corporate logo.

3. **dimension** n., a measure of width, height, or length
   a. What are the dimensions of the ballroom?
   b. We need the dimensions of the meeting rooms before we can determine how many chairs each will hold.

4. **exact** adj., characterized by accurate measurements or inferences
   a. We will need an exact head count by noon tomorrow.
   b. The exact measurements of the room are unknown, but we can guess.

5. **general** adj., involving only the main features rather than precise details
   a. We have a general idea of how many guests will attend.
   b. In general, about half the guests will bring their spouses.

6. **ideally** adj., perfectly; conforming to an ideal
   a. Ideally, the location for the concert would have plenty of parking.
   b. Lucy explained that ideally her wedding would take place on the beach, but she realized it might be difficult to arrange.

7. **lead time** n., the time between the initial stage of a project and the appearance of results
   a. The lead time for reservations is unrealistic.
   b. We will need to give the caterer enough lead time to cut the cake.

8. **plan** v., to formulate a scheme
   a. We plan to get together tomorrow to discuss the menu.
   b. Planning their wedding was a source of tension for the young couple.

9. **proximity** n., the state, quality, sense, or fact of being near or next to; closeness
   a. The fans were worried by the proximity of the storm clouds.
   b. An important factor in selecting the site was its close proximity to a parking garage.

10. **regulate** v., to control
    a. The state strictly regulates the preparation of food for public consumption.
    b. The site staff closely regulates how many cars can be brought on the grounds.

11. **site** n., a place or setting
    a. Once we saw the site, we knew it would be perfect for the event.
    b. The manager of the site was most helpful.

12. **stage** v., to exhibit or present
    a. The gazebo outside was the perfect location from which to stage the cutting of the cake.
    b. A historic house can be the perfect site to stage a small reception.

Word Families

verb	assist	Let me assist you with planning your next event.
noun	assistance	Dennis's idea of assistance is to call a professional firm for advice.
noun	assistant	In light of the number of events she had to run this year, Annu asked her boss for an assistant.

verb	coordinate	Ralph had a hard time coordinating the schedules of everybody involved in planning the event.
noun	coordination	Edna is a very good organizer, and coordination of events is one of her specialties.
noun	coordinator	The staff chose Marcel to be the coordinator for the company picnic.

verb	generalize	When we generalize, we must be aware of the many exceptions.
adjective	general	I need a general idea of what you want before I can provide specific answers.
adverb	generally	Although I cannot speak for every case, generally it is less expensive to buy in quantity.

verb	idealize	Rhoda idealized the location until she could no longer see any flaws in it.
adjective	ideal	A hotel with a large garden would be the ideal site for the reception.
adverb	ideally	Ideally, the site would be within our budget and have an outdoor area.

verb	plan	The committee planned to hold the luncheon in the office conference room rather than at a restaurant.
noun	plan	The finalized plans for the event will be presented at the staff meeting tomorrow.
noun	planner	Since she wanted to have a large wedding, Matilda decided to hire a wedding planner to help her make the arrangements.

verb	regulate	The state will regulate the food-handling precautions.
noun	regulation	Please obey the state regulations regarding serving alcohol to minors.
adjective	regulatory	Even though it is private, the country club's kitchen is subject to the rules of regulatory agencies.

Incomplete Sentences

Choose the word that best completes the sentence.

1. Do you need our _____ with any of the evening's details?
   (A) assist
   (B) assisting`
   (C) assistance
   (D) assistant

2. The event did not go off well because the _____ did a poor job of organizing it.
   (A) coordinator
   (B) coordination
   (C) coordinated
   (D) coordinates

3. _____ speaking, the event was poorly organized.
   (A) General
   (B) Generally
   (C) Generality
   (D) Generalizations

4. When the event planner saw the hotel ballroom, she knew that the size wasn't _____, but the price was right.
   (A) ideal
   (B) ideally
   (C) idealize
   (D) idealist

5. Joshua quit his job and started his own business as an events _____.
   (A) planned
   (B) plans
   (C) planner
   (D) planning

6. Like restaurants, caterers are subject to _____ concerning safe food handling.
   (A) regulate
   (B) regulations
   (C) regulatory
   (D) regulating

Error Recognition

Choose the underlined word or phrase that should be rewritten and rewrite it.

7. The hotel manager gave Natasha <u>assisting</u> in <u>planning</u> her first reception, especially in <u>coordinating</u> all the
                                                     A   **B**   **C**
   details and preparing the <u>site</u>.
                                    D

   _____

8. Boris wanted to <u>stage</u> a fund-raising event, but the <u>ideally</u> locations either did not have the <u>dimensions</u> to
                                 A   **B**   **C**
   accommodate the crowd he expected, or they were not in reasonable <u>proximity</u> to downtown.
                                                                                         D

   _____

9. In choosing a <u>site</u> for the reception, Ms. Benson had special criteria that had to be met, including close
                                 A
   <u>proximity</u> to public transportation, so she needed a lot of <u>lead time</u> to meet her <u>exactly</u> needs.
     B   **C**   **D**

   _____

10. In order to <u>coordination</u> the event, we had to have a <u>general</u> idea of how many guests would attend, and <u>plan</u>
                            A   **B**   **C**
    an <u>ideal</u> menu to satisfy the needs and tastes of everyone who attended.
        D

    _____

Reading Comprehension

Read the following passage and write the words in the blanks below.

assist	exact	lead time	regulations
coordinated	general	planning	site
dimensions	ideally	proximity	stage

Planning an event is not simple. There are hundreds of details that have to be (11.) _____, whether it is a wedding or a business conference. Early in the (12.) _____ process, you need to decide on the (13.) _____. If you know where you want to (14.) _____ the event, you should contact the site representative for an (15.) _____ description of the facility. The staff will provide you with information about room (16.) _____; food and beverage arrangements, including whether there are local (17.) _____ or restrictions for serving alcoholic beverages; and required (18.) _____ for reserving the site.

If you decide that the first site is not (19.) _____ suited for your specific requirements, a guidebook will (20.) _____ you in finding an alternative setting. In considering location, you should also think about its (21.) _____ to public transportation.

With a (22.) _____ idea of how many people will attend, and how much money you can spend, you can narrow down the available sites to the ones that best accommodate the needs of your group.

LISTENING COMPREHENSION

Listen to Track 35 of the Compact Disc to hear the statements for Lesson 35

Part I Picture

Look at the picture and listen to the sentences. Choose the sentence that best describes the picture.

23. Ⓐ Ⓑ Ⓒ Ⓓ

Part II Question—Response

Listen to the question and the three responses. Choose the response that best answers the question.

24. Ⓐ Ⓑ Ⓒ   25. Ⓐ Ⓑ Ⓒ

Part III Short Conversations

Listen to the short dialogs. Then read the question and choose the best answer.

26. What are the speakers discussing?
    (A) The wedding coordinator.
    (B) The place for the wedding reception.
    (C) The decorations for the reception.
    (D) The wedding date.

27. Where will the reception take place?
    (A) At a nightclub.
    (B) At a museum.
    (C) At a theater.
    (D) At a restaurant.

Part IV Short Talks

Listen to the short talk. Then read the questions and choose the best answer.

28. When will the office party take place?
    (A) Next week.
    (B) Next month.
    (C) In the afternoon.
    (D) Next weekend.

29. What kind of site are they looking for?
    (A) One that is near the office.
    (B) A small one.
    (C) One that has a stage.
    (D) An inexpensive one.

Word Review #7

Lessons 31–35 Resaurants and Events

Choose the word that best completes the sentence.

1. The aroma coming from the restaurant was so _____ that the tourists did not hesitate before entering.
   (A) appeal
   (B) appealed
   (C) appealing
   (D) appeals

2. Because the menu was not in his native language, the visitor asked the waiter for

   _____.
   (A) guide
   (B) guided
   (C) guiding
   (D) guidance

3. The waiter _____ that the customer would enjoy the duck.
   (A) predict
   (B) predicted
   (C) predicting
   (D) prediction

4. Food critics are also expected to _____ a restaurant's service and atmosphere.
   (A) judge
   (B) judges
   (C) judging
   (D) judgment

5. The host usually _____ the check for his guest.
   (A) picks over
   (B) picks on
   (C) picks off
   (D) picks up

6. Sometimes diners request _____, or "separate," checks.
   (A) individuality
   (B) Individually
   (C) individual
   (D) individualize

7. The most _____ customers seem to be the worst tippers.
   (A) demand
   (B) demanded
   (C) demanding
   (D) demandingly

8. Food preparation is not just frying hamburgers; it is a respected _____.
   (A) profess
   (B) professing
   (C) profession
   (D) professional

9. An event planner must _____ the entire affair, not just choose the menu.
   (A) coordinated
   (B) coordinating
   (C) coordinator
   (D) coordinate

10. The planner must also ensure that participants observe all local _____.
    (A) regulated
    (B) regulations
    (C) regulating
    (D) regulate

Choose the underlined word or phrase that should be rewritten and rewrite it.

11. Although most of us <u>settle</u> for a <u>familiar</u> restaurant, a <u>daringly</u> diner will listen to other <u>suggestions</u>.
                       A   B   C   D

    _____

12. A <u>site</u> for a national <u>culinary</u> event should be in close <u>proximity</u> to <u>elegantly</u> restaurants and cooking supply
      A   B   C   D
    stores.

    _____

13. <u>Ingredients</u> are not added <u>randomly</u> to a dish; a <u>mixed up</u> in the order during food preparation could change
        A   B   C
    the <u>flavor</u>.
       D

    _____

14. I enjoy a restaurant that <u>mixes</u> its offerings and <u>relies</u> on flavor and <u>elegance</u> to bring <u>patronize</u> back.
                              A   B   C   D

    _____

15. Although a <u>general</u> concept of the <u>ideal</u> event is all right at the beginning, the outline must become more

A   B
    <u>exacted</u> as <u>planning</u> continues.

C   D

    _____

16. <u>Accustom to</u> impressing patrons, the chef taught his <u>apprentice</u> how to use <u>culinary</u> tricks to <u>incorporate</u> the

A   B   C   D
    best flavors and textures.

    _____

17. While even the most <u>demanding</u> chefs draw on traditional <u>methods</u>, new technology has <u>multiplied</u> ways to

A   B   C
    improve flavor without <u>compromise</u> quality.

D

    _____

18. <u>Securing</u> reservations doesn't guarantee seating on <u>arrived</u>, but it does <u>narrow</u> the chances of a long wait if

A   B   C
    there is a sudden <u>influx</u> of diners.

D

    _____

19. Some restaurants require a long <u>lead time</u> for <u>staging</u> a large event, but that time will allow you to add any-

A   B
    thing you had <u>forgetting</u> and <u>settle</u> matters you hadn't thought about.

C   D

    _____

20. Offering to pay the tip while your host <u>settles</u> the bill is a way to <u>reminder</u> someone who has <u>forgotten</u> that a

A   B   C
    tip, although <u>subjective</u>, should be at least 15 percent of the bill.

D

    _____

Lesson 36

General Travel

Words to learn

agent
announcement
beverage
blanket
board
claim
delay
depart
embarkation
itinerary
prohibit
valid

1. **agent** n., a representative of a company
   a. A travel agent can usually find you the best deals on tickets and hotels.
   b. You can buy your ticket from the ticket agent at the train station right before you get on the train.
2. **announcement** n., a public notification
   a. Did you hear an announcement about our new departure time?
   b. I expect an announcement any time now about a snow emergency at the airport.
3. **beverage** n., a drink other than plain water
   a. The flight attendant offered all passengers a cold beverage during the flight.
   b. The restaurant had a range of beverages on the drinks menu, including soft drinks and juices.
4. **blanket** n., a covering for keeping warm, especially during sleep; any full coverage; v., to cover uniformly
   a. It's going to be a cold night so I'll ask housekeeping to send an extra blanket for our bed.
   b. The snow blanketed the windshield, making it difficult to see the roads.
5. **board** v., to enter a boat, plane, or train
   a. For security reasons, visitors are not allowed in the area of the airport where passengers board the planes.
   b. We will board the train for New York in ten minutes.
6. **claim** v., to take as rightful; to retrieve
   a. Please proceed directly to the baggage arrival area to claim your luggage.
   b. Lost luggage can be claimed at the airline office.
7. **delay** v., to postpone until a later time
   a. The bus was delayed due to inclement weather.
   b. The heavy traffic delayed our arrival at the train station.
8. **depart** v., to go away or leave; to vary from a regular course of action.
   a. After the wedding, the married couple departed for their honeymoon in Morocco.
   b. We're going to depart from our usual policy and allow you to leave work early one day a week.
9. **embarkation** n., the process of getting on a plane or ship
   a. Cruise passengers are given a pass for embarkation when they check in at the dock.
   b. The flight crew must check the passengers' documents before embarkation.
10. **itinerary** n., a proposed route for a journey, showing dates and means of travel
    a. He reviewed the itinerary the travel agent had faxed him before purchasing the ticket.
    b. I had to change my itinerary when I decided to add two more countries to my vacation.
11. **prohibit** v., to forbid by authority or to prevent
    a. We were prohibited from wearing casual clothes in the office.
    b. Airline regulations prohibit the passengers from having beverages open during takeoff and landing.
12. **valid** adj., having legal efficacy or correctness
    a. I need to make certain that my passport is valid if we plan to go overseas this December.
    b. The officer's argument for increased airport security seemed valid at the time.

Word Families

verb	announce	The captain announced that the flight would be landing in approximately 15 minutes.
noun	announcement	The flight attendant made an announcement reminding the passengers that this was a no-smoking flight.
noun	announcer	The announcer gave the instructions for boarding, in three languages.

verb	board	You can't board the flight without an embarkation card.
noun	board	The board of directors met to discuss problems with the striking pilots.
adjective	onboard	The onboard telephone was expensive to use, but a true time-saver.

verb	claim	International passengers must proceed to customs as soon as they claim their baggage.
noun	claim	If the airline has lost your luggage, you can file a claim with the insurance company.
noun	claimant	There was a long line of claimants waiting at the lost luggage office.

verb	delay	Please don't delay me; I need to get to my gate immediately.
noun	delay	The delay in takeoff times was caused by a bad storm.

verb	depart	The flight will depart from Gate 25.
noun	departure	The pilot always reminds the flight attendants to make sure that all passengers are ready for departure.
adjective	departed	The house felt empty without the departed guests.

verb	validate	You can get your parking ticket validated at the concierge desk.
noun	validation	The restaurant received three stars, which is quite a validation of the chef's skills.
adjective	valid	Your ticket is no longer valid because it was issued over a year ago.

Incomplete Sentences

Choose the word that best completes the sentence.

1. The desk clerk _____ the change in gate numbers at least an hour ago.
    (A) announcement
    (B) announcing
    (C) announcer
    (D) announced

2. When it's time to _____ the flight, an announcement will be made.
    (A) boarded
    (B) boarding
    (C) board
    (D) boarder

3. As soon as John _____ his luggage, he went outside to look for a taxi.
    (A) claim
    (B) claimed
    (C) claimant
    (D) claims

4. The man had to _____ his travel plans because an emergency came up at work.
    (A) delay
    (B) delaying
    (C) delayed
    (D) delays

5. The train's _____ was delayed because of a problem on the track.
    (A) departed
    (B) departure
    (C) departs
    (D) depart

6. The airport applied a blanket rule that all passengers must be in possession of _____ tickets in order to enter the waiting area.
    (A) valid
    (B) validity
    (C) validate
    (D) validation

Error Recognition

Choose the underlined word or phrase that should be rewritten and rewrite it.

7. Once we heard that the <u>departing</u> flight would be <u>delaying</u> for several hours, because of the fog that <u>blanketed</u>
          A   B   C
    the coast, we exercised by walking around the baggage <u>claim</u> area.
                                                            D

    _____

8. Because he had lost the <u>itinerary</u> that his travel <u>agent</u> had given him, Mr. Peacock looked at the <u>embark</u> card
                              A   B   C
    to check the exact time that his flight would <u>depart</u>.
                                                   D

    _____

9. The man had to show the gate attendant his <u>validation</u> passport and <u>itinerary</u>, in addition to his <u>embarkation</u>
                                                 A   B   C
    card, before he was allowed to <u>board</u> the flight.
                                    D

    _____

10. The <u>announcement</u> reminded all <u>boarding</u> passengers that carrying on <u>beverages</u> was <u>prohibition</u> on this
        A   B   C   D
    airline.

    _____

Reading Comprehension

Read the following passage and write the words in the blanks below.

agent	blanket	delayed	itinerary
announcements	board	depart	prohibited
beverage	claims	embarkation	valid

When Ms. Tan has to go on business travel, she calls her favorite travel (11.) _____. He reminds her to make sure that she takes a (12.) _____ passport on her trip. Once her reservations have been made and confirmed, the travel agent will issue a ticket and an (13.) _____. Before leaving for the airport, she calls the airline to check if the flight is on time and has not been (14.)_____.

At the airport, after checking in her suitcase at the check-in counter, since she is (15.) _____ from taking more than one piece of carry-on luggage onto the plane, Ms. Tan receives her (16.) _____ card. She will present this at the gate when it is time to (17.) _____ her flight. She is told to be at the gate 15 minutes before the flight is to (18.) _____. During the flight, the attendant may offer her a (19.) _____, and she can even request a (20.) _____ if she is cold. The captain will make (21.) _____ during the flight to let the passengers know at what altitude they are flying, and when they may expect to arrive at their destination.

Once the flight has landed, Ms. Tan disembarks and must go through customs after she (22.) _____ her baggage. After this, she will take a cab to the hotel where she is staying, so she can rest and prepare for her meeting the next day. She will also reconfirm her return flight a day or two before she leaves to return home.

LISTENING COMPREHENSION

Listen to Track 36 of the Compact Disc to hear the statements for Lesson 36

Part I Picture

Look at the picture and listen to the sentences. Choose the sentence that best describes the picture.

23. Ⓐ Ⓑ Ⓒ Ⓓ

Part II Question—Response

Listen to the question and the three responses. Choose the response that best answers the question.

24. Ⓐ Ⓑ Ⓒ   25. Ⓐ Ⓑ Ⓒ

Part III Short Conversations

Listen to the short dialogs. Then read the question and choose the best answer.

26. Why will the woman's trip be delayed?
    (A) It's too late to get a ticket.
    (B) The travel agent won't accept her credit card.
    (C) She needs to renew her passport.
    (D) She's afraid of flying.

27. Who is the man speaking with?
    (A) A pilot.
    (B) A hotel clerk.
    (C) A travel agent.
    (D) A flight attendant.

Part IV Short Talks

Listen to the short talk. Then read the questions and choose the best answer.

28. What do passengers have to show the flight attendant?
    (A) An embarkation card.
    (B) A passport.
    (C) A trip itinerary.
    (D) A boarding pass.

29. When will the flight leave?
    (A) At 1:15.
    (B) In twenty minutes.
    (C) At nine o'clock.
    (D) In five minutes.

Airlines

1. **deal with** v. phrase, to attend to; to manage; to see to
    a. Ticket agents must deal courteously with irate customers.
    b. Sick passengers, frightened children, and rude pilots are just a few of the things cabin attendants have to deal with.
2. **destination** n., the place to which one is going or directed
    a. The Great Barrier Reef is a popular tourist destination this year.
    b. Once you have determined your desired destination, we can work toward getting the best airfare.
3. **distinguish** v., to make noticeable or different
    a. Suki was able to distinguish between the different types of jets on the runway.
    b. My travel agent has distinguished herself as being one of the best in our area.
4. **economize** v., to be careful about spending money
    a. My travel agent knows I like to economize and always looks out for the best prices for me.
    b. We decided to economize this year and take our vacation during the off season, when prices are lower.
5. **equivalent** adj., equal
    a. Carlos used the Internet to search for hotels of equivalent dollar value to the one recommended.
    b. The food the airline serves in coach class is equivalent to that served in first class.
6. **excursion** n., a pleasure trip; a trip at a reduced fare
    a. With some time between meetings in London, the company president enjoyed an excursion to Stonehenge.
    b. The finance officer was pleased to find an excursion for the entire consulting team.
7. **expense** n., something requiring payment
    a. A luxury vacation involves many expenses.
    b. If we keep our expenses down, we might have enough money to take a longer trip.
8. **extend** v., to make longer; to offer
    a. We extended our vacation by a day.
    b. Our wonderful travel agent extended the full services of her firm to us.
9. **prospective** adj., likely to become or be
    a. The airline had a reception to impress travel agents who might be prospective clients.
    b. I narrowed my list of prospective destinations to my three top choices.
10. **situation** n., the combination of circumstances at a given moment
    a. The airline suggested I check with the State Department regarding the political situation in the country I'm flying to.
    b. The vast number of different airfares available makes for a complicated situation.
11. **substantially** adj., significantly
    a. The airline I work for had a substantially higher rating for customer satisfaction than our competitors had.
    b. The airfares charged by different airlines are not substantially different.
12. **system** n., a functionally related group of elements
    a. The airline system covers the entire world with flights.
    b. We need a better system to keep track of how much money we are spending on this vacation.

Word Families

verb	distinguish	I can't distinguish any difference in the two airlines, since their fares are the same.
adjective	distinguishable	The airline's planes were easily distinguishable by the bright logo on the planes' tails.
adverb	distinguishably	Even though you have paid a lower fare, we won't be distinguishably different than the other passengers on the plane.

verb	economize	We no longer fly first class, since our company is trying to econmize.
adjective	economical	Without hesitation, we chose the more economical of the two airline tickets.
adverb	economically	A good travel agent can help you plan your trip economically.

noun	expense	To stay within our travel budget, we must keep all our expenses as low as possible.
adjective	expensively	The first-class seats are for those who travel expensively but with great style.
adverb	expensive	Only the most expensive fares were still available.

verb	extend	When people travel to an interesting destination for business, they often extend their trip by a few days in order to enjoy the place as a tourist.
noun	extent	Larry has traveled to Japan many times and the extent of his knowledge of that country is impressive.
adjective	extensive	Pamela is taking six months off from work in order to take an extensive tour of South America.

noun	prospect	The prospects of getting a seat on this evening's flight are not good.
adjective	prospective	The travel agency offered special deals in order to attract prospective customers.

noun	substance	I couldn't recognize the substance that was on my meal tray and that the airlines called dinner.
adjective	substantial	Ms. Qin found there was a substantial difference in the price quoted for the plane ticket, depending on which day she flew.
adverb	substantially	There is substantially no difference in the quality of food served in first class and in economy class.

Incomplete Sentences

Choose the word that best completes the sentence.

1. Let me point out the features of our service that _____ our airline from our competitors.
   (A) distinguishably
   (B) distinguishable
   (C) distinguishing
   (D) distinguish

2. Let's shop around until we find a more _____ airfare.
   (A) economical
   (B) economize
   (C) economy
   (D) economically

3. We need to keep our _____ down so you'll have to find us better prices on airline tickets.
   (A) expensiveness
   (B) expensively
   (C) expenses
   (D) expensive

4. I decided not to _____ my trip since I felt so tired by the time I finished my business meetings.
   (A) extended
   (B) extent
   (C) extensive
   (D) extend

5. My travel agent said there were good _____ of finding a reasonably priced airfare.
   (A) prospective
   (B) prospectively
   (C) prospectors
   (D) prospects

6. Unless the airfares differ _____, you should book seats on the airline with which you have frequent flyer miles.
   (A) substance
   (B) substantially
   (C) substantial
   (D) substantiality

Error Recognition

Choose the underlined word or phrase that should be rewritten and rewrite it.

7. For travelers looking for economical **(A)** fares, you get substantially **(B)** savings with special excursion **(C)** rates to your destination **(D)**.

   _____

8. Due to the expense **(A)** of flights to our travel destination **(B)**, our travel agent suggests we extensive **(C)** our stay to get the most out of the difficult situation **(D)**.

   _____

9. The airline system **(A)** is so complex that it is difficult to distinguishable **(B)** between equivalent **(C)** fares on different airlines; that is why most people appreciate the expertise of a travel agent used to dealing **(D)** with the airlines.

   _____

10. A prospect **(A)** traveler may need to compromise to get an economical **(B)** excursion **(C)** fare to a vacation destination **(D)**.

    _____

Reading Comprehension

Read the following passage and write the words in the blanks below.

deal with	equivalent	extending	situation
destination	excursion	distinguishable	substantial
economical	expensive	prospective	system

If you travel, you most likely will have to (11.) _____ flying. Flying is the quickest, most convenient means of travel between countries, and often between different parts of one country. Flying is (12.) _____, but when all costs are taken into account for traveling any (13.) _____ distance, air travel is usually less expensive than driving by car. It is also the most (14.) _____ way to go in terms of time. You'll miss the scenery en route, but you'll have more time at your vacation (15.) _____ with air travel.

Airlines sell seats at a variety of prices under a (16.) _____ of requirements and restrictions. Full-fare tickets are the most expensive, but give you the most flexibility in terms of making changes. A (17.) _____ traveler can buy a ticket up to takeoff time as long as a seat is available.

Fares change rapidly, and even travel experts find it difficult to keep up. The changing (18.) _____ is due to many factors, including increased competition. As a general rule, the less you pay for the ticket, the more restrictions you can expect. If you are trying to save money, look for (19.) _____ fares. These are the airline's (20.) _____ of a special sale. Most excursion fares are for round-trip travel and have strict regulations and a minimum and maximum length of stay, so don't count on (21.) _____ your vacation or staying less time than required. However, once you are on the plane, you are not (22.) _____ from passengers who paid higher fares.

LISTENING COMPREHENSION

Listen to Track 37 of the Compact Disc to hear the statements for Lesson 37

Part I Picture

Look at the picture and listen to the sentences. Choose the sentence that best describes the picture.

23. Ⓐ Ⓑ Ⓒ Ⓓ

Part II Question—Response

Listen to the question and the three responses. Choose the response that best answers the question.

24. Ⓐ Ⓑ Ⓒ   25. Ⓐ Ⓑ Ⓒ

Part III Short Conversations

Listen to the short dialogs. Then read the question and choose the best answer.

26. How can the traveler get a lower airfare?
    (A) By being flexible about dates.
    (B) By arriving on Sunday.
    (C) By changing the destination.
    (D) By paying before noon today.

27. What are the speakers discussing?
    (A) The length of the trip.
    (B) The schedule of the airline.
    (C) The cost of the ticket.
    (D) The quality of the airline.

Part IV Short Talks

Listen to the short talk. Then read the questions and choose the best answer.

28. How can a client find out about tickets to another country?
    (A) Call back later.
    (B) Press two.
    (C) Use the computer.
    (D) Press one.

29. What can a client do by pressing three?
    (A) Make hotel reservations.
    (B) Purchase airline tickets.
    (C) Find out about excursion rates.
    (D) Connect with the agency's computer.

Trains

1. **comprehensive** adj., covering broadly; inclusive
   a. The conductor has a comprehensive knowledge of rail systems from all over the world.
   b. Our travel agent gave us a comprehensive travel package, including rail passes.

2. **deluxe** adj., noticeably luxurious
   a. My parents decided to splurge on deluxe accommodations for their trip.
   b. The train station is not near any of the deluxe hotels, so we will have to take a taxi.

3. **directory** n., a book or collection of information or directions
   a. We consulted the directory to see where the train station was located.
   b. By calling directory assistance, Mr. Scannel was able to get the phone number for the train station.

4. **duration** n., the time during which something lasts
   a. Mother lent me her spare jacket for the duration of the trip.
   b. Despite our personal differences, my roommate and I agreed to be as pleasant as possible for the duration of the train ride.

5. **entitle** v., to allow or qualify
   a. During the holiday rush, a train ticket entitled the passenger to a ride, but not necessarily a seat.
   b. The mess the train line made of Pedro's sleeping room reservations entitled him to a free upgrade to a better room.

6. **fare** n., the money paid for transportation
   a. The train fare has increased since I rode last.
   b. Pay your fare at the ticket office and you will get a ticket to board the train.

7. **offset** v., to counterbalance
   a. The high cost of the hotel room offset the savings we made by taking the train instead of the plane.
   b. By reducing her transportation costs once in the United States, Mrs. Sato offset the cost of getting to this country.

8. **operate** v., to perform a function
   a. The train operates on a punctual schedule.
   b. The train only operates in this area at the height of the tourist season.

9. **punctually** adv., promptly
   a. Please be on time; the train leaves punctually at noon.
   b. The train usually arrives punctually; I can't imagine what is delaying it today.

10. **relatively** adv., somewhat
    a. The train is relatively empty for this time of day.
    b. The train station has been relatively busy for a weekday.

11. **remainder** n., the remaining part
    a. The Alaskan frontier has train service in the summer, but for the remainder of the year the tracks are impassable.
    b. We will move you to a less expensive room and credit the remainder of what you've already paid to your charge card.

12. **remote** adj., far removed
    a. I was surprised to find train service to such a remote location.
    b. We took the train out of the city and found a remote hotel in the country for the weekend.

Word Families

noun	comprehensiveness	Due to the comprehensiveness of the train system, the complete timetable was a thick document.
adjective	comprehensive	Due to the comprehensive reach of the rail system, the train can take you to every major city and many smaller ones.
adverb	comprehensively	The surveyors comprehensively studied the terrain before planning the site for the new train tracks.

verb	direct	We were unfamiliar with the city, so the hotel manager directed us to the train station.
noun	direction	The ticket agent at the train station gave us directions to the nearest restaurant.
noun	directory	At the train station you can pick up a free directory to local restaurants, museums, and other places of interest to visitors.

verb	operate	Trains don't operate in this town after the summer tourism season is over.
noun	operation	The train system is a massive operation with thousands of large and small stations across the country.
adjective	operational	As the operational expenses for the train system rose, the managers were forced to either cut services or raise prices.

noun	punctuality	The Swiss trains are legendary for their punctuality.
adjective	punctual	For a transportation service to have any credibility, it must be punctual.
adverb	punctually	The conductor arrived punctually at the train station.

verb	remain	It is safer for all passengers to remain in their seats until the train comes to a complete stop.
noun	remains	The waiter cleared off the remains of our meal after we left the dining car.
noun	remainder	After our exciting stay in New York, the remainder of the trip seemed dull.

noun	remoteness	The remoteness of the state park was part of its attraction, but since it's not served by a train line, I couldn't get to it.
adjective	remote	The remote cabin in the woods can only be reached by car; the nearest train station or airport is more than 100 miles away.
adverb	remotely	I wasn't remotely interested in taking a cross-country trip by train since I can't stand to be confined for a long time.

Incomplete Sentences

Choose the word that best completes the sentence.

1. Do you have a _____ map that shows all the station stops west of the Mississippi?
   (A) comprehension
   (B) comprehensively
   (C) comprehensive
   (D) comprehensiveness

2. We got lost in the train station and had to ask for _____ to the gate that our train was leaving from.
   (A) directions
   (B) directed
   (C) directory
   (D) directs

3. The train has stopped because of a malfunction, but we expect it to be _____ again within minutes.
   (A) operational
   (B) operate
   (C) operation
   (D) operationally

4. John never arrives _____, so I am always anxious when we travel together for fear of missing a train.
   (A) punctualness
   (B) punctually
   (C) punctual
   (D) punctuality

5. Sylvia's family _____ with her in the station until she was ready to board the train.
   (A) remains
   (B) remainder
   (C) remained
   (D) remaining

6. With this traffic, there isn't even a _____ chance that we will get to the train station on time.
   (A) remotely
   (B) remote
   (C) remoteness
   (D) remotest

Error Recognition

Choose the underlined word or phrase that should be rewritten and rewrite it.

7. If the train is <u>punctuality</u> to the time schedule listed in the <u>directory</u>, we can <u>offset</u> the previous delay and be

A   B   C
   back on schedule for the <u>remainder</u> of the trip.

D

   _____

8. The lesser <u>fare</u> does not necessarily <u>entitle</u> you to a seat, so there is a <u>remotely</u> chance you will have to stand

      A   B   C
   when the train <u>operates</u> on a busy holiday.

D

   _____

9.. The train has a <u>comprehensively</u> array of sleeping accommodations, ranging from <u>deluxe</u> suites to <u>relatively</u>

           A   B   C
   small rooms, with a range of <u>fares</u>.

D

   _____

10. The transcontinental train ride, which is 12 days in <u>duration</u>, <u>operating</u> through some of the more <u>remote</u> parts

         A   B   C
    of Canada; then the <u>remainder</u> of your trip is in the beautiful city of Vancouver.

D

    _____

Reading Comprehension

Read the following passage and write the words in the blanks below.

comprehensive	duration	offset	relatively
deluxe	entitle	operate	remainder
directories	fares	punctual	remote

Trains are among the best ways to see a lot of a country in a (11.) _____ short amount of time. In addition to the consideration of time, traveling by train allows you to really see the country you are passing through. You need only get to the station on time; after that you can relax and watch from the window.

Most trains are on time and run on a (12.) _____ schedule. Routes, schedules, and (13.) _____ are listed in a timetable available at a train station, in many travel (14.) _____, or posted on the World Wide Web. Directories that are (15.) _____ list all the trains, the cities they serve, the stations they depart from, and the class of services available. A few (16.) _____ travel destinations are accessible only during the peak tourist season; the train does not (17.) _____ there the (18.) _____ of the year.

The fare is based on how far you travel and the quality of your accommodations. The basic fare buys you a seat for the (19.) _____ of the trip. To be more precise, an unreserved seat guarantees a passenger transportation only; seats are allocated on a first-come, first-served basis. On busy holidays, it is possible that you could stand for at least some of your trip. For long trips, you will want to reserve a seat.

If you are traveling overnight, the cost of your room accommodation will depend on how (20.) _____ your room is. Although taking the train is less expensive than flying, the savings may be (21.) _____ by the cost of booking a sleeping room.

Travelers coming to the United States can take advantage of special rates not available in the United States. These passes (22.) _____ the bearer to unlimited coach travel on trains for a fixed period of days, usually a month.

LISTENING COMPREHENSION

Listen to Track 38 of the Compact Disc to hear the statements for Lesson 38

Part I Picture

Look at the picture and listen to the sentences. Choose the sentence that best describes the picture.

23. Ⓐ Ⓑ Ⓒ Ⓓ

Part II Question—Response

Listen to the question and the three responses. Choose the response that best answers the question.

24. Ⓐ Ⓑ Ⓒ   25. Ⓐ Ⓑ Ⓒ

Part III Short Conversations

Listen to the short dialogs. Then read the question and choose the best answer.

26. Why do the speakers have to stand?
    (A) They bought their tickets late.
    (B) The trip isn't long.
    (C) They didn't pay a high fare.
    (D) The train is crowded.

27. What are the speakers discussing?
    (A) The operator of the train.
    (B) The comfort of the train ride.
    (C) The directions to the train station.
    (D) The time the train leaves.

Part IV Short Talks

Listen to the short talk. Then read the questions and choose the best answer.

28. What is an advantage of riding a high-speed train?
    (A) It is always on time.
    (B) It goes to many cities.
    (C) You can get off anytime you want.
    (D) It is cheaper than a plane.

29. What is true about a high-speed train?
    (A) It is just as fast as a plane.
    (B) It is almost as slow as a traditional train.
    (C) It is almost as fast as a plane in some cases.
    (D) It's just as fast as a traditional train.

Hotels

1. **advanced** adj., highly developed; at a higher level
   a. Since the hotel installed an advanced computer system, all operations have been functioning more smoothly.
   b. Pablo has been promoted to assistant manager and he is happy with his advanced position.

2. **chain** n., a group of enterprises under a single control
   a. Budget-priced hotel chains have made a huge impact in the industry.
   b. The hotel being built in Seoul is the newest one in the chain.

3. **check in** v., to register at a hotel; to report one's presence
   a. Patrons check in at the hotel immediately upon their arrival.
   b. To know that the conference guests have arrived, we ask them to check in at the registration desk.

4. **confirm** v., to validate
   a. Jorge called the hotel to confirm that he had a room reservation.
   b. We automatically send a postcard to let you know that your travel dates have been confirmed.

5. **expect** v., to consider probable or reasonable
   a. You can expect a clean room when you check in at a hotel.
   b. Mr. Kim expected that the bed linens would be changed daily.

6. **housekeeper** n., someone employed to do domestic work
   a. Eloise's first job at the hotel was as a housekeeper and now she is the manager.
   b. The desk clerk is sending the housekeeper to bring more towels to your room.

7. **notify** v., to report
   a. They notified the hotel that they had been delayed in traffic and would be arriving late.
   b. Lydia notified the hotel in writing that she was canceling her reservation.

8. **preclude** v., to make impossible; to rule out
   a. The horrible rainstorm precluded us from traveling any further.
   b. The unexpected cost of the room precluded a gourmet dinner for the travelers.

9. **quote** v., to give exact information on; n., a quotation
   a. We were quoted a price of $89 for the room for one night.
   b. Call ahead and get a price quote for a week-long stay.

10. **rate** n., the payment or price according to a standard
    a. The rate for the hotel room is too high considering how few services are available on-site.
    b. The sign in the lobby lists the seasonal rates.

11. **reservation** n., an arrangement to set something aside
    a. I know I made a reservation for tonight, but the hotel staff has no record of it in the system.
    b. It is difficult, if not impossible, to get reservations at this hotel at the height of the summer season.

12. **service** n., useful functions
    a. The hotel has a number of luxury services like the on-site gym, sauna, pool, and beauty salon.
    b. Mr. Rockmont called room service to order a late-night snack.

Word Families

verb	advance	We are advancing steadily toward our goal of improving customer service at every hotel in the chain.
noun	advance	Clarissa booked the bridal suite in advance of the hotel's official opening.
adjective	advanced	All hotel employees who do well at their jobs will be given the opportunity to move up to an advanced position.

verb	confirm	It is wise to confirm your reservation before you leave for your trip.
noun	confirmation	The confirmation code given to Suzanne when she booked her room made it easy for her to resolve her problem.
adjective	confirmed	The concierge had the confirmed helpful manner that is necessary in her position.

verb	expect	We expect to reach our destination by dinner.
noun	expectation	The guest's expectations were not met, so he complained to the manager.
adjective	expectant	The expectant travelers, loaded with luggage, left the hotel for their scheduled flight.

verb	notify	Please notify the front desk clerk if there are any problems with your room.
noun	notification	Written notification is required for any changes in reservations.

verb	quote	When customers ask for the room rate, just quote them the prices listed on this sheet.
noun	quotation	The quotation given to me didn't make sense, so I called again to verify it.
adjective	quotable	Our manager instructed us that the current room rates would be quotable only until the end of the month, when a rate increase would go into effect.

verb	reserve	We reserved a room well in advance.
noun	reservation	Seeing the crowds on the highway, I decided to pull over and telephone the hotel to make a reservation.
noun	in reserve	Like many other businesses, a hotel must keep some cash in reserve to pay for emergencies.

Incomplete Sentences

Choose the word that best completes the sentence.

1. We paid a lot of money for this room and we expect an _____ level of service.
   (A) advance   (C) advanced
   (B) advances   (D) advancing

2. Gladys _____ her reservation by calling in advance.
   (A) confirmation   (C) confirming
   (B) confirmed   (D) confirmative

3. The Chamber of Commerce had high _____ for the amount of business the new hotel would bring to the town.
   (A) expectancy   (C) expect
   (B) expected   (D) expectations

4. The hotel received the _____ of our early arrival and had everything ready for us.
   (A) notified   (C) notification
   (B) notifies   (D) notify

5. I expect the rate that I was _____ over the phone and I will not accept any changes.
   (A) quoted   (C) quotable
   (B) quotation   (D) quotes

6. Since we had made our _____ so far in advance, we saved considerably on the room rate.
   (A) reserve   (C) reserved
   (B) reservation   (D) reservable

Error Recognition

Choose the underlined word or phrase that should be rewritten and rewrite it.

7. By making <u>reserve</u> three months in <u>advance</u>, Cleo was able to take advantage of a special <u>rate</u> that was
          A   **B**   **C**
   cheaper than the price <u>quoted</u> in the hotel brochure.
                     D

   _____

8. With multiple locations in every major city, the dominant hotel <u>chains</u> offer low <u>rates</u> and extensive <u>services</u>
                                            A   **B**   **C**
   that many small hotels are <u>preclusion</u> from offering.
                          D

   _____

9. Even before you <u>check in</u> at the registration desk, you can <u>expectation</u> that the hotel <u>housekeeper</u> has made
                     A   **B**   **C**
   your room ready in <u>advance</u> of your arrival.
                     D

   _____

10. Before departing for his trip, Jacques called the hotel in <u>advance</u> to <u>confirm</u> the <u>rate</u> and to make sure the staff
                                                 A   **B**   **C**
    had been <u>notification</u> that he needed a wheelchair-accessible room.
                D

    _____

Reading Comprehension

Read the following passage and write the words in the blanks below.

advance	confirm	notify	rates
chains	expect	preclude	reservations
check in	housekeeper	quoted	service

People stay in hotels for business and personal travel. But with room rates being so high, many travelers are staying home. Since high costs can (11.) _____ travel, smart travelers know they can save money and get the best (12.) _____ for a room by making (13.) _____ well in (14.) _____ of the beginning of their trip. When you make a reservation, the hotel staff will ask you to (15.) _____ them as soon as there is any change in your travel plans. To avoid any surprises, it's a good idea to call and (16.) _____ the availability of your room and the rate you were (17.) _____.

In selecting a hotel, first think about the kinds of (18.) _____ you will need or like to have. You naturally (19.) _____ a clean, well-lit room. You naturally expect that a (20.) _____ will clean your room daily even in the smallest hotels. Large hotel (21.) _____ offer the most services, such as a pool, health club, or money exchange. The front desk clerks will tell you about such services when you (22.) _____ at the hotel.

LISTENING COMPREHENSION

Listen to Track 39 of the Compact Disc to hear the statements for Lesson 39

Part I Picture

Look at the picture and listen to the sentences. Choose the sentence that best describes the picture.

23. Ⓐ Ⓑ Ⓒ Ⓓ

Part II Question—Response

Listen to the question and the three responses. Choose the response that best answers the question.

24. Ⓐ Ⓑ Ⓒ   25. Ⓐ Ⓑ Ⓒ

Part III Short Conversations

Listen to the short dialogs. Then read the question and choose the best answer.

26. When will Mrs. Kim arrive at the hotel?
    (A) Today.
    (B) This weekend.
    (C) Next winter.
    (D) In several weeks.

27. When must a customer notify the hotel?
    (A) When she wants to leave a deposit.
    (B) When she will arrive several hours early.
    (C) When she expects to return to the hotel.
    (D) When she wants to cancel a reservation.

Part IV Short Talks

Listen to the short talk. Then read the questions and choose the best answer.

28. Who is the speaker addressing?
    (A) New hotel employees.
    (B) Regular hotel customers.
    (C) Experienced hotel managers.
    (D) Hotel chain owners.

29. What is the goal of the hotel chain?
    (A) To get more customers.
    (B) To provide the best service.
    (C) To charge higher rates.
    (D) To hire more employees.

Lesson

40

Car Rentals

Words to learn

busy
coincide
confusion
contact
disappoint
intend
license
nervously
optional
tempt
thrill
tier

1. **busy** adj., engaged in activity
   a. Alfred was busy getting ready for his vacation.
   b. The airport was busy, with people catching planes and heading for car rental companies.
2. **coincide** v., to happen at the same time
   a. My cousin's wedding coincided with a holiday weekend, so it was a perfect time to rent a car and go for a drive.
   b. Sean was hoping that the days for the special discount on car rentals would coincide with his vacation, but they did not.
3. **confusion** n., a lack of clarity, order, or understanding
   a. There was some confusion about which rental discount coupons applied to which car rental agency.
   b. To avoid any confusion about renting the car, Yolanda asked her travel agent to make the arrangements on her behalf.
4. **contact** v., to get in touch with
   a. Manuel contacted at least a dozen car rental agencies to get the best deal.
   b. Last night I was contacted by my travel agent who said he had found a better price on a car rental.
5. **disappoint** v., to fail to satisfy the hope, desire, or expectation of
   a. Leila was disappointed to discover that no rental cars were available the weekend she wished to travel.
   b. I hate to disappoint you, but I can't allow you to rent a car unless you have a major credit card.
6. **intend** v., to have in mind
   a. I never intended to drive to Los Angeles until my brother suggested we do it together.
   b. Do you intend to return the car to this location or to another location?
7. **license** n., the legal permission to do or own a specified thing
   a. First, I'll need to see your driver's license and a major credit card.
   b. You will need a license in order to run this business.
8. **nervously** adv., in a distressed or uneasy manner
   a. As we approached the city Lonnie started driving nervously, so I volunteered to drive that part of the trip.
   b. I looked around nervously the entire time I was in the dark parking garage.
9. **optional** adj., not compulsory or automatic
   a. Check this box if you wish to have this optional insurance.
   b. Having a driver's license is not optional.
10. **tempt** v., to be inviting or attractive to
    a. I am tempted by the idea of driving across the country instead of flying.
    b. Gina is tempted to rent the smaller car to save a few dollars.
11. **thrill** n., the source or cause of excitement or emotion
    a. The thought of renting a sports car gave John a thrill.
    b. Just taking a vacation is thrill enough, even if we are driving instead of flying.
12. **tier** n., a rank or class
    a. The car rental company had a few tiers of cars, each one costing more than the previous tier.
    b. If you are on a budget, I suggest you think about renting a car from our lowest tier.

Word Families

verb	confuse	These long car rental contracts always confuse me.
noun	confusion	The crowds at the car rental office resulted in a lot of confusion.
adjective	confusing	Driving in an unfamiliar city can be quite confusing.

verb	coincide	This year, my vacation coincides with a national holiday, which will make renting a car more expensive.
noun	coincidence	By coincidence, I ran into an old friend in line waiting to rent a car.
adverb	coincidentally	Coincidentally, we are offering a special discount if you are over age 65.

verb	disappoint	The service at that car rental agency always disappoints me, so next time I plan to use a different agency.
noun	disappointment	The poor condition of the car we rented was an unexpected disappointment.
adjective	disappointing	The weather during our trip was so disappointing that we came home early.

noun	intention	I have every intention of paying by cash even though I reserved the car with my credit card.
adjective	intent	Intent on avoiding an accident, Zola drove cautiously through the rush hour traffic.
adverb	intently	The tourist intently studied the road map.

noun	nervousness	I hope my nervousness did not show when I was filling out the forms.
adjective	nervous	This was Jane's first time renting a car, so she was somewhat nervous.
adverb	nervously	Mr. Lane nervously parallel parked the rental car between two others in the parking garage.

verb	tempt	Can I tempt you to rent a larger car with a special discount?
noun	temptation	The temptation to drive the sports car fast was too great for Karl to resist.
adjective	tempting	As tempting as it sounds to drive to Florida, I think I'd rather fly.

Incomplete Sentences

Choose the word that best completes the sentence.

1. The constant road repair work made driving through the city _____.
   (A) confuse
   (B) confuses
   (C) confusion
   (D) confusing

2. I don't think it is a _____ that the special discount rate for renting a car expires right before the holiday weekend.
   (A) coincidental
   (B) coincidentally
   (C) coincidence
   (D) coincide

3. It was _____ to discover that the car rental company had only compact cars available.
   (A) disappointing
   (B) disappointed
   (C) disappointment
   (D) disappoints

4. Our _____ is to rent a comfortable car and spend several weeks driving through the mountains.
   (A) intent
   (B) intently
   (C) intention
   (D) intend

5. Tito _____ drove the rental car through the crowded garage following the signs to the car rental return location.
   (A) nerve
   (B) nervousness
   (C) nervous
   (D) nervously

6. The new car rental company _____ me to try them by offering a discount coupon toward my next rental.
   (A) tempted
   (B) tempting
   (C) temptation
   (D) temptress

Error Recognition

Choose the underlined word or phrase that should be rewritten and rewrite it.

7. Due to the <u>busy</u> weekend, by <u>coincidence</u> both a government and a religious holiday, travelers who had not
       A   B
   reserved ahead were <u>disappointment</u> when they <u>contacted</u> car rental agencies and found no cars available.
                    C   D

   _____

8. I'm sure the car rental agent did not <u>intend</u> to <u>confuse</u> me with the various insurance coverage <u>options</u>, but
                  A   B   C
   I was <u>nervousness</u> weighing my options and became overwhelmed.
         D

   _____

9. Carlos found the signs directing him to the car rental drop-off location so <u>confusion</u> that he drove <u>nervously</u>
                                       A   B
   around the parking garage until he finally used his cell phone to <u>contact</u> a <u>busy</u> agent and get directions.
                                               C   D

   _____

10. After inspecting the customer's credit card and driver's <u>license</u>, Luisa tried to <u>temptation</u> the customer into
                                             A   B
    renting a more expensive car by promoting the <u>thrill</u> of a sports car ride, but he chose a car from the rental
                                            C
    agency's budget <u>tier</u>.
             D

    _____

Reading Comprehension

Read the following passage and write the words in the blanks below.

busy	contacted	license	tempted
coincided	disappointment	nervous	thrill
confusing	intended	optional	tier

Many travelers taking a driving vacation simply rent a car. Yoko called ahead to rent a car at her vacation destination. Although she was (11.) _____ to book a car once she arrived at her destination, Yoko was (12.) _____ about not having a reservation. Her vacation (13.) _____ with a holiday, so she knew many other people would also be renting cars. Yoko wanted to avoid the (14.) _____ of finding that a car was not available at this (15.) _____ travel time.

There are a lot of car rental firms, so Yoko (16.) _____ several of them to compare rates and requirements. At each company she called, she learned she would need a valid driver's (17.) _____ and a major credit card to rent a car.

Yoko found the many different rates for renting cars (18.) _____. Some companies offered substantial discounts provided that the car was reserved for a certain number of days. One company offered her a great daily rate, but it was based on a three-day rental. Since she only (19.) _____ to rent the car for two days, the discount did not apply to her. Also, the base price did not cover (20.) _____ costs, like collision insurance or gas refills.

Another factor influencing the rate was the type of car. Rentals are based on a (21.) _____ price system. The more luxurious or sporty, or the larger the car, the higher the daily rate. Since Yoko needed only a small reliable car, she found a reasonable rate—although she would have liked the (22.) _____ of driving a convertible!

LISTENING COMPREHENSION

Listen to Track 40 of the Compact Disc to hear the statements for Lesson 40

Part I Picture

Look at the picture and listen to the sentences. Choose the sentence that best describes the picture.

23. Ⓐ Ⓑ Ⓒ Ⓓ

Part II Question—Response

Listen to the question and the three responses. Choose the response that best answers the question.

24. Ⓐ Ⓑ Ⓒ   25. Ⓐ Ⓑ Ⓒ

Part III Short Conversations

Listen to the short dialogs. Then read the question and choose the best answer.

26. Why are there no rental cars available?
    (A) All the cars have been rented because it's a busy holiday.
    (B) The rental company is closed for the weekend.
    (C) The staff of the rental company is on vacation.
    (D) The rental company has gone out of business.

27. Who is the man speaking with?
    (A) An insurance agent.
    (B) A police officer.
    (C) Another customer.
    (D) A car rental agent.

Part IV Short Talks

Listen to the short talk. Then read the questions and choose the best answer.

28. Who is the audience for this talk?
    (A) People who work in travel agencies.
    (B) People who rent cars locally.
    (C) People who work in car rental agencies.
    (D) People who travel to other countries.

29. When should a traveler get an international driver's license?
    (A) After arriving in another country.
    (B) After contacting a local rental agency.
    (C) Before leaving on a trip.
    (D) When signing a car rental contract.

Word Review #8   Lessons 36–40 Travel

Choose the word that best completes the sentence.

1. When _____ your luggage, be sure to check the name on the tag.
   (A) claim
   (B) claimed
   (C) claimant
   (D) claiming

2. The plane's _____ was delayed until the wings were defrosted.
   (A) depart
   (B) departed
   (C) departure
   (D) departing

3. Many airlines _____ courtesy discounts to senior citizens.
   (A) extend
   (B) extending
   (C) extension
   (D) extensive

4. It is easier to _____ making reservations if you are specific about your requirements.
   (A) deal in
   (B) deal from
   (C) deal out
   (D) deal with

5. Trains are generally more _____ than airlines.
   (A) punctuality
   (B) punctually
   (C) punctual
   (D) punctuate

6. Some travel agencies _____ on a very tight budget.
   (A) operating
   (B) operation
   (C) operates
   (D) operate

7. Even if you pay cash, you need a credit card just to _____ to a hotel.
   (A) check in
   (B) checks in
   (C) checking in
   (D) checked in

8. Sometimes when you arrive, there is no room for you, even with a _____ reservation.
   (A) confirm
   (B) confirms
   (C) confirmed
   (D) confirmation

9. Without a reservation, renting a car could be a big _____.
   (A) disappoint
   (B) disappointed
   (C) disappointing
   (D) disappointment

10. No one will allow someone who doesn't have a _____ to rent a car.
    (A) licensed
    (B) license
    (C) licensing
    (D) licensee

Choose the underlined word or phrase that should be rewritten and rewrite it.

11. Before <u>reservation</u> a hotel room, ask the agent to <u>quote</u> the lowest <u>rate</u>; then make a <u>confirmed</u> reservation.
          A   B   C   D

12. An airline can be <u>economical</u> and still <u>distinguishing</u> itself with more comfortable <u>blankets</u> or a wider choice of
                        A   B   C
    <u>beverages</u>.
    D

13. Before <u>boarding</u>, check the <u>valid</u> of your passport, that you have an extra copy of your <u>itinerary</u>, and that you
          A   B   C
    are not carrying any <u>prohibited</u> items.
                        D

14. The rental agency was so <u>busy</u> that people caught in the <u>confusion</u> were <u>tempted</u> to <u>contacting</u> another
                            A   B   C   D
    agency.

15. Finding an <u>economically</u> <u>excursion</u> fare does not mean that your trip must be <u>substantially</u> different from a
                A   B   C
    more <u>expensive</u> one.
          D

16. If your hotel accommodations do not meet your <u>expecting</u>, <u>notify</u> the <u>housekeeper</u>, who will immediately

A   B   C
    <u>service</u> the room.

D

    _____

17. Trains offer <u>comprehensive</u> services at very different <u>fares</u>, from the <u>deluxe</u> to the <u>relativity</u> basic.

A   B   C   D

    _____

18. Travel agencies are <u>notified</u> in <u>advance</u> of bargains and receive regular <u>announcing</u> about dangerous

A   B   C
    <u>situations</u>.

D

    _____

19. No matter what the rental rate, when you start selecting <u>options</u> equipment, you should be a little <u>nervous</u>

A   B
    about whether the value is <u>equivalent</u> to the <u>expense</u>.

C   D

    _____

20. At the point of <u>embarkation</u>, listen for <u>announcements</u> about when you may <u>board</u> or whether there will be a

A   B   C
    <u>delayed</u>.

D

    _____

Movies

1. **attainment** n., achievement
   a. The actress received a lot of attention for her many professional attainments.
   b. The attainment of an Academy Award validates a performer's career.

2. **combine** v., to come together
   a. The director combined two previously separate visual techniques.
   b. The new production company combines the talents of three of Hollywood's best known teams.

3. **continue** v., to maintain without interruption
   a. The film continues the story set out in an earlier film.
   b. The search for a star will continue until one is found.

4. **description** n., a representation in words or pictures
   a. The description of the film did not match what we saw on screen.
   b. The critic's description of the film made it sound very appealing.

5. **disperse** v., to spread widely, to scatter
   a. The reporters dispersed after the press agent cancelled the interview with the film director.
   b. The crowd outside the movie premiere would not disperse until they had seen the movie stars.

6. **entertainment** n., a diverting performance or activity
   a. The movie was provided for our entertainment.
   b. There was no entertainment for children of guests at the hotel.

7. **influence** v., to alter or affect
   a. The editor's style influenced a generation of film editors.
   b. The producer was able to influence the town council to allow her to film in the park.

8. **range** n., the scope
   a. The range of the director's vision is impressive.
   b. What is the price range you are willing pay for a ticket to the premiere?

9. **release** v., to make available to the public; to give permission for performance
   a. The film was finally released to movie theaters after many delays.
   b. The producers of the film are hoping to release it in time for the holidays.

10. **representation** n., exemplification; symbolization
    a. The actor's representation of his character did not seem authentic.
    b. The film's representation of world poverty through the character of the hungry child was quite moving.

11. **separately** adv., apart
    a. Each scene of the movie was filmed separately from the others.
    b. The theater was very crowded so we had to sit separately.

12. **successive** adj., following in order
    a. The script went through successive rewrites.
    b. Somehow the successive images were interrupted and had to be edited again.

Word Families

verb	attain	The film quickly attained a reputation as a "must-see" movie.
noun	attainment	The technical attainments in the movie's special effects were impressive.
adjective	attainable	The director's goal of having an unlimited budget was not attainable.

verb	continue	Continue giving out movie passes until I tell you to stop.
noun	continuation	The continuation of the film will be shown after the intermission.
adjective	continual	The actors' continual demands slowed down the pace of production.

verb	describe	Please describe the new movie theater to me.
noun	description	The description of Africa in the film was not as I remembered it.
adjective	descriptive	The writer's descriptive account of the war is shocking and saddening.

verb	entertain	The comedian worked hard to entertain the children in the hospital.
noun	entertainment	Movies are one of the most popular forms of entertainment.
adjective	entertaining	The light comedy was entertaining, if not memorable.

verb	represent	The actor represented the ideals of the culture.
noun	representation	We felt that the movie's representation of the effects of war was very realistic.
noun	representative	The actress couldn't attend the awards ceremony so she had a representative accept the award for her.

verb	separate	Some movie fans can't separate fantasy from reality and confuse an actor with the character he plays.
adjective	separate	Moviemaking combines several separate processes.
adverb	separately	The actors rehearsed their lines separately before filming the scene together.

Incomplete Sentences

Choose the word that best completes the sentence.

1. Do you think this actor will _____ the heights of his famous father?
   (A) attain
   (B) attaining
   (C) attainable
   (D) attainment

2. A sequel is a _____ of a story set in motion by a previous film.
   (A) continuity
   (B) continuing
   (C) continuation
   (D) continues

3. Each director has a uniquely _____ style of storytelling.
   (A) descriptive
   (B) describe
   (C) description
   (D) descriptively

4. _____ is one of the fastest growing sectors of the economy.
   (A) Entertained
   (B) Entertainment
   (C) Entertain
   (D) Entertainingly

5. We were impressed by the director's _____ of the conflict between good and evil.
   (A) representative
   (B) represented
   (C) represents
   (D) representation

6. The actors left the hotel _____ in order to avoid attracting a lot of attention.
   (A) separate
   (B) separately
   (C) separation
   (D) separating

Error Recognition

Choose the underlined word or phrase that should be rewritten and rewrite it.

7. Part of the <u>entertainment</u> of seeing a movie is understanding how the director <u>combination</u> a <u>range</u> of different
   A   **B**   **C**
   styles to <u>attain</u> an artistic goal.
              D

   _____

8. The director's early films, which showed the classic French <u>influential</u> of <u>combining</u> tragedy and comedy in a
                                                                  A   **B**
   broad <u>range</u> of story material, were finally <u>released</u> on video.
          C   **D**

   _____

9. The film <u>described</u> the poverty of the city in a <u>succession</u> of stark images that <u>continuation</u> the director's famil-
              A   **B**   **C**
   iar theme of how good and evil are <u>dispersed</u> throughout society.
                                       D

   _____

10. The award-winning film <u>combined</u> the frequently <u>separate</u> worlds of critical success and popular appeal that
                            A   **B**
    other films fail to <u>attain</u> by <u>representation</u> the full range of human emotions.
                         C   **D**

    _____

Reading Comprehension

Read the following passage and the words in the blanks below.

attain	descriptions	influence	represent
combines	disperse	range	separate
continues	entertaining	released	successive

The popularity of the movies began early in the 20th century and (11.) _____ today. People of all ages find movies (12.) _____. Movies are a worldwide phenomenon, as the internationalism of movie distribution has helped to (13.) _____ ideas around the globe. One movie can quickly (14.) _____ other movies. But why are movies so popular?

Movies are a kind of storytelling. They try to describe an idea or record an observation about our culture. These (15.) _____ are recorded using moving visual images. Some movies portray the situation accurately and realistically, whereas other movies find visual symbols to (16.) _____ those situations.

On the most simple level, movies are a succession of moving images. These (17.) _____ images are captured on film. Directors film a wide (18.) _____ of shots—long, medium, and close up—to create a visual composition. The visual images, along with plot, characterization, and sound, produce the desired narrative. The shots are joined together in any number of combinations in a process called editing.

Making a film is a massive, complex, and expensive task that (19.) _____ art and business. Making a movie involves the talents of hundreds, and sometimes thousands, of artists, producers, and business people. It can take months, even years, for a film to be (20.) _____ into a movie theater.

Like a novel, a movie is not just a story, but a story told a certain way. A film director may want to make a movie that tells a meaningful story or one that is primarily entertaining, and will use different filming techniques to (21.) _____ that goal. It is impossible to (22.) _____ what is told in a movie from how it is told. A director's artistic vision can range from improvised to carefully controlled. Think about the complexity of a movie the next time you see one.

LISTENING COMPREHENSION

Listen to Track 41 of the Compact Disc to hear the statements for Lesson 41

Part I Picture

Look at the picture and listen to the sentences. Choose the sentence that best describes the picture.

23. Ⓐ Ⓑ Ⓒ Ⓓ

Part II Question—Response

Listen to the question and the three responses. Choose the response that best answers the question.

24. Ⓐ Ⓑ Ⓒ   25. Ⓐ Ⓑ Ⓒ

Part III Short Conversations

Listen to the short dialogs. Then read the question and choose the best answer.

26. What do the speakers say about the film?
    (A) It was too simple.
    (B) It wasn't descriptive enough.
    (C) It wasn't good.
    (D) It was very suspenseful.

27. What are the speakers discussing?
    (A) The lighting in the theater.
    (B) The price of entertainment.
    (C) Shows on TV.
    (D) An actress's acting style.

Part IV Short Talks

Listen to the short talk. Then read the questions and choose the best answer.

28. Who is the speaker talking about?
    (A) A director.
    (B) A movie producer.
    (C) An actress.
    (D) An interviewer.

29. When will the movie be released?
    (A) Next month.
    (B) In several weeks.
    (C) Next year.
    (D) In several years.

Theater

Words to learn

action
approach
audience
creative
dialogue
element
experience
occur
perform
rehearse
review
sell out

1. **action** n., the series of events that form the plot of a story or play
   a. The director decided that the second act needed more action and asked the playwright to review the work.
   b. The action on stage was spellbinding.

2. **approach** v., to go near; to move toward
   a. The performance approaches perfection.
   b. The director approached the play from an unusual angle.

3. **audience** n., the spectators at a performance
   a. The audience cheered the actors as they walked off the stage.
   b. The playwright expanded his audience by writing for film as well as for stage.

4. **creative** adj., imaginative or artistic
   a. The writer's creative representation of the Seven Deadly Sins was astounding.
   b. There are a number of creative people writing for the theater these days.

5. **dialogue** n., a conversation between two or more persons
   a. The actors performed the dialogue without using scripts.
   b. The written dialogue seemed great, but was hard to perform.

6. **element** n., fundamental or essential constituent
   a. The audience is an essential element of live theater.
   b. By putting together all the elements of theater into one play, he overwhelmed the critics.

7. **experience** n., an event or a series of events participated in or lived through
   a. The experience of live theater is very thrilling.
   b. Going to the theater was not part of Claude's experience growing up.

8. **occur** v., to take place; to come about
   a. The murder in the play occurs in the second act.
   b. It never occurred to me that the wife whom the character referred to was imaginary.

9. **perform** v., to act before an audience, to give a public presentation of
   a. The theater group performed a three-act play.
   b. Juan performed the role without forgetting any lines.

10. **rehearse** v., to practice in preparation for a public performance; to direct in rehearsal
    a. The players rehearsed for only three weeks before the show opened.
    b. The director rehearses with the actors ten hours each day.

11. **review** n., a critical estimate of a work or performance; v., writing a criticism of a performance
    a. The critic's influential review of the play was so negative that it sank the entire production.
    b. The newspaper sent a rank amateur to review the play.

12. **sell out** v., to sell all the tickets
    a. The Broadway opening sold out months in advance.
    b. We expect that this play will be a smash and sell out quickly.

Word Families

verb	act	Roger's dream is to act in a Broadway play.
noun	action	There isn't much action in the play, but it is captivating nonetheless.
noun	actor	There are quite a few well-known actors in the cast.

verb	approach	The actress approached me with the idea for a new play.
noun	approach	The informal approach to the play was unconventional.
adjective	approachable	Despite his great fame, the director was friendly and approachable.

verb	create	The playwright created a realistic town and townspeople with the scenery and dialogue.
noun	creation	The creation of the elaborate costumes took months.
adjective	creative	The director is one of the most creative people I know.

verb	experience	The actor experienced great self-doubt before he became famous.
noun	experience	Directors bring their experience of the world onto the stage.
adjective	experienced	The experienced make-up artist transformed Maxine into an old woman in a matter of minutes.

verb	perform	The popular actress was hired to perform Shakespeare on a world tour.
noun	performance	I booked tickets for the performance the day they went on sale.
noun	performer	The performers each had three costume changes.

verb	rehearse	The cast had to rehearse the scene over and over again until the director was finally satisfied.
noun	rehearsal	The actors spent several months in rehearsal before they performed the play.
adjective	rehearsed	Lydia's acceptance speech for her award sounded more rehearsed than natural.

Incomplete Sentences

Choose the word that best completes the sentence.

1. The director's creativity showed in everything from her _____ to the literary quality of the play to the costumes and sets.
   (A) approaching   (C) approachable
   (B) approach   (D) approachability

2. Edward is a very talented _____ although he can't sing or dance well at all.
   (A) actor   (C) action
   (B) acts   (D) acting

3. As your director, I call upon you to bring your life _____ into your role.
   (A) experienced   (C) experiential
   (B) experiencing   (D) experience

4. I am not _____ enough to work in the theater, but I certainly enjoy attending it.
   (A) create   (C) creative
   (B) creativeness   (D) creativity

5. I look forward to the annual _____ of *The Nutcracker* ballet.
   (A) performance   (C) perform
   (B) performer   (D) performable

6. There isn't much time left to _____ before the play opens.
   (A) rehearsals   (C) rehearsing
   (B) rehearse   (D) rehearsed

Error Recognition

Choose the underlined word or phrase that should be rewritten and rewrite it.

7. Under a <u>creation</u> hand, common <u>elements</u> come together to make a special <u>experience</u> for the <u>audience</u>.
        A   B   C   D

   _____

8. The <u>reviews</u> of the new play were all very positive, so the <u>performing</u> <u>sold out</u> quickly as <u>audiences</u> spread the
      A   B   C   D
   good word.

   _____

9. The <u>action</u> of the play was very unconventional, so its meaning could be <u>approached</u> from different levels;
      A   B
   when this <u>occurrence</u>, <u>audiences</u> have a lot to talk about.
                  C   D

   _____

10. Even before the <u>rehearsals</u> were completed, the <u>dialogues</u> between the characters had been heard and seen
                   A   B
    on television, so the performance was <u>sold out</u> before the <u>reviewing</u> ran in the papers.
                                       C   D

    _____

Reading Comprehension

Read the following passage and write the words in the blanks below.

action	created	experiences	rehearsal
approach	dialogue	occurs	reviews
audience	elements	performance	sell out

Many people find nothing as exciting as an evening of live theater. The theater combines great works of literature written for the stage, the talents of great actors, and the efforts of hundreds of skilled artisans who work to create a mood. This mood, (11.) _____ by the actors, director, and playwright with the supporting (12.) _____ of sets, lighting, and costumes, is what makes a theatrical (13.) _____ magical. When the curtain goes up, this magic (14.) _____ right before your eyes.

The director of a play will (15.) _____ the work from his or her own artistic perspective. Each director has a different vision and this shapes how he or she directs the movement or (16.) _____ between the characters. Directors use not only their theatrical training, but real-life experiences to create a meaningful, realistic evening. Actors also bring their own artistic and personal (17.) _____ to their work. This is why every staging of a play is unique.

Plays construct another world before your eyes. Ordinary words turn into meaningful (18.) _____. Costumes and sets can be realistic or symbolic. Everything in a play looks easy, but it takes many weeks of (19.) _____ to get everything in place.

Watching a play from the (20.) _____ is great fun. To find out if a play is good, look for (21.) _____ in the newspapers or ask friends. When plays are really popular, the available seats can fill up quickly and the play will (22.) _____.

LISTENING COMPREHENSION

Listen to Track 42 of the Compact Disc to hear the statements for Lesson 42

Part I Picture

Look at the picture and listen to the sentences.
Choose the sentence that best describes the picture.

23. Ⓐ Ⓑ Ⓒ Ⓓ

Part II Question—Response

Listen to the question and the three responses. Choose the response that best answers the question.

24. Ⓐ Ⓑ Ⓒ   25. Ⓐ Ⓑ Ⓒ

Part III Short Conversations

Listen to the short dialogs. Then read the question and choose the best answer.

26. What do the speakers say about the play?
    (A) They've heard that the play is funny.
    (B) Tickets are still on sale.
    (C) The play got a bad review.
    (D) The dialogue is hard to understand.

27. What are the speakers discussing?
    (A) The size of the theater.
    (B) The meaning of the play.
    (C) The directions to the theater.
    (D) The length of the play.

Part IV Short Talks

Listen to the short talk. Then read the questions and choose the best answer.

28. When can a performance of *Romeo and Juliet* be seen?
    (A) Today.
    (B) On Thursday afternoon.
    (C) On Sunday morning.
    (D) On Thursday evening.

29. How can you get tickets to the play?
    (A) Call the Shakespeare Organization.
    (B) Call 656-9025.
    (C) Write to the theater.
    (D) Order them by e-mail.

Music

Words to learn

available
broaden
category
disparate
divide
favor
instinct
prefer
reason
relaxation
taste
urge

1. **available** adj., ready for use; willing to serve
    a. In order to understand all the words to the opera, Sue Lin kept an Italian dictionary available at all times.
    b. I checked the list of available compact discs before ordering.

2. **broaden** v., to make wider
    a. Dominique wants to broaden her knowledge of opera history.
    b. You will appreciate music more if you broaden your tastes and listen to several types of music.

3. **category** n., a division in a system of classification; a general class of ideas
    a. Jazz is one of many categories of music.
    b. The works of Mozart are in a category by themselves.

4. **disparate** adj., fundamentally distinct or different
    a. In the song, the disparate voices hauntingly join a blended chorus.
    b. Religious songs cut across disparate categories of music.

5. **divide** v., to separate into parts
    a. The music class was evenly divided between those who liked country and western music and those who do not.
    b. The broad topic of music can be divided into manageable parts, such as themes, styles, or centuries.

6. **favor** v., to be partial to
    a. Sam enjoys the works of several composers but he tends to favor Mozart.
    b. I'd favor an evening at a jazz concert over an evening at the opera any time.

7. **instinct** n., an inborn pattern that is a powerful motivation
    a. The student's ability to play the cello was so natural, it seemed an instinct.
    b. The music lover followed his instincts and collected only music that he enjoyed.

8. **prefer** v., to like someone or something more than another or others
    a. He preferred contemporary music to any other type.
    b. Ms. Lanet prefers to get a seat near the aisle when she attends a concert.

9. **reason** n., the basis or motive for an action; an underlying fact or cause
    a. We'll never understand the reason why some music is popular and some is not.
    b. There is every reason to believe that Beethoven will still be popular in the next century.

10. **relaxation** n., the act of relaxing or the state of being relaxed; refreshment of body or mind
    a. Listening to soothing music before bedtime provides good relaxation.
    b. He played the piano for relaxation and pleasure.

11. **taste** n., the ability to discern what is excellent or appropriate
    a. Ella had the taste required to select a musical program for the visiting dignitaries.
    b. This music does not appeal to my tastes; but I'm old-fashioned.

12. **urge** v., to advocate earnestly
    a. His mother urged him to study the piano; the rest is musical history.
    b. Despite my reluctance, my friends urged me to attend an opera.

Word Families

verb	broaden	Connie would like to broaden her collection of CDs and add a few more music categories to it.
adjective	broad	We'll cover a broad range of music in the music appreciation class.
adverb	broadly	The orchestra director travels broadly in search of new musical talent.

verb	categorize	Some singers have a broad range of styles and are difficult to categorize.
noun	category	Most of Sam's compact discs fall into the category of classical music.
adjective	categorical	The sheet music follows the categorical system used in most libraries.

verb	favor	The music critic clearly favors some musicians over others.
adjective	favorite	The teenager had an extensive collection of music by all her favorite groups.
adjective	favorable	The favorable reviews of the group's new album helped to push the album up the sales charts.

verb	prefer	I would prefer tickets for Saturday's concert, but will accept Sunday tickets if that is all that is available.
noun	preference	Jazz is his preference, but he is usually happy to hear anything playing locally.
adjective	preferential	The stage manager gave the opera diva preferential treatment, fearing her famous temper.

verb	relax	After a long concert tour, the singer liked to relax by the pool.
noun	relaxation	Listening to music is an enduring form of relaxation.
adjective	relaxing	There is nothing more relaxing than listening to music.

verb	urge	My music teacher urged me not to give up the violin even though I was having such a hard time with it.
noun	urge	Richard gets the urge to play the guitar every time he passes a music store window.
adjective	urgent	It's urgent to order those concert tickets as soon as possible because they will sell out quickly.

Incomplete Sentences

Choose the word that best completes the sentence.

1. My friends have urged me to _____ my tastes to include more classical music.
   (A) broad   (C) broaden
   (B) broadly   (D) broadened

2. I don't know how to _____ my taste in music.
   (A) categorize (C) categorical
   (B) categories (D) categorically

3. The string quartet received a _____ comparison to the best of the genre.
   (A) favor   (C) favorably
   (B) favoritism (D) favorable

4. The symphony members _____ to travel abroad only once a year.
   (A) prefer   (C) preference
   (B) preferable (D) preferential

5. After a hard day at work, we like to _____ to soothing music.
   (A) relaxation (C) relaxing
   (B) relaxes   (D) relax

6. Sometimes I get an _____ to learn how to play a musical instrument.
   (A) urgent   (C) urges
   (B) urge   (D) urgently

Error Recognition

Choose the underlined word or phrase that should be rewritten and rewrite it.

7. Although my friends have <u>urged</u> me to change my <u>taste</u> in music, I still <u>favor</u> country-western music, which is
            A   B   C
   always <u>availability</u> on the radio.
          D

   _____

8. The basic <u>categories</u> of music can be <u>division</u> into a few <u>broad</u> groups that appeal to many different musical
           A   B   C
   <u>tastes</u>.
    D

   _____

9. The <u>reasons</u> for the <u>disparate</u> kinds of music in the world reflect not only personal <u>preferable</u> but also people's
       A   B   C
   <u>instinctive</u> need to express themselves.
     D

   _____

10. Every night, Chester <u>prefers</u> to <u>relaxation</u> and forget the workday by indulging his <u>urge</u> to listen to his <u>favorite</u>
                        A   B   C   D
    music.

    _____

Reading Comprehension

Read the following passage and write the words in the blanks below.

available	disparate	instinctive	relax
broad	divided	prefer	taste
category	favorite	reason	urge

Everyone loves music, it seems. And there's little (11.) _____ to wonder why. There is so much music (12.) _____ from which to choose, and there is a (13.) _____ of music to appeal to every (14.) _____. The major groups of music are (15.) _____ broadly into classical, popular, and jazz. Within these (16.) _____ groups are many other subcategories. For example, such (17.) _____ types of music as movie sound tracks, rhythm and blues, rock, and rap all fit within the category of popular music.

The (18.) _____ to make and enjoy music may be (19.) _____. Even small children will (20.) _____ certain kinds of music.

Another reason that music is so popular is the variety of settings in which one can enjoy his or her (21.) _____ kind of music. You can go to a church to hear great religious music, or to a concert hall to hear a well-known classical symphony. On another night, you might go to a small club to listen to an up-and-coming jazz group while you enjoy a drink. A few nights later, you might go with some friends to join thousands of other people in a stadium to hear your favorite rock band play in your city on a world tour. And, back at your house or apartment, you can (22.) _____ while you put in a tape or CD and listen to your favorite artists again and again in your own home.

LISTENING COMPREHENSION

Listen to Track 43 of the Compact Disc to hear the statements for Lesson 43

Part I Picture

Look at the picture and listen to the sentences. Choose the sentence that best describes the picture.

23. Ⓐ Ⓑ Ⓒ Ⓓ

Part II Question—Response

Listen to the question and the three responses. Choose the response that best answers the question.

24. Ⓐ Ⓑ Ⓒ   25. Ⓐ Ⓑ Ⓒ

Part III Short Conversations

Listen to the short dialogs. Then read the question and choose the best answer.

26. What does the man say about the music at the store?
    (A) It matches his tastes.
    (B) It is boring.
    (C) It sounds pretty.
    (D) It is interesting.

27. What does the man want to do?
    (A) Get a new radio set.
    (B) Listen to relaxing music.
    (C) Explain the kind of music he prefers.
    (D) Adjust the volume on the radio.

Part IV Short Talks

Listen to the short talk. Then read the questions and choose the best answer.

28. What is the class about?
    (A) The history of music.
    (B) Playing musical instruments.
    (C) Music appreciation.
    (D) Reading music.

29. What does the speaker urge the listeners to do?
    (A) Buy the text right away.
    (B) Try a musical instrument.
    (C) Take a test.
    (D) Start listening to music every day.

Museums

Words to learn

acquire
admire
collection
criticism
express
fashion
leisure
respond
schedule
significant
specialize
spectrum

1. **acquire** v., to gain possession of; to get by one's own efforts
   a. The museum acquired a van Gogh during heavy bidding.
   b. The sculptor acquired metalworking skills after much practice.

2. **admire** v., to regard with pleasure; to have esteem or respect for
   a. Raisa, admiring the famous smile, stood before the Mona Lisa for hours.
   b. I admire all the effort the museum put into organizing this wonderful exhibit.

3. **collection** n., a group of objects or works to be seen, studied, or kept together
   a. The museum's collection contained many works donated by famous collectors.
   b. The museum's collection kept two full-time curators busy.

4. **criticism** n., an evaluation, especially of literary or other artistic works
   a. According to the criticism of the Victorian era, the painting was a masterpiece; now it is considered merely a minor work.
   b. The revered artist's criticism of the piece was particularly insightful.

5. **express** v., to give an opinion or depict emotion
   a. The sculptor was able to express his feelings better through the use of clay rather than words.
   b. The photograph expresses a range of emotions.

6. **fashion** n., the prevailing style or custom
   a. According to the fashion of the day, the languid pose of the sculpture was high art.
   b. The museum's classical architecture has never gone out of fashion.

7. **leisure** n., freedom from time-consuming duties; free time
   a. The woman took up painting in her retirement, when she had more leisure time.
   b. We can go to the permanent collection at our leisure.

8. **respond** v., to make a reply; to react
   a. You should respond to the invitation to attend the museum gala.
   b. The visitors who viewed those poignant photographs responded emotionally.

9. **schedule** v., to enter in a planner or diary
   a. We didn't schedule enough time to see all the exhibits that we were interested in.
   b. The museum is scheduling a collection of works by Japanese masters.

10. **significant** adj., meaningful; having a major effect; important
    a. The use of lambs to symbolize innocence is significant in Western art.
    b. The rash of new acquisitions represented a significant change in the museum's policies.

11. **specialize** v., to concentrate on a particular activity
    a. The art historian specialized in Navajo rugs.
    b. The museum shop specializes in Ming vases.

12. **spectrum** n., a range of related qualities, ideas, or activities
    a. The painting crosses the spectrum from symbolic to realistic representation.
    b. The whole spectrum of artistic expression was represented in the exhibit.

Word Families

verb	admire	People from all around the world visit the museum to admire the great works of art on display.
noun	admiration	I have great admiration for anyone who can create art.
adjective	admired	Monet is one of the most admired artists of the Impressionist movement.

verb	collect	The enthusiast began to collect Shaker furniture in the 1960s.
noun	collection	My parents' collection of crystal had outgrown their dining room cupboard.
noun	collector	The avid collector spent weekends at estate sales looking for rare art objects.

verb	criticize	The sculptor was criticized for his lack of perspective.
noun	critic	The art critic gave the show a poor review, which saddened the exhibition team.
noun	criticism	The writer's elegant essays on the use of light in Flemish painting were landmarks in art criticism.

verb	respond	When Mr. Hon did not respond to the invitation to the opening, we assumed he was not able to attend.
noun	response	The response to the request for assistance was overwhelming.
adjective	responsive	The director was not responsive to any of the staff's suggestions, which made them both annoyed and anxious.

verb	schedule	The museum has scheduled a lecture series to accompany the special exhibit.
noun	schedule	Several local artists are featured on the gallery's winter schedule.
adjective	scheduled	There are several scheduled events at the museum this weekend.

verb	specialize	The art student decided to specialize in French and English paintings of the 1860s.
noun	specialist	The curator is a specialist in native Caribbean art.
adjective	specialized	The museum hired specialized personnel to adjust the humidity and light for the display of ancient books.

Incomplete Sentences

Choose the word that best completes the sentence.

1. The museum was lucky to be given a collection of works by such an _____ artist.
   (A) admiration   (C) admired
   (B) admire   (D) admires

2. Once Mimi began _____ pottery, her husband gave her pieces as gifts.
   (A) collection   (C) collecting
   (B) collectable   (D) collector

3. The curator's _____ of the museum's fund-raising plan seemed shortsighted.
   (A) criticism   (C) critical
   (B) critic   (D) criticize

4. We have been asked to _____ to the proposal by the end of the month.
   (A) responsive   (C) respond
   (B) response   (D) responding

5. The museum offers a _____ of guided tours.
   (A) schedules   (C) scheduling
   (B) scheduled   (D) schedule

6. After becoming a _____ in Egyptian tomb painting, the art historian lost her interest in other kinds of art.
   (A) specialize   (C) specially
   (B) specialist   (D) special

Error Recognition

Choose the underlined word or phrase that should be rewritten and rewrite it.

7. Delores <u>admired</u> the wonderful <u>collection</u> of nature photographs that seemed to <u>expressive</u> the wide <u>spectrum</u>
        A   B   C   D
   of design found in nature.

   _____

8. The city's newest museum, which <u>specializes</u> in art by African-Americans, has <u>acquisition</u> works that are
                                A   B
   <u>significant</u> in how they <u>respond</u> to the American experience.
     C   D

   _____

9. Even though the paintings had once been very <u>fashionable</u>, art <u>critics</u> now find them to be <u>insignificant</u> and
                                        A   B   C
   unworthy of being in a museum <u>collect</u>.
                                   D

   _____

10. The museum has <u>acquired</u> so many new paintings that I will have to <u>schedule</u> a day to <u>admire</u> them at my
                  A   B   C
    <u>leisurely</u>.
      D

    _____

Reading Comprehension

Read the following passage and write the words in the blanks below.

acquire	criticism	leisure	significant
admire	expressing	responded	specialize
collected	fashion	schedule	spectrum

Museums are places to view and (11.) _____ the great works of art. All large cities, and even many small cities, have good art museums in which you will find a wide (12.) _____ of paintings, sculptures, drawings, and prints.

Museums attempt to collect and display a broad range of examples of how, throughout time, men and women have (13.) _____ to what they have seen, thought, and felt by (14.) _____ themselves through materials like stone, clay, and paint, or ink and paper. The artist imposes an order on these materials that is (15.) _____. Some styles of art or particular objects are in (16.) _____ for only a while, and others earn positive (17.) _____ over time and are seen as enduring classics. Museums collect the best of these works for the public to see.

When you go to a museum, be sure to (18.) _____ plenty of time to see the art without feeling rushed. If you are lucky enough to live near a museum, you can come back again at your (19.) _____. Some museums show a broad collection of art from different times and cultures, often (20.) _____ and donated by their generous patrons. Other museums (21.) _____ in displaying art from a certain period, say from the ancient world, or by a certain group or nationality of people, like by Native Americans.

The operations of many museums are paid for by the government and these museums are often free to the public; other museums must charge each person upon entry. These fees help the museum operate and (22.) _____ more works.

LISTENING COMPREHENSION

Listen to Track 44 of the Compact Disc to hear the statements for Lesson 44

Part I Picture

Look at the picture and listen to the sentences. Choose the sentence that best describes the picture.

23. Ⓐ Ⓑ Ⓒ Ⓓ

Part II Question—Response

Listen to the question and the three responses. Choose the response that best answers the question.

24. Ⓐ Ⓑ Ⓒ   25. Ⓐ Ⓑ Ⓒ

Part III Short Conversations

Listen to the short dialogs. Then read the question and choose the best answer.

26. What are the speakers discussing?
(A) A drawing.
(B) A sculpture.
(C) A painting.
(D) A photograph.

27. What is the speakers' opinion of the museum's art collection?
(A) It has too many works by minority artists.
(B) It is good because the staff has done a lot of work.
(C) It is too big.
(D) It needs to have a diverse range of works.

Part IV Short Talks

Listen to the short talk. Then read the questions and choose the best answer.

28. When does the lecture series at the museum begin?
(A) Next month.
(B) Next week.
(C) This month.
(D) This week.

29. How can you find out the schedule of guided tours?
(A) Visit the main gallery.
(B) Press two.
(C) Go on-line.
(D) Speak with an operator.

Media

1. **assignment** n., v., something, such as a task, that is assigned
   a. This assignment has to be turned in before midnight.
   b. When the reporter is on assignment, research piles up on her desk.

2. **choose** v., to select one thing over another
   a. Alan chooses to read *The New York Times* over the *Wall Street Journal*.
   b. I did not choose that candidate to be the editor of our student newspaper.

3. **constantly** adv., continually
   a. An advantage of Internet news reports is that they can be constantly updated.
   b. People constantly look to the news to keep up-to-date on what is going on in the world.

4. **constitute** v., to be the elements or parts of
   a. All the different news sources constitute the media industry.
   b. A talented staff, adequate printing facilities, and sufficient distribution points constitute a successful newspaper.

5. **decision** n., judgment or choice
   a. The court made the decision to allow the newspaper to print the controversial story.
   b. Newspaper editors often have to make quick decisions about which stories to publish.

6. **disseminate** v., to scatter widely; to distribute
   a. The media disseminates news across the world.
   b. The computer virus was disseminated through the newsroom by reporters sharing terminals.

7. **impact** n., a strong, immediate impression
   a. The story of the presidential scandal had a huge impact on the public.
   b. The impact of the news coverage is yet to be known.

8. **in-depth** adj., in complete detail; thorough
   a. The newspaper gave in-depth coverage of the tragic bombing.
   b. Ivan's in-depth story on the spread of the disease received praise from many of his colleagues.

9. **investigate** v., to uncover and report hidden information
   a. Reporters need to thoroughly investigate the facts before publishing their stories.
   b. Michelle's editor sent her to the capital to investigate the story behind the government scandal.

10. **link** n., an association; a relationship
    a. The computer links will take you to today's headlines.
    b. The father-daughter team of reporters is just one example of many family links at this newspaper.

11. **subscribe** v., to receive a periodical regularly on order
    a. Jill subscribes to a gardening magazine.
    b. It is convenient to subscribe to the newspaper because it is delivered to your house daily.

12. **thorough** adj., exhaustively complete
    a. The reporters were thorough in their coverage of the event.
    b. The story was the result of thorough research.

Word Families

verb	choose	No one was surprised when the student decided to choose a career in journalism.
noun	choice	It's your choice whether we use a color or black and white photo.
adjective	choosy	The editor was famous for being choosy about whom she wanted on her staff.

noun	constancy	The reporter's constancy in writing thorough news reports earned her a loyal following of readers.
adjective	constant	The constant ringing of the telephone distracted Susan from writing her report.
adverb	constantly	The editor constantly asks the reporters to recheck their facts.

verb	decide	The editor decided not to publish the story because the facts were unreliable.
noun	decision	The decision to lay off several reporters was made for financial reasons alone.
adjective	decisive	Newspaper editors must be decisive when determining which stories go on the front page.

verb	investigate	Alban was excited about his first chance to investigate a story.
noun	investigation	The investigation into the president's past was covered by the media worldwide.
adjective	investigative	After turning up details in the crime that even the police had missed, Helen became well known as an investigative reporter.

verb	subscribe	I subscribe to the local newspaper to stay current.
noun	subscription	Buying a subscription to the magazine was much less expensive than buying individual issues.
noun	subscribers	The magazine went out of business because it did not have enough subscribers.

noun	thoroughness	A newspaper cannot survive long without a reputation for thoroughness.
adjective	thorough	Toshi is famous for her thorough and fair reporting of the issues.
adverb	thoroughly	The reporter thoroughly checked all his facts to avoid any potential embarrassment.

Incomplete Sentences

Choose the word that best completes the sentence.

1. I don't want to pressure you, but you need to _____ the reporter who will cover the mayor's race this year.
(A) chosen (C) choose
(B) choosy (D) choice

2. By _____ asking questions, Harry was able to get the information he wanted for his report.
(A) constant (C) consistence
(B) constancy (D) constantly

3. Georgette _____ to stop subscribing to the newspaper because she felt the quality of the reporting had deteriorated.
(A) decision (C) decides
(B) decided (D) decisive

4. The reporters followed the official _____ by interviewing all the witnesses to the crime.
(A) investigate (C) investigative
(B) investigation (D) investigational

5. I need to renew my _____ for cable television, but I can't find the form.
(A) subscribing (C) subscriber
(B) subscription (D) subscribe

6. The editor was impressed with how _____ the reporter was in getting the details from his sources.
(A) thorough (C) thoroughly
(B) thoroughness (D) thoroughbred

Error Recognition

Choose the underlined word or phrase that should be rewritten and rewrite it.

7. The <u>decision</u> and <u>thorough</u> way the reporter handled every <u>assignment</u> made her a natural candidate for the
    A   B   C
<u>investigative</u> news desk.
    D

8. The avid reader was so impressed with the <u>in-depth</u> information the magazine <u>disseminated</u> about terrorist
                                      A   B
training camps that he immediately became a <u>subscriber</u> in order to ensure he had a <u>constancy</u> supply of news.
                                          C   D

9. The media, which is <u>comprised</u> of newspapers, magazine, television and radio news, and Internet news
                          A
services, <u>investigator</u> and <u>disseminates</u> news in an impartial fashion and serves as our <u>link</u> to the world.
          B   C   D

10. The TV anchor knew the <u>impact</u> the tragic story would have so he <u>assignment</u> a junior reporter to develop a
                      A   B
<u>thorough</u>, <u>in-depth</u> story on the tragedy.
   C   D

Reading Comprehension

Read the following passage and write the words in the blanks below.

assignments	constitutes	impact	links
chooses	decisions	in-depth	subscribes
constant	disseminated	investigative	thoroughly

Chen likes to get his news from the paper. Lemma turns on the television to find out what's going on in the world. Eve (11.) _____ to more magazines than she can keep track of, whereas Kobi (12.) _____ to listen to radio talk shows that cover issues (13.) _____ to tap into what's going on in the world. All these people are touched by the media.

What is the media? What (14.) _____ the media? The media consists of all the ways that news and information is (15.) _____ to a mass audience. The media covers everything from hard news, which is (16.) _____ reporting, to stories that are purely entertaining, such as whether your favorite movie star was on the "Best Dressed/Worst Dressed" list. Whether in print or broadcast on TV, the stories are the product of the reporting of many journalists who write the stories, and editors who give out the (17.) _____, assess the quality of the writing and research, and make the (18.) _____ about where and when the stories run.

The news has an immediate (19.) _____. The Internet puts global news onto the personal computer on your desk. Almost all browsers have (20.) _____ to up-to-the-minute news stories from various news services. You can get (21.) _____ news updates from a variety of sources via your personal computer, providing you with the most up-to-date and (22.) _____ coverage.

LISTENING COMPREHENSION

Listen to Track 45 of the Compact Disc to hear the statements for Lesson 45

Part I Picture

Look at the picture and listen to the sentences. Choose the sentence that best describes the picture.

23. Ⓐ Ⓑ Ⓒ Ⓓ

Part II Question—Response

Listen to the question and the three responses. Choose the response that best answers the question.

24. Ⓐ Ⓑ Ⓒ   25. Ⓐ Ⓑ Ⓒ

Part III Short Conversations

Listen to the short dialogs. Then read the question and choose the best answer.

26. According to the speakers, why are newspapers better than TV news?
    (A) Newspaper editors are decisive.
    (B) Newspaper coverage is more thorough.
    (C) Newspaper stories are more interesting.
    (D) Newspapers cover better stories.

27. What are the speakers discussing?
    (A) Public opinion of the media.
    (B) Places that sell newspapers.
    (C) The best way to disseminate the news.
    (D) The Internet as a news source.

Part IV Short Talks

Listen to the short talk. Then read the questions and choose the best answer.

28. What is the topic of the news report?
    (A) A speech made by the country's president.
    (B) The state of the national economy.
    (C) Fraud committed by a company president.
    (D) An industry report.

29. At what time can this news report be heard?
    (A) 5:00.
    (B) 12:00.
    (C) 6:00.
    (D) 10:00.

Word Review #9   **Lessons 41–45 Entertainment**

Choose the word that best completes the sentence.

1. Movies are probably the most popular form of _____ in the United States.
   (A) entertain
   (B) entertained
   (C) entertaining
   (D) entertainment

2. Television has seriously _____ society.
   (A) influence
   (B) influenced
   (C) influencing
   (D) influential

3. Actors can spend too much time _____ as well as too little.
   (A) rehearse
   (B) rehearsed
   (C) rehearsing
   (D) rehearsal

4. Even when a show is _____, it is sometimes possible to get in.
   (A) sell out
   (B) sell on
   (C) sold off
   (D) sold out

5. Orchestra music is wonderfully conducive to _____.
   (A) relaxation
   (B) relaxed
   (C) relaxes
   (D) relax

6. There is no good or bad music, only that which does or does not appeal to your _____.
   (A) taste
   (B) tastes
   (C) tasted
   (D) tasting

7. New _____ are one of the most exciting aspects of museum work.
   (A) acquire
   (B) acquisitions
   (C) acquires
   (D) acquisitive

8. Sometimes I look at a famous painting and wonder why it is considered more _____ than the ones on either side of it.
   (A) signify
   (B) signified
   (C) significant
   (D) significantly

9. The Internet _____ information faster than any other medium.
   (A) disseminate
   (B) disseminates
   (C) dissemination
   (D) disseminating

10. In any news medium, the only news is what the editor _____ is news.
    (A) decide
    (B) decides
    (C) decision
    (D) decisions

Choose the underlined word or phrase that should be rewritten and rewrite it.

11. The <u>dialogue</u> between <u>collectors</u> and art <u>specialize</u> <u>influences</u> the shape of a museum's collection.
        A   B   C   D
    _____

12. The <u>range</u> of <u>critical</u> of the film reflects the <u>tastes</u> of a diverse <u>audience</u>.
        A   B   C   D
    _____

13. <u>Critics'</u> <u>reviews</u> have a great <u>impacted</u> on the <u>entertainment</u> industry.
      A   B   C   D
    _____

14. Music is <u>available</u> in a <u>broad</u> range of <u>categories</u> to suit individual <u>prefers</u>.
            A   B   C   D
    _____

15. Some writers <u>choose</u> to specialize in <u>in-depth</u> <u>investigated</u> <u>assignments</u>.
          A   B   C   D
    _____

16. Rave <u>reviewed</u> can <u>create</u> <u>sold-out</u> <u>performances</u> for the run of the show.
           A   B   C   D

_____

17. I prefer to <u>admire</u> art <u>collections</u> at <u>leisurely</u>, especially paintings that have an <u>impact</u> on me.
               A   B   C   D

_____

18. Some critics <u>express</u> <u>criticisms</u> that reflect their <u>instinctive</u> <u>responsive</u>, not analysis.
                   A   B   C   D

_____

19. Many newspapers have on-line <u>links</u> to <u>constantly</u> updates or <u>in-depth</u> analysis; some send a news summary
                                 A   B   C
to <u>subscribers</u>.
   D

_____

20. Editors face constant <u>decisions</u> about what <u>constituting</u> news, and <u>schedule</u> stories according to their <u>instinct</u>
                          A   B   C   D
and experience.

_____

Doctor's Office

Words to learn

annually
appointment
assess
diagnose
effective
instrument
manage
prevent
recommendation
record
refer
serious

1. **annually** adv., yearly
   a. Everyone should get a physical exam annually.
   b. A number of tests are provided annually by my insurance plan.
2. **appointment** n., arrangements for a meeting; a position in a profession
   a. To get the most out of your appointment, keep a log of your symptoms and concerns.
   b. The psychiatrist holds an academic appointment at the university hospital as well as having a private practice.
3. **assess** v., to determine the value or rate of something
   a. The physical therapist assessed the amount of mobility Ms. Crowl had lost after her stroke.
   b. The insurance rate Mr. Victor was assessed went up this year after he admitted that he had started smoking again.
4. **diagnose** v., to recognize a disease; to analyze the nature of something
   a. After considering the patient's symptoms and looking at his test results, the doctor diagnosed the lump as benign.
   b. She diagnosed the problem as a failure to follow the directions for taking the medication.
5. **effective** adj., producing the desired effect; being in effect
   a. Howard was pleased to find that the diet recommended by his doctor was quite effective.
   b. The new policies, effective the beginning of the fiscal year, change the amount charged to see the physician.
6. **instrument** n., a tool for precise work; the means whereby something is achieved
   a. The pediatrician tried not to frighten the children with her strange-looking instruments.
   b. The senior physician carried his instruments in a black leather bag.
7. **manage** v., to handle; to deal with; to guide
   a. The head nurse's ability to manage her staff through a difficult time caught the hospital administrator's attention.
   b. By carefully managing their limited resources, the couple found the money for the elective surgery.
8. **prevent** v., to keep from happening; to hinder
   a. By encouraging teenagers not to smoke, doctors are hoping to prevent many cases of cancer.
   b. His full caseload prevented the doctor from taking on new patients.
9. **recommendation** n., advice; endorsement
   a. It is important to follow the doctor's recommendations if you want to improve your health.
   b. The professor gave her former student a recommendation when he applied for a job at the hospital.
10. **record** n., an official copy of documents
    a. Ms. Han typed a written request for her medical records.
    b. The official records kept in the city archives showed that an unusually high number of babies are born in the summer months.
11. **refer** v., to direct for treatment or information; to mention
    a. I was referred to this specialist by the family practice nurse.
    b. As soon as Agnes referred to the failed treatment, everyone's mood soured.
12. **serious** adj., weighty
    a. The impact of the serious news could be read on everyone's face.
    b. For her dissertation, she made a serious study of women's health care needs in developing nations.

Word Families

verb	assess	He was able to assess her health problems with the help of her detailed medical history.
noun	assessment	The specialist's assessment of the patient's condition was consistent with the general practioner's.
adjective	assessable	That medical condition is not assessable by this laboratory test.

verb	diagnose	Her symptoms are overlapping, making it difficult to diagnose the exact cause of her chest pain.
noun	diagnosis	Phil did a much better job of taking care of himself once his father had a diagnosis of lung cancer.
adjective	diagnostic	The new X-ray suite has all the latest diagnostic equipment.

verb	prevent	By stopping smoking now, you may be able to prevent lung cancer.
noun	prevention	He made a career of disease prevention through mass vaccinations.
adjective	preventive	Eloise took preventive steps against gum disease by more thorough toothbrushing.

verb	recommend	I recommend that you have this test annually starting at age 40.
noun	recommendation	Against my doctor's recommendation, I decided to purchase the generic brand of medication.
adjective	recommendable	There is nothing particularly recommendable about this therapy over the other therapy I mentioned.

verb	record	The doctor records the patient's description of her symptoms in the patient's medical chart.
noun	record	When you apply for health insurance, the insurance company will probably want to look at your medical records.
adjective	recorded	After office hours there is a recorded message on the doctor's answering machine that gives an emergency telephone number.

noun	seriousness	Martha's doctor tried to make her understand the seriousness of her condition.
adjective	serious	Mr. Kim was relieved to find out that his disease was not serious.
adverb	seriously	The doctor spoke seriously with Arthur about the need to lose weight.

Incomplete Sentences

Choose the word that best completes the sentence.

1. Luckily, the test results show no _____ damage from the accident.
   (A) assess
   (B) assessment
   (C) assessing
   (D) assessable

2. This is not an easy _____ to make without the benefit of numerous test results.
   (A) diagnosis
   (B) diagnose
   (C) diagnostic
   (D) diagnosed

3. The most effective way to treat illness is to _____ it from ever occurring.
   (A) prevention
   (B) preventable
   (C) preventing
   (D) prevent

4. Gabriela did not consistently follow her doctor's _____ and her condition did not improve.
   (A) recommendations
   (B) recommendable
   (C) recommended
   (D) recommending

5. Jane's doctor asked her to _____ everything she ate for a week.
   (A) records
   (B) record
   (C) recording
   (D) recorded

6. Public health officials are just now realizing the _____ of this disease.
   (A) seriousness
   (B) serious
   (C) seriously
   (D) series

Error Recognition

Choose the underlined word or phrase that should be rewritten and rewrite it.

7. Li had visited his doctor <u>annually</u>, and his thorough medical <u>record</u> helped the new doctor <u>assessment</u> Li's
   A   B   C
   overall health and <u>recommend</u> a weight loss strategy.
                         D

   _____

8. The doctor's <u>instruments</u>, such as scopes and lights for seeing into ears and down throats, help the doctor
                   A
   make an accurate <u>diagnose</u> in the office, without <u>referring</u> patients to a lab for further tests, thus eliminating
                      B   C
   further <u>appointments</u>.
             D

   _____

9. An emergency room is most <u>effectiveness</u> in treating a <u>serious</u> problem, like a heart attack, because it has
                               A   B
   many technical and staff resources to <u>diagnose</u> and <u>manage</u> a crisis.
                                           C   D

   _____

10. Working with your doctor, you can <u>prevent</u> or minimize health problems with a plan that <u>recommendation</u>
                                        A   B
    certain screening tests that can <u>diagnose</u> disease early when it is most easily <u>managed</u>.
                                       C   D

    _____

Reading Comprehension

Read the following passage and write the verify words in the blanks below.

annually	diagnosing	manage	record
appointment	effective	preventing	refer
assessment	instruments	recommend	serious

Sooner or later, everyone needs to go to the doctor's office. In fact, it's in your best interest to see your doctor at least (11.) _____. The better he or she knows you and your health, the more (12.) _____ your doctor can be. Most people need help in (13.) _____ routine medical problems they are experiencing, such as symptoms of colds and the flu, allergies, rashes, and ear aches. Other times, people visit a doctor for help in (14.) _____ health problems from ever occurring, through lowering their risk of heart attack or stroke by dieting or exercising.

When you arrive for your (15.) _____, the doctor's office staff will have ready a (16.) _____ of all your visits, so that the doctor has a complete reference of your health. The visit will begin with an (17.) _____ of your general health and a discussion of any problems that are of concern you.

The doctors may use a variety of (18.) _____ to get a closer look at you. The doctor will (19.) _____ your problem and (20.) _____ a treatment plan. The doctor may prescribe medication, (21.) _____ you to a specialist more experienced in treating your condition, or order tests to gain more information. In (22.) _____ cases, he or she may send you to the hospital for care.

LISTENING COMPREHENSION

Listen to Track 46 of the Compact Disc to hear the statements for Lesson 46

Part I Picture

Look at the picture and listen to the sentences. Choose the sentence that best describes the picture.

23. Ⓐ Ⓑ Ⓒ Ⓓ

Part II Question—Response

Listen to the question and the three responses. Choose the response that best answers the question.

24. Ⓐ Ⓑ Ⓒ   25. Ⓐ Ⓑ Ⓒ

Part III Short Conversations

Listen to the short dialogs. Then read the question and choose the best answer.

26. Who is the woman speaking with?
    (A) An insurance broker.
    (B) An office manager.
    (C) A receptionist.
    (D) A doctor.

27. What does the doctor recommend that the man do?
    (A) Research treatment options.
    (B) Be patient.
    (C) See a specialist.
    (D) Check into the best hospital.

Part IV Short Talks

Listen to the short talk. Then read the questions and choose the best answer.

28. What kind of job is being advertised?
    (A) Doctor.
    (B) Office manager.
    (C) Director.
    (D) Office assistant.

29. How can someone apply for this job?
    (A) Send in a résumé.
    (B) Make an appointment.
    (C) Telephone the office.
    (D) Submit records.

Dentist's Office

1. **aware** adj., having knowledge
   a. I was not aware that flossing my teeth could prevent a buildup of plaque.
   b. My dentist made me aware that I should have an appointment twice a year.

2. **catch up** v., to bring up to date
   a. My dentist likes to take time to catch up before she starts the examination.
   b. The dental assistant caught up on her paperwork in between patients.

3. **distraction** n., the act of being turned away from the focus
   a. To provide a distraction from the noise, Luisa's dentist offered her a pair of earphones.
   b. My dentist is kind enough to provide distractions like television, which take my mind off the procedure.

4. **encouragement** n., inspiration or support
   a. The perfect checkup was certainly encouragement to keep up my good dental hygiene.
   b. Let me offer you some encouragement about your crooked teeth.

5. **evident** adj., easily seen or understood; obvious
   a. The presence of a wisdom tooth was not evident until the dentist started to examine the patient.
   b. Unfortunately, his poor dental hygiene is evident from a distance.

6. **habit** n., a customary manner or practice
   a. The toddler's father stressed the importance of toothbrushing in hopes of establishing a good habit.
   b. The patient had a habit of grinding his teeth during his sleep.

7. **illuminate** v., to provide or brighten with light
   a. The dark recesses of the mouth can only be seen clearly when illuminated with a lamp.
   b. Let me turn on more lights to properly illuminate the back teeth.

8. **irritate** v., to chafe or inflame, to bother
   a. The broken tooth rubbed against my tongue, irritating it.
   b. Hannah's gums are irritated by foods that are very cold or very hot.

9. **overview** n., a summary; a survey; a quick look
   a. I did a quick overview of your teeth and they look in good shape.
   b. An overview of your dental records shows a history of problems.

10. **position** n., the right or appropriate place
    a. Let me tilt your head to a more comfortable position for you.
    b. The position of the chair can be adjusted to a range of heights.

11. **regularly** adv., occurring at fixed intervals
    a. She brushes regularly after every meal.
    b. I have to remind my son regularly to brush his teeth.

12. **restore** v., to bring back to an original condition
    a. The cleaning restored the whiteness of my teeth.
    b. I will talk to my dentist about whether she knows any procedure to restore the parts of my teeth that I have ground away.

Word Families

verb	distract	The child is frightened by the instruments. Try to distract his attention while I get ready.
noun	distraction	The soothing background music was a pleasant distraction from the drilling sounds at the dentist's office.
adjective	distracted	The distracted patient left the office without paying her bill.

verb	encourage	My dentist has been encouraging me to see a specialist about my gum problem.
noun	encouragement	Although the cleaning routine recommended by the dentist was tedious, with some encouragement, Richard was able to follow it regularly.
adjective	encouraging	It was encouraging to find out that I had no serious problems at my last dental checkup.

noun	evidence	The dentist found evidence of decay on my wisdom tooth.
adjective	evident	My lack of dental hygiene was evident without a checkup.
adverb	evidently	Proper flossing evidently worked, since my gums are now in good health.

noun	habit	I'm trying to start the habit of flossing at least once a day.
adjective	habitual	His habitual coffee drinking stained his teeth.
adverb	habitually	Jack is habitually late for his appointments, which forced the receptionist to scold him.

verb	irritate	My dentist was late for my appointment, which irritated me, especially since he did not apologize.
noun	irritation	I have an irritation on the inside of my mouth that won't heal.
adjective	irritating	Matthew decided to visit the dentist because of an irritating gum problem.

verb	regulate	We cannot regulate the temperature in the waiting room today because the thermostat is broken.
adjective	regular	Many dental problems can be avoided by following a regular cleaning routine.
adverb	regularly	I haven't been visiting the dentist regularly.

Incomplete Sentences

Choose the word that best completes the sentence.

1. I don't want to _____ you, but there is a phone call waiting for you at the front desk.
    (A) distractedly
    (B) distractible
    (C) distraction
    (D) distract

2. My dentist always _____ me to floss more regularly.
    (A) encouraging
    (B) encouragement
    (C) encourages
    (D) encourage

3. It was _____ from the X-rays that I needed dental work.
    (A) evident
    (B) evidently
    (C) evidence
    (D) evidential

4. Knowing his _____ tidiness, I'm not surprised to learn that David flosses three times a day.
    (A) habit
    (B) habitual
    (C) habitually
    (D) habitualness

5. An _____ at the gum line can be nothing serious or the symptom of a larger problem.
    (A) irritate
    (B) irritable
    (C) irritation
    (D) irritability

6. _____ visits to the dentist are necessary for maintaining good dental health.
    (A) Regularly
    (B) Regular
    (C) Regulate
    (D) Regulates

Error Recognition

Choose the underlined word or phrase that should be rewritten and rewrite it.

7. Most parents are <u>aware</u> that they can prevent dental problems by <u>encouragement</u> their children to get in the
                A   B

    <u>habit</u> of brushing <u>regularly</u>.
     C   D

    _____

8. You cannot <u>catch up</u> overnight after months of bad dental <u>habits</u>; the damage to your teeth is already <u>evident</u>
                A   B   C

    and it will be hard to <u>restoration</u> them to health.
                            D

    _____

9. The sound of the drill <u>irritated</u> the patient, so her dentist gave her earphones to <u>distraction</u> her, a <u>habit</u> she
                             A   B   C

    <u>encouraged</u> him to repeat.
     D

    _____

10. The dentist settled Marcus into a <u>position</u> where the light could <u>illuminate</u> his back teeth; although the intensity
                                         A   B

    of the light is <u>irritation</u>, it makes problems with the back teeth more <u>evident</u>.
                        C   D

    _____

Reading Comprehension

Read the following passage and write the words in the blanks below.

aware	encourage	illuminates	position
catch up	evident	irritates	regularly
distraction	habit	overview	restores

At least twice a year, Toshiro makes an appointment with his dentist. He's (11.) _____ that taking good care of his teeth and seeing a dentist can help prevent the buildup of tartar and plaque that could cause serious problems later.

The dentist starts the appointment by looking over Toshiro's chart, which details all the work that has been done on his teeth, as a way to (12.) _____ on Toshiro's dental health. Toshiro brushes (13.) _____, but is not so regular about daily flossing. His dentist is trying to (14.) _____ a better flossing (15.) _____, by demonstrating some easy-to-use techniques.

When the dentist is ready to look into Toshiro's mouth, she adjusts the height and (16.) _____ of the chair to make sure she can see all of Toshiro's teeth. A bright light (17.) _____ Toshiro's eyes, but (18.) _____ the dark places in the back of his mouth. The dentist does a quick (19.) _____ of Toshiro's mouth, looking for any obvious problems, such as a cavity or a broken tooth. The dentist asks if Toshiro has been having any problems, like tooth pain, bleeding, or soreness.

Sometimes, problems in the mouth are quite (20.) _____ and can be seen by the dentist's trained eye. But other times, the dentist will take X-rays to make certain there are no problems in areas she cannot see, such as under the gum line or inside a tooth.

The dentist then goes to work, repairing any damage. She then (21.) _____ the natural color to his teeth with a thorough cleaning. The noise of the drills and cleaners can upset some patients, so Toshiro's dentist is kind enough to supply earphones to provide a (22.) _____.

LISTENING COMPREHENSION

Listen to Track 47 of the Compact Disc to hear the statements for Lesson 47

Part I Picture

Look at the picture and listen to the sentences. Choose the sentence that best describes the picture.

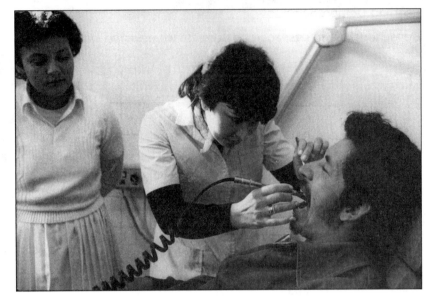

23. Ⓐ Ⓑ Ⓒ Ⓓ

Part II Question—Response

Listen to the question and the three responses. Choose the response that best answers the question.

24. Ⓐ Ⓑ Ⓒ   25. Ⓐ Ⓑ Ⓒ

Part III Short Conversations

Listen to the short dialogs. Then read the question and choose the best answer.

26. What is the man's problem?
    (A) Dentist appointments are very expensive.
    (B) His teeth need cleaning.
    (C) He can't get a dentist appointment.
    (D) His tooth is irritating him.

27. What does the patient want?
    (A) He wants shinier teeth.
    (B) He wants a cup of coffee.
    (C) He wants to see his dental records.
    (D) He wants all his cavities filled.

Part IV Short Talks

Listen to the short talk. Then read the questions and choose the best answer.

28. What product is advertised?
    (A) False teeth.
    (B) A tooth whitener.
    (C) Chewing gum.
    (D) A toothbrush.

29. What are the customers asked to do?
    (A) Use the product for just two days.
    (B) Change their cleaning habits.
    (C) Use the product every night.
    (D) Visit the dentist.

Health Insurance

1. **allow** v., to let do or happen; to permit
   a. My insurance does not allow me to choose my own hospital.
   b. The health plan made an exception by allowing me to go directly to a dermatologist.

2. **alternative** adj., allowing a choice; other
   a. To lower the cost of health insurance, my employer chose an alternative method of insuring us.
   b. I'd like to discuss alternative treatments before I agree to anything.

3. **aspect** n., a feature element; an appearance
   a. The right to chose their own doctor is an important aspect of health coverage for many people.
   b. The aspect of HMOs that people most dislike is the lack of personal service.

4. **concern** n., anxiety; worry
   a. Whenever I have health concerns, I call my doctor.
   b. The rising cost of health care is of great concern to many people.

5. **emphasize** v., to stress
   a. The nurse emphasized the importance of eating a balanced diet.
   b. The new insurance plan emphasizes wellness by providing reimbursement for health club memberships.

6. **incur** v., to become subject to
   a. I incurred substantial expenses that my health plan does not cover.
   b. Dominic incurs the cost of a co-payment at each doctor's visit.

7. **personnel** n., a group of employees or workers
   a. The office manager insisted that she needed more personnel to finish the project on time.
   b. The employee went to see the director of personnel about taking an extended leave of absence.

8. **policy** n., a set of rules and regulations
   a. Company policy did not provide for overtime pay.
   b. The company's insurance policy did not cover cosmetic surgery.

9. **portion** n., a section or quantity within a larger thing; a part of a whole
   a. A portion of my benefits is my health care coverage.
   b. I am keeping a record of the portion of my income I spend on health care.

10. **regardless** adv., in spite of
    a. Regardless of the cost, we all need health insurance.
    b. I keep going to the same doctor, regardless of the fact that she does not take my pain seriously.

11. **salary** n., a fixed compensation paid regularly for work done; one's pay
    a. The receptionist believed that he worked too hard for such a small salary.
    b. The technician was pleased to have a raise in salary after only six months on the job.

12. **suit** v., to be appropriate; to satisfy
    a. This insurance plan doesn't suit our family as it doesn't cover well-baby care.
    b. I have finally found a health plan that suits my needs.

Word Families

verb	allow	The insurance policy did not allow multiple prescription refills.
noun	allowance	The policy is liberal in its allowance for optometry services.
adjective	allowable	A maximum of two dental visits is allowable under the plan.

verb	alternate	We alternate turns in taking the kids to the doctor.
noun	alternative	Our medical insurance was too expensive, so we sought a cheaper alternative.
adjective	alternative	We need to find an alternative health plan as this one is too expensive.

verb	concern	It concerns me that we haven't been able to find a suitable health insurance plan.
noun	concern	A good doctor will pay attention to any and all concerns the patient expresses about his or her health.
adjective	concerned	I am concerned about the limited benefits this insurance plan offers.

verb	emphasize	The plan representative emphasized the need for a second medical opinion.
noun	emphasis	The emphasis of the health plan is on staying well.
adjective	emphatic	Hassan made an emphatic appeal to the medical insurance director.

verb	regard	We regard this health insurance plan as one of the best options available.
adjective	regardful	The company was not regardful of the needs of most of the employees when it chose this health insurance plan.
adverb	regardless	I took the job regardless of the poor health benefits the company offers.

verb	suit	I'm dropping my health plan because it does not suit my needs.
adjective	suitable	Not every kind of health insurance is suitable for every family.
adverb	suitably	The errors on my insurance statement were caught and suitably fixed.

Incomplete Sentences

Choose the word that best completes the sentence.

1. Office policy does not _____ employees to leave the office for medical appointments.
   (A) allow
   (B) allowing
   (C) allowable
   (D) allowance

2. You should investigate to see if there are any _____ to costly hospital stays.
   (A) alternate
   (B) alternatively
   (C) alternatives
   (D) alternating

3. It _____ me that our company is not willing to look for an alternative to our current health insurance plan.
   (A) concern
   (B) concerned
   (C) concerns
   (D) concerning

4. I'm really pleased that my health plan provider is paying for my gym membership as a way to _____ its concern for my health.
   (A) emphasis
   (B) emphasize
   (C) emphatic
   (D) emphasizing

5. I _____ health insurance as an indispensable job benefit.
   (A) regardless
   (B) regardful
   (C) regarding
   (D) regard

6. The employee's goal is to find her family _____ health coverage.
   (A) suit
   (B) suitable
   (C) suitably
   (D) suitability

Error Recognition

Choose the underlined word or phrase that should be rewritten and rewrite it.

7. One <u>aspect</u> of the health plan that Vivianne likes is the <u>emphasize</u> on wellness; this means the plan will pay a
       A   B

   large <u>portion</u> of her annual physical, allowing her to keep more of her <u>salary</u>.
        C   D

   _____

8. <u>Concerned</u> about <u>incurred</u> large costs for health premiums, employers found ways to lower the cost, such as
    A   B

   having <u>personnel</u> contribute more to the premium and aligning with <u>alternative</u> providers like HMOs.
        C   D

   _____

9. The HMOs will not <u>allow</u> their subscribers to use medical <u>personnel</u> they do not find <u>suitability</u>; for example,
           A   B   C

   seeing a specialist without a referral is discouraged, <u>regardless</u> of the cause.
                                              D

   _____

10. Finding a <u>suitable</u> health <u>policy</u> is difficult, since most place the <u>emphasis</u> on cost and are not <u>concern</u> with the
            A   B   C   D

   quality of care.

   _____

Reading Comprehension

Read the following passage and write the words in the blanks below.

allow	concerns	personnel	regardless
alternatives	emphasize	policy	salary
aspect	incurs	portion	suitable

The cost and availability of health insurance is one of the greatest (11.) _____ of company (12.) _____. A covered employee should be familiar with the terms and conditions of the insurance (13.) _____. Although the insured pays a (14.) _____ of the cost of his or her coverage through (15.) _____ deductions, the employer generally covers most of the cost.

Self-employed persons can arrange for their own insurance or join an association of those performing similar work in order to get lower premiums. Traditionally, the insurance carrier will (16.) _____ most of the charges related to medical care, although the insured might be responsible for a small portion.

Although the company or association negotiates the most (17.) _____ terms they can, most experts (18.) _____ that employees should be on the lookout for (19.) _____ that might better suit their needs. (20.) _____ of the cost of premiums, the most important (21.) _____ of good health insurance is that it meets the needs of the insured and (22.) _____ the least possible cost for necessary procedures.

LISTENING COMPREHENSION

Listen to Track 48 of the Compact Disc to hear the statements for Lesson 48

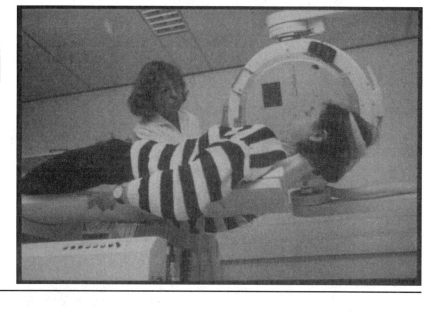

Part I Picture

Look at the picture and listen to the sentences. Choose the sentence that best describes the picture.

23. Ⓐ Ⓑ Ⓒ Ⓓ

Part II Question—Response

Listen to the question and the three responses. Choose the response that best answers the question.

24. Ⓐ Ⓑ Ⓒ   25. Ⓐ Ⓑ Ⓒ

Part III Short Conversations

Listen to the short dialogs. Then read the question and choose the best answer.

26. What will happen if the man sees a specialist without a referral?
    (A) He won't be able to get an appointment immediately.
    (B) He will only see a portion of the bill.
    (C) He won't be provided with good care.
    (D) He will pay a higher percentage of the cost.

27. What do the speakers say about the new health plan?
    (A) It's very expensive.
    (B) It has few benefits.
    (C) It pays for health club membership.
    (D) It's traditional.

Part IV Short Talks

Listen to the short talk. Then read the questions and choose the best answer.

28. Why has a new health plan been chosen?
    (A) To help people save money.
    (B) Because the old plan is no longer available.
    (C) To get more benefits.
    (D) Because people are interested in alternative medicine.

29. Who will the new plan be available to?
    (A) Only people who earn a low salary.
    (B) Anyone who is interested.
    (C) Only people who have special health concerns.
    (D) Just those who have worked at the company for a long time.

Hospitals

1. **admit** v., to permit to enter
   a. The injured patient was admitted to the unit directly from the emergency room.
   b. The staff refused to admit the patient until he had proof of insurance.

2. **authorize** v., to approve
   a. The doctor suggested that she check with her insurance company to make sure it would authorize a lengthened hospital stay.
   b. We cannot share the test results with you until we have been authorized to do so by your doctor.

3. **designate** v., to indicate or specify
   a. The labels on the bags designated the type of blood they contained.
   b. On her admittance form, Grandmother designated Aunt Tessa as her chief decision-maker.

4. **escort** n., a person accompanying another to guide or protect
   a. Let's see if there is an escort available to take you to the parking garage.
   b. You cannot leave the unit on your own; you'll have to wait for an escort.

5. **identify** v., to ascertain the name or belongings of
   a. The tiny bracelets identified each baby in the nursery.
   b. Your medical records are all marked with your patient number to identify them in case of a mix-up.

6. **mission** n., an inner calling to pursue an activity or perform a service
   a. The hospital chaplain took as his mission to visit every patient admitted each day.
   b. The nurse explained that the mission of everyone in the unit was to make sure the patients got well as soon as possible.

7. **permit** v., to allow
   a. Smoking is not permitted anywhere inside the hospital.
   b. Would you check with the nurse to see if I am permitted to eat before surgery?

8. **pertinent** adj., having relevance to the matter at hand
   a. You should mention any pertinent health issues to the staff before you are admitted for surgery.
   b. The patient's health record contained pertinent information, like the dates of all his inoculations.

9. **procedure** n., a series of steps taken to accomplish an end
   a. The surgical procedure can now be done in half the amount of time it took even five years ago.
   b. Call the hospital to schedule this procedure for tomorrow.

10. **result** n., an outcome
    a. Your lab results won't be ready for hours.
    b. The scientific results prove that the new procedure is not significantly safer than the traditional one.

11. **statement** n., an accounting showing an amount due; a bill
    a. The billing statement was filed with the insurance company last month.
    b. Check with your doctor's office for an original statement; we cannot process a faxed copy.

12. **usually** adv., customarily
    a. That kind of surgery is usually performed on an outpatient basis.
    b. The insurance company does not usually pay for procedures that are considered elective or optional.

Word Families

verb	admit	The patients lined the hospital corridors waiting to be admitted.
noun	admittance	Your admittance to the hospital is dependent on your showing proof that you can pay the bills.
noun	admission	Take these records down to Admissions and have them duplicate the files for you.

verb	authorize	Your doctor has to authorize these tests before we can proceed with them.
noun	authority	Before major surgery, it is a good idea to give decision-making authority to a close relative in case something happens to you.
noun	authorization	The nurse could not submit an authorization over the phone; it had to be done in writing.

verb	designate	The hospital administrator designated a team to create an emergency preparedness plan.
noun	designation	The designation of the hospital as one of the best in the region certainly helped its marketing efforts.
noun	designator	The national health service is the sole designator of which hospitals will get the grants.

verb	identify	If you will identify your valuables, the nurse will give them back to you.
noun	identification	Please remember to bring some form of identification with you when you check in at the hospital.
adjective	identifiable	The red cross on the hospital's helicopter landing pad was identifiable from the air.

verb	permit	I can't permit more than one visitor at a time in the intensive care unit.
noun	permission	Mohammed got his insurance company's permission to stay another day in the hospital.
adjective	permissible	It is not permissible to smoke inside the hospital.

adjective	usual	It is usual for health insurance companies to require patients to make co-payments for hospital stays.
adjective	unusual	Because of her unusual condition, Martha's doctor sent her to a specialist for treatment.
adverb	usually	These days, patients usually stay in the hospital for only a few days at a time.

Incomplete Sentences

Choose the word that best completes the sentence.

1. Before my father was _____ to the hospital, he had to undergo a series of tests.
   (A) admit
   (B) admitted
   (C) admittance
   (D) admissions

2. Will your insurance company _____ a visit to a specialist?
   (A) authorize
   (B) authorization
   (C) authority
   (D) authorizing

3. As a precaution, it's wise to _____ someone in your family to make health care decisions for you in case there is a time that you cannot.
   (A) designation
   (B) designate
   (C) designator
   (D) designated

4. Your X-rays will have your name and social security number printed on them, so we can easily _____ them as yours.
   (A) identifiably
   (B) identification
   (C) identifiable
   (D) identify

5. Before we can begin the surgery, we will need your signed _____ authorizing us to perform the procedure.
   (A) permit
   (B) permissive
   (C) permission
   (D) permissible

6. Is it _____ for a doctor to order so many tests?
   (A) usual
   (B) usually
   (C) unusually
   (D) used

Error Recognition

Choose the underlined word or phrase that should be rewritten and rewrite it.

7. Jose's <u>authorization</u> for the surgical <u>procedure</u> had expired, so the hospital would not <u>admission</u> him until they
        A   B   C
   had <u>permission</u> to do so from his health plan.
       D

   _____

8. When delayed test <u>results</u> became a <u>usually</u> occurrence, the hospital administrator <u>identified</u> it as a problem
                 A   B   C
   that could damage the <u>mission</u> of the hospital.
           D

   _____

9. In an official <u>statement</u>, the hospital <u>authorized</u> all nursing units to <u>designation</u> a staff member to <u>escort</u>
           A   B   C   D
   patients to their cars.

   _____

10. The <u>admissions</u> office asked Ruby for all her <u>pertinent</u> personal data, such as <u>identification</u> and health plan
        A   B   C
    <u>authorized</u>, before she could check into her hospital room.
     D

    _____

Reading Comprehension

Read the following passage and write the words in the blanks below.

admitting	escort	permitted	results
authorization	identification	pertinent	statement
designated	mission	procedures	usually

Hospitals have a (11.) _____ to provide patients with high-quality medical care. Everyone on staff will make sure that you get the best possible treatment for your condition.

When you arrive at the hospital, you should have with you all the (12.) _____ information needed to be admitted, like your insurance information and copies of X-rays and other test (13.) _____, even if they were taken at another facility. Bring your insurance card and any referral or (14.) _____ form from your doctor. You should also have some form of (15.) _____ with a photo. You will also need to sign an agreement regarding treatment consent. Once you arrive, there is usually a concierge who will assist you with the (16.) _____ process.

Many elective surgeries and other (17.) _____ are (18.) _____ done on the same day. Usually a hospital staff member will (19.) _____ you to the exit and make sure you get into the car safely. After you leave the hospital, you will receive a (20.) _____ from the hospital for the charges your insurer does not cover. Your insurance policy will outline any amount for which you may be responsible.

You will find that smoking is not (21.) _____ in any hospital building. Often, hospitals have (22.) _____ smoking areas outside for patients, families, and staff who wish to smoke.

LISTENING COMPREHENSION

Listen to Track 49 of the Compact Disc to hear the statements for Lesson 49

Part I Picture

Look at the picture and listen to the sentences. Choose the sentence that best describes the picture.

23. Ⓐ Ⓑ Ⓒ Ⓓ

Part II Question—Response

Listen to the question and the three responses. Choose the response that best answers the question.

24. Ⓐ Ⓑ Ⓒ   25. Ⓐ Ⓑ Ⓒ

Part III Short Conversations

Listen to the short dialogs. Then read the question and choose the best answer.

26. What does the woman's mother need?
   (A) An overnight hospital stay.
   (B) Special permission from her surgeon.
   (C) Money to pay the hospital.
   (D) A surgical procedure.

27. What is the woman's complaint?
   (A) The records weren't delivered on time.
   (B) Her husband didn't get an identification card.
   (C) The computer system broke down.
   (D) Her husband's records got mixed up.

Part IV Short Talks

Listen to the short talk. Then read the questions and choose the best answer.

28. Who is the speaker?
   (A) A doctor.
   (B) A lab technician.
   (C) A nurse.
   (D) An insurance agent.

29. When will the surgery take place?
   (A) In eight days.
   (B) In a week.
   (C) In ten days.
   (D) In 23 days.

Pharmacy

1. **consult** v., to seek advice or information of
    a. The doctor consulted with a specialist before writing a new prescription.
    b. May I consult with you about a drug interaction case I have?
2. **control** v., to exercise authoritative or dominating influence over
    a. To control the cost of this medication, you may get the generic version.
    b. Please take your medication every day to control your high blood pressure.
3. **convenient** adj., suited or favorable to one's purpose; easy to reach
    a. Is this a convenient location for you to pick up your prescription?
    b. It is convenient to have a pharmacy right across the street from my doctor's office.
4. **detect** v., to discover or ascertain
    a. My doctor put me through some simple tests to detect if I have asthma.
    b. I have to keep track of my sleep patterns to detect how many times I get up in the night.
5. **factor** n., a contribution to an accomplishment, a result, or a process
    a. Taking medications as directed is an important factor in getting well.
    b. Could my cat be a factor contributing to my asthma?
6. **interaction** n., a mutual activity
    a. My pharmacist was concerned about the interaction of the two medications I was prescribed.
    b. The interaction between the patient and the doctor showed a high level of trust.
7. **limit** n., the point beyond which something cannot proceed
    a. My prescription has a limit of three refills.
    b. My health plan authorization sets a limit on which health care providers I can see without their permission.
8. **monitor** v., to keep track of
    a. The nurse practitioner carefully monitors the number of medications her patients are taking.
    b. The patient had weekly appointments so that the doctor could monitor her progress.
9. **potential** adj., capable of being but not yet in existence; possible
    a. To avoid any potential side effects from the medication, be sure to tell your doctor all the drugs you are currently taking.
    b. Given the potential delay in getting reimbursed by the health plan, why don't we just fill one prescription today?
10. **sample** n., a portion, piece, or segment that is representative of a whole
    a. The pharmacist gave Myra a few free samples of the allergy medication.
    b. A sample of the population taking the new medicine was surveyed to determine whether it caused side effects.
11. **sense** n., a judgment; an intellectual interpretation
    a. The doctor had a good sense about what the problem was but wanted to get a second opinion.
    b. I got the sense it would be better to get my prescription filled right away.
12. **volunteer** v., to perform as a volunteer
    a. My doctor volunteered to call the drugstore, so my medication would be waiting for me.
    b. Since Tom was feeling so unwell, his son volunteered to pick up his prescription at the pharmacy for him.

Word Families

verb	consult	Beatrice consulted her pharmacist about the number of different medications she is taking.
noun	consultation	Let me arrange a consultation with a specialist to discuss your heart problem and some possible medications.
adjective	consultative	This is a consultative process and you probably won't have a definitive answer immediately.

noun	convenience	The convenience of a 24-hour neighborhood pharmacy is not to be underestimated.
adjective	convenient	Many people shop there because of its convenient location.
adverb	conveniently	The pharmacy is conveniently located on my way home from work.

verb	detect	The laboratory test detected the presence of medication in his blood.
noun	detection	Early detection of diseases usually means that medications can be more effective.
adjective	detectable	After he took his medication faithfully for a few months and exercised more, Jack's disease was no longer detectable.

verb	limit	My health insurance company has severely limited the amount of money it will pay out for prescription medicine.
noun	limit	Even though that headache medicine does not require a prescription, there is a limit to how many times a day you should take it.
adjective	limited	The new drugstore on the corner really isn't convenient because of its limited hours of operation.

noun	potential	Be careful when taking this medication because it has the potential to make you feel sleepy.
adjective	potential	Margaret decided not to take the medicine the doctor had prescribed because of its potential side effects.
adverb	potentially	Many medications are potentially dangerous so it is important to take them exactly as prescribed by the doctor.

verb	volunteer	The pharmacist volunteers his services monthly at the free clinic for homeless people.
noun	volunteer	Volunteers bring filled prescriptions from the pharmacy to the homes of shut-ins.
adjective	voluntary	Your compliance with this new policy is completely voluntary, but we think it is in the public interest that you do so.

Incomplete Sentences

Choose the word that best completes the sentence.

1. Would you please schedule the patient for a medical _____ tomorrow afternoon?
    (A) consult
    (B) consultation
    (C) consulting
    (D) consultative

2. Your prescription will be ready in an hour, if that's _____ for you.
    (A) conveniences
    (B) conveniently
    (C) convenience
    (D) convenient

3. The procedure _____ a slight problem, but the doctor assured us not to be alarmed.
    (A) detected
    (B) detect
    (C) detection
    (D) detectable

4. My doctor has decided to _____ the amount of medication I am taking.
    (A) limit
    (B) limited
    (C) limiting
    (D) limits

5. Inform the pharmacist of any other medications you are taking to avoid any _____ drug interactions.
    (A) potentially
    (B) potential
    (C) potentiality
    (D) potency

6. We desperately need _____ to help at the free clinic next month.
    (A) voluntary
    (B) volunteer
    (C) volunteers
    (D) volunteerism

Error Recognition

Choose the underlined word or phrase that should be rewritten and rewrite it.

7. By <u>consultative</u> with her pharmacist, Lydia was able to establish a computer record that <u>monitored</u> the kinds of
    A
    B
    drugs she took to prevent the <u>potential</u> for harmful <u>interactions</u>.
    C
    D
    _____

8. The <u>limited</u> pharmacy hours were not <u>convenient</u> for me, so I was grateful when my doctor <u>voluntary</u> to give
    A
    B
    C
    me free drug <u>samples</u>.
    D
    _____

9. Gladys's symptoms grew increasingly difficult to <u>control</u>, so her doctor wrote a prescription for a <u>convenience</u>
    A
    B
    strap-on heart <u>monitor</u> that would immediately <u>detect</u> an irregular heartbeat.
    C
    D
    _____

10. It made <u>sense</u> to Sanjay that the pharmacist should <u>monitor</u> drug <u>interactive</u> and other <u>factors</u> that could be
    A
    B
    C
    D
    harmful.
    _____

Reading Comprehension

Read the following passage and the words in the blanks below.

consulting	detection	limit	samples
control	factors	monitor	sense
convenient	interactions	potential	volunteers

Yoko is having trouble with seasonal allergies this fall. After (11.) _____ with her doctor, they decide she should take medication on a regular basis to (12.) _____ her symptoms. Her doctor recommends the medication he thinks will work best and offers her a handful of (13.) _____ at no charge. For her long-term needs, Yoko will need to have a prescription filled. Her doctor (14.) _____ to call the pharmacy Yoko uses to order a supply, which will (15.) _____ the time she spends waiting for the prescription to be filled.

Yoko is new in town and does not know which pharmacy she wants to use. She knows that there is a drugstore near her apartment and one near where she works, but does not remember the operating hours for either. Yoko knows that (16.) _____ hours and location are important (17.) _____ in selecting a pharmacy. Although she can fill different prescriptions at different drugstores, it makes more (18.) _____ to Yoko to fill all of her medications at one location.

Occasionally, some drugs will have harmful (19.) _____. Usually, your doctor will prevent a drug interaction problem before it starts. But, if you see more than one doctor, it is hard to (20.) _____ the various medications you are taking. Having all your prescriptions filled at one location increases the chances that the pharmacist will detect a (21.) _____ drug interaction problem. This timely (22.) _____ can save your life.

LISTENING COMPREHENSION

Listen to Track 50 of the Compact Disc to hear the statements for Lesson 50

Part I Picture

Look at the picture and listen to the sentences. Choose the sentence that best describes the picture.

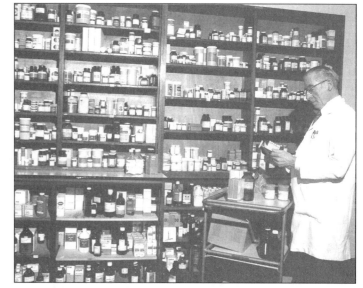

23. Ⓐ Ⓑ Ⓒ Ⓓ

Part II Question—Response

Listen to the question and the three responses. Choose the response that best answers the question.

24. Ⓐ Ⓑ Ⓒ   25. Ⓐ Ⓑ Ⓒ

Part III Short Conversations

Listen to the short dialogs. Then read the question and choose the best answer.

26. When will the patient fill the prescription?
   (A) Right away.
   (B) Within two days.
   (C) On the way to work.
   (D) After trying the samples.

27. What will the man do now?
   (A) Talk with his wife.
   (B) Call the pharmacy.
   (C) Pick up his wife.
   (D) Go to the pharmacy.

Part IV Short Talks

Listen to the short talk. Then read the questions and choose the best answer.

28. What is a possible side effect of the medication?
   (A) Sleepiness.
   (B) Stomachaches.
   (C) Fatigue.
   (D) Headaches.

29. How often should the patient take the medication?
   (A) Once a day.
   (B) Two times a day.
   (C) Three times a day.
   (D) Four times a day.

Word Review #10   Lessons 46–50 Health

Choose the word that best completes the sentence.

1. Your doctor's _____ are as important as his prescriptions.
    (A) recommend
    (B) recommended
    (C) recommending
    (D) recommendations

2. Dentists are as concerned with your dental _____ as with the condition of your teeth.
    (A) habits
    (B) habitual
    (C) habitually
    (D) habituated

3. To avoid _____ any additional charges, you should ask to be discharged from the hospital.
    (A) incur
    (B) incurs
    (C) incurred
    (D) incurring

4. It is as fast and efficient to _____ with your pharmacist as with your physician.
    (A) consult
    (B) consulting
    (C) consulted
    (D) consultation

5. Although an annual checkup is important, you should also make an _____ whenever you have a health concern.
    (A) appoint
    (B) appointed
    (C) appointment
    (D) appointments

6. A dentist can perform dental _____ as well as routine maintenance.
    (A) restore
    (B) restored
    (C) restoring
    (D) restoration

7. A good medical insurance will _____ preventive health programs as well as treatment.
    (A) emphasize
    (B) emphasis
    (C) emphasizing
    (D) emphasized

8. The most difficult part of hospitalization is being _____.
    (A) admit
    (B) admitted
    (C) admissions
    (D) admitting

9. A pharmacist will _____ the customer's medications.
    (A) monitor
    (B) monitors
    (C) monitoring
    (D) monitored

10. I don't understand most of what I read in a hospital's billing _____.
    (A) state
    (B) stated
    (C) stating
    (D) statement

Choose the underlined word or phrase that should be rewritten and rewrite it.

11. Your pharmacist is a <u>conveniently</u> <u>factor</u> in <u>monitoring</u> your prescription <u>record</u>.
    　　　　　　　　　　　　A　　　　　　B　　　　　C　　　　　　　　　　　　　　　　D

    _____

12. At your <u>annual</u> <u>appointment</u>, your doctor can most <u>effective</u> <u>diagnose</u> you if you tell her everything.
    　　　　　　A　　　　　B　　　　　　　　　　　　　　　　C　　　　　D

    _____

13. Any doctor can help you to <u>management</u> your medical health by helping you <u>prevent</u> risky behavior and
    　　　　　　　　　　　　　　　A　　　　　　　　　　　　　　　　　　　　　　B

    eliminate bad <u>habits</u> or by <u>referring</u> you to a specialist.
    　　　　　　　　C　　　　　　D

    _____

14. Before being <u>admission</u> to a hospital, you need to have all <u>pertinent</u> documents as <u>evidence</u> of insurance
    　　　　　　　　A　　　　　　　　　　　　　　　　　　　　B　　　　　　　　　　C

    <u>authorization</u>.
    　　D

    _____

15. <u>Regardless</u> of how minor, any <u>procedure</u> can <u>resulting</u> in <u>serious</u> complications.
       A   B   C   D

    _____

16. Once a doctor <u>assesses</u> your condition, his <u>alternatives</u> include <u>referral</u> you to another physician
                    A   B   C
    or <u>recommending</u> special exercise or diet.
         D

    _____

17. Even when a dental problem is not <u>evident</u>, a dentist's powerful <u>illumination</u> and specialized <u>instruments</u>
                                  A   B   C
    can make him <u>awareness</u> of a potential problem.
               D

    _____

18. Some insurance <u>policies</u> do not <u>allowed</u> for certain procedures <u>designated</u> cosmetic instead of <u>restorative</u>.
               A   B   C   D

    _____

19. Some physicians <u>voluntarily</u> information about generic drugs or give <u>samples</u>, always alert to <u>potential</u>
                   A   B   C
    <u>interactions</u>.
       D

    _____

20. <u>Distracting</u> by multiple <u>policy</u> regulations, insurance <u>personnel</u> do not always respond accurately to a patient's
     A   B   C
    <u>concerns</u>.
     D

    _____

Answer Key

Lessons 1–5 General Business
Lesson 1 Contracts: 1. A 2. A 3. B 4. D 5. B 6. D 7. A,
resolution 8. C, determine 9. C, cancel 10. A, establishes
11. agreement 12. parties 13. specifies 14. obligates
15. assurance 16. establishment 17. determine 18. provide
19. resolve 20. engaging 21. abide by 22. cancel 23. B
24. C 25. A 26. D 27. C 28. A 29. A

Lesson 2 Marketing: 1. C 2. A 3. C 4. A 5. D 6. B 7. B,
inspire 8. B, persuade 9. D, compared 10. B, attracting
11. product 12. market 13. persuaded 14. consumers
15. attract 16. satisfied 17. current 18. inspire 19. convince
20. compared 21. competes 22. fad 23. C 24. A 25. B
26. C 27. C 28. D 29. C

Lesson 3 Warranties: 1. D 2. B 3. D 4. C 5. A 6. D 7. D,
expired 8. D, vary 9. A, consequences 10. A, consider
11. promise 12. required 13. frequently 14. consider
15. characteristics 16. vary 17. coverage 18. implies
19. expire 20. protect 21. reputations 22. consequences
23. A 24. B 25. A 26. A 27. B 28. B 29. A

Lesson 4 Business Planning: 1. A 2. A 3. C 4. D 5. C
6. A 7. B, demonstrate 8. D, offering 9. D, evaluate 10. B,
risks 11. develop 12. primary 13. avoid 14. strength
15. substitute 16. strategy 17. evaluation 18. offered
19. risks 20. gathering 21. demonstrate 22. address 23. A
24. A 25. B 26. D 27. B 28. A 29. B

Lesson 5 Conferences: 1. B 2. C 3. B 4. A 5. A 6. D 7.
B, register 8. A, selecting 9. C, holding 10. C, attendees
11. associations 12. get in touch 13. take part in
14. sessions 15. attending 16. select 17. arrangements
18. accommodate 19. hold 20. overcrowded 21. location
22. register 23. D 24. B 25. B 26. C 27. C 28. A 29. D

Word Review #1: 1. C 2. D 3. D 4. D 5. A 6. B 7. A 8. B
9. A 10. A 11. B, inspire 12. A, select 13. D, satisfy
14. D, resolve 15. B, selecting 16. C, implies 17. B, assurance 18. A, attract 19. B, registered 20. B, products

Lessons 6–10 Office Issues
Lesson 6 Computers: 1. A 2. B 3. B 4. B 5. B 6. C 7. C,
delete 8. C, figured out 9. D, warning 10. C, compatible
11. shut down 12. warning 13. figure out 14. access
15. search 16. deleted 17. duplicate 18. ignore 19. display
20. failed 21. allocate 22. compatible 23. C 24. A 25. A
26. D 27. D 28. B 29. C

Lesson 7 Office Technology: 1. D 2. C 3. A 4. B 5. D
6. B 7. C, physically 8. A, as needed 9. C, recurring 10. A,
initiated 11. is in charge of 12. durable 13. affordable
14. reduce 15. capacity 16. physical 17. initiates
18. stays on top of 19. recurring 20. provider 21. as needed
22. stock 23. A 24. B 25. C 26. A 27. D 28. D 29. B

Lesson 8 Office Procedures: 1. A 2. B 3. B 4. D 5. A
6. B 7. C, casual 8. D, practices 9. D, warning 10. B, had
been exposed to 11. appreciation 12. made of
13. reinforced 14. casually 15. code 16. out of
17. verbalize 18. practices 19. outdated 20. been exposed
to 21. brought in 22. glimpse 23. B 24. C 25. C 26. B
27. B 28. A 29. B

Lesson 9 Electronics: 1. C 2. D 3. B 4. A 5. C 6. A 7. D,
sharply 8. D, software 9. B, revolutionized 10. C, technology
11. sharply 12. networks 13. facilitates 14. processing
15. disks 16. technical 17. storage 18. software 19. replace
20. popular 21. revolutionize 22. skills 23. C 24. C 25. B
26. D 27. A 28. A 29. C

Lesson 10 Correspondence: 1. A 2. B 3. A 4. A 5. B
6. C 7. C, proofed 8. A, revised 9. C, complicated
10. D, folded 11. proofed 12. revision 13. beforehand
14. assemble 15. folding 16. courier 17. express
18. registered 19. layout 20. mention 21. complicated
22. petition 23. C 24. B 25. C 26. C 27. B 28. A 29. B

Word Review #2: 1. C 2. D 3. B 4. D 5. B 6. A 7. B 8. B
9. C 10. B 11. D, as needed 12. A, affordability 13. D, display
14. D, practices 15. B, proof 16. D, shut down 17. A, recurring,
recurrent 18. B, assembled 19. B, revolution 20. C, reduce

Lessons 11–15 Personnel
Lesson 11 Job Advertising and Recruiting: 1. C 2. A
3. A 4. B 5. D 6. A 7. B, recruiters 8. B, candidates 9. C,
qualified 10. C, match 11. time-consuming 12. match
13. recruit 14. accomplishments 15. bring together
16. abundant 17. candidates 18. qualifications 19. Coming
up with 20. profile 21. commensurate 22. submit 23. D
24. A 25. B 26. D 27. C 28. D 29. A

Lesson 12 Applying and Interviewing: 1. D 2. C 3. A
4. D 5. B 6. A 7. A, applicant's 8. B, be ready for
9. B, confident 10. D, constantly 11. experts 12. confidence
13. weaknesses 14. constantly 15. follow up 16. abilities
17. apply 18. backgrounds 19. called in 20. are ready for
21. present 22. hesitant 23. A 24. A 25. C 26. B 27. D
28. D 29. B

Lesson 13 Hiring and Training: 1. B 2. B 3. C 4. A 5. D
6. B 7. B, conducted 8. A, hire 9. D, updates
10. D, successful 11. conducted 12. rejected
13. successfully 14. generate 15. hires 16. training
17. update 18. keep up with 19. set up 20. mentor
21. look up to 22. on track 23. B 24. A 25. B 26. D 27. B
28. D 29. B

Lesson 14 Salaries and Benefits: 1. C 2. C 3. C 4. B 5. B
6. A 7. D, flexible 8. A, vested 9. B, delicate 10. C, eligible
11. negotiated 12. benefits 13. compensated 14. delicate
15. be aware of 16. wage 17. flexibility 18. basis 19. raise
20. retirement 21. eligible 22. vested 23. C 24. B 25. A
26. C 27. D 28. A 29. A

Lesson 15 Promotions, Pensions, and Awards: 1. C 2. C
3. C 4. C 5. B 6. A 7. C, dedication 8. A, valuable
9. C, obvious 10. C, productive 11. recognizes
12. contributions 13. achievements/merits 14. promotions
15. merits/achievements 16. loyalty 17. obvious
18. look to 19. productivity 20. value 21. look forward
22. dedicate 23. C 24. A 25. C 26. D 27. C 28. B 29. C

Word Review #3: 1. A 2. A 3. B 4. C 5. D 6. C 7. B 8. B
9. D 10. A 11. D, successful 12. B, training 13. B, recognition
14. A, recruited 15. B, promotion 16. B, compensate
17. A, negotiating 18. D, flexible 19. C, on track 20. B, set up

Lessons 16–20 Purchasing
Lesson 16 Shopping: 1. C 2. A 3. D 4. A 5. C 6. C 7. B,
behavior 8. A, bear 9. C, expand 10. B, items 11. bear
12. behavior 13. mandatory 14. strictly 15. items
16. expand 17. exploring 18. comforting 19. merchandise
20. bargains 21. checkout 22. trend 23. C 24. B 25. B
26. A 27. D 28. B 29. C

Lesson 17 Ordering Supplies: 1. C 2. C 3. C 4. C 5. B
6. A 7. A, maintaining 8. D, essential 9. D, diversity
10. A, smoothly 11. everyday 12. stationery 13. obtained
14. diverse 15. maintaining 16. essential 17. prerequisite
18. smooth 19. functioning 20. enterprise 21. source
22. quality 23. C 24. C 25. C 26. C 27. D 28. B 29. A

Lesson 18 Shipping: 1. A 2. C 3. A 4. A 5. C 6. B
7. A, accurate 8. A, fulfill 9. D, minimize 10. A, remember
11. integral 12. catalog 13. Shipping 14. minimize
15. accurate 16. carrier 17. inventory 18. sufficient
19. fulfill 20. on hand 21. remember 22. supplies 23. C
24. B 25. A 26. A 27. B 28. D 29. D

Lesson 19 Invoices: 1. B 2. B 3. C 4. D 5. A 6. A
7. C, rectified 8. A, imposed 9. C, discount 10. A, efficient
11. efficient 12. order 13. compiled 14. Charges
15. customer 16. estimated 17. terms 18. imposed
19. discount 20. mistake 21. rectified 22. promptly 23. A
24. A 25. C 26. D 27. A 28. C 29. D

Lesson 20 Inventory: 1. B 2. A 3. A 4. D 5. D 6. A
7. A, verify 8. B, running 9. C, subtracts 10. C, reflect
11. verifies 12. crucial 13. liability 14. running 15. subtracts
16. adjusted 17. automatically 18. scanning 19. reflect
20. tedious 21. discrepancies 22. disturbances 23. A 24. A
25. C 26. A 27. B 28. D 29. D

Word Review #4: 1. A 2. B 3. A 4. A 5. C 6. C 7. B 8. A
9. D 10. B 11. B, efficiently 12. A, bargain 13. B, essential
14. B, accuracy 15. D, discount 16. A, tedious 17. C, promptly
18. D, quality 19. B, strictly 20. D, disturbing

Lessons 21–25 Financing and Budgeting
Lesson 21 Banking 1. A 2. D 3. B 4. B 5. C 6. D
7. B, accepted 8. B, restrictions 9. C, deducted, deductible
10. B, cautious 11. transact 12. borrow 13. mortgages
14. cautious 15. down payment 16. dividends 17. restrict
18. take out 19. balance 20. deductions 21. accept
22. signature 23. D 24. A 25. C 26. D 27. A 28. B 29. A

Lesson 22 Accounting 1. D 2. A 3. B 4. B 5. C 6. C
7. B, reconcile 8. A, accumulation 9. D, profits
10. C, budget 11. accumulated 12. budget 13. clients
14. outstanding 15. profitable 16. audited 17. accounting
18. building up 19. turnover 20. reconcile 21. debt
22. assets 23. A 24. B 25. A 26. A 27. C 28. C 29. B

Lesson 23 Investments 1. C 2. B 3. A 4. A 5. C 6. D
7. C, returns 8. B, commitment 9. A, aggressive
10. C, pull out 11. invest 12. resources 12. wise
14. portfolio 15. pull out 16. return 17. committed 18. long
term 19. fund 20. attitude 21. conservative (or aggressive)
22. aggressive (or conservative) 23. A 24. A 25. C 26. B
27. A 28. D 29. B

Lesson 24 Taxes 1. A 2. B 3. B 4. D 5. B 6. C 7. C,
file 8. D, refunded 9. B, withheld 10. C, calculation
11. prepares 12. deadline 13. fill out 14. filed 15. spouse
16. joint 17. refund 18. calculated 19. owe 20. gave up
21. withhold 22. penalized 23. D 24. A 25. C 26. B 27. B
28. A 29. D

Lesson 25 Financial Statements 1. C 2. C 3. B 4. A
5. D 6. A 7. B, desired 8. A, projected 9. C, realistic
10. C, translated 11. level 12. target 13. forecasts
14. overall 15. projected 16. desired 17. yield 18. translate
19. realistic 20. perspective 21. detailed 22. typical 23. A
24. C 25. A 26. B 27. B 28. C 29. A

Word Review #5. 1. A 2. B 3. D 4. B 5. C 6. C 7. D 8. A
9. D 10. D 11. B, accept 12. D, budget 13. C, conservative
14. C, detailed 15. A, caution 16. D, pulling out
17. B, return 18. C, yield 19. D, owing 20. A, filling out

Lessons 26–30 Management Issues
Lesson 26 Property and Departments 1. B 2. B 3. A 4. C
5. A 6. C 7. B, scrutiny 8. C, collaboration 9. B, disruption
10. D, inconsiderate 11. disruptive 12. adjacent 13. lobby
14. inconsiderate 15. collaboration 16. hampered 17. move
up 18. scrutinized 19. opting 20. conducive
21. concentrate 22. open to 23. A 24. A 25. C 26. D 27. D
28. D 29. C

Lesson 27 Board Meetings and Committees 1. A 2. A
3. B 4. C 5. B 6. B 7. A, adhering to 8. D, progress
9. B, priority 10. A, matters 11. waste 12. agenda
13. matters 14. goals 15. lengthy 16. adhered to
17. brought up 18. priority 19. go ahead 20. periodically
21. progress 22. concluded 23. D 24. C 25. C 26. D 27. B
28. A 29. D

Lesson 28 Quality Control 1. C 2. C 3. A 4. C 5. C 6. A
7. D, defects 8. A, inspector 9. B, enhanced 10. C, repelled
11. conform 12. defects 13. garment 14. inspect
15. throws out 16. enhance 17. repel 18. take back
19. brand 20. uniform 21. wrinkle 22. perceive 23. C 24. B
25. B 26. D 27. C 28. D 29. B

Lesson 29 Product Development 1. A 2. A 3. C 4. B
5. B 6. B 7. D, solving 8. B, responsibilities 9. D, ascertain
10. A, examine 11. anxious 12. decade 13. supervisor
14. responsible 15. logical 16. systematic 17. ascertain
18. solve 19. researched 20. examining 21. experiments
22. assume 23. B 24. C 25. A 26. C 27. A 28. D 29. C

Lesson 30 Renting and Leasing 1. B 2. A 3. D 4. C 5. B
6. C 7. B, lease 8. C, apprehensive 9. B, fluctuations
10. B, get out of 11. apprehensive 12. lease 13. Occupancy
14. indicator 15. fluctuations 16. due to 17. condition
18. lock themselves into 19. get out of 20. circumstances
21. options 22. subject to 23. A 24. B 25. A 26. D 27. A
28. D 29. D

Word Review #6: 1. C 2. A 3. C 4. A 5. C 6. D 7. D 8. C
9. B 10. D 11. C, disruption 12. A, adhere to 13. C, throwing out
14. A, circumstances 15. B, ascertaining 16. C, wastes
17. D, conclude 18. D, conform 19. B, moving up
20. C, uniformly

Lessons 31–35 Restaurants and Events
Lesson 31 Selecting a Restaurant 1. B 2. C 3. D 4. D
5. C 6. A 7. C, suggest 8. D, subjectivity 9. B, mixes
10. D, compromise 11. secure 12. relies 13. guidance
14. suggestion 15. subjective 16. daring 17. appeal
18. majority 19. compromise 20. mix 21. familiar 22. arrive
23. A 24. A 25. A 26. B 27. C 28. A 29. B

Lesson 32 Eating Out 1. A 2. C 3. D 4. C 5. A 6. D
7. C, mixed up 8. D, predicted 9. B, remind 10. B, flavorful
11. random 12. patrons 13. predict 14. forget 15. remind
16. mix up 17. complete 18. judged 19. excite 20. basic
21. flavor 22. ingredients 23. B 24. B 25. C 26. A 27. C
28. D 29. C

Lesson 33 Ordering Lunch 1. D 2. C 3. B 4. A 5. B
6. C 7. C, impressed 8. C, multiple 9. D, common
10. D, delivered 11. falls to 12. burdensome 13. multiple
14. narrow 15. common 16. individual 17. settled 18. list
19. delivered 20. pick up 21. impress 22. elegant 23. C
24. A 25. B 26. D 27. B 28. C 29. A

Lesson 34 Cooking as a Career 1. D 2. D 3. C 4. B 5. B
6. A 7. C, methods 8. B, profession 9. B, relinquish
10. C, incorporate 11. outlet 12. drawn 13. profession
14. demanding 15. influx 16. incorporate 17. methods
18. themes 19. accustomed 20. relinquish 21. culinary
22. apprenticeship 23. A 24. C 25. B 26. D 27. C 28. C
29. B

Lesson 35 Events 1. C 2. A 3. B 4. A 5. C 6. B
7. A, assistance 8. B, ideal 9. D, exact 10. A, coordinate
11. coordinated 12. planning 13. site 14. stage 15. exact
16. dimensions 17. regulations 18. lead time 19. ideally
20. assist 21. proximity 22. general 23. A 24. B 25. C
26. B 27. B 28. B 29. A

Word Review #7: 1. C 2. D 3. B 4. A 5. D 6. C 7. C 8. C
9. D 10. B 11. C, daring 12. D, elegant 13. C, mix-up
14. D, patrons 15. C, exact 16. A, Accustomed to
17. D, compromising 18. B, arrival 19. C, forgotten
20. B, remind

Lessons 36–40 Travel
Lesson 36 General Travel 1. D 2. C 3. B 4. A 5. B 6. A
7. B, delayed 8. C, embarkation 9. A, valid 10. D, prohibited
11. agent 12. valid 13. itinerary 14. delayed 15. prohibited
16. embarkation 17. board 18. depart 19. beverage
20. blanket 21. announcements 22. claim 23. A 24. A
25. B 26. C 27. D 28. B 29. B

Lesson 37 Airlines 1. D 2. A 3. C 4. D 5. D 6. B 7. B,
substantial 8. C, extend 9. B, distinguish 10. A, prospective
11. deal with 12. 6, expensive 13. substantial
14. economical 15. destination 16. system 17. prospective
18. situation 19. excursion 20. equivalent 21. extending
22. distinguishable 23. D 24. C 25. C 26. A 27. C 28. B
29. A

Lesson 38 Trains 1. C 2. A 3. A 4. B 5. C 6. B 7. A,
punctual 8. C, remote 9. A, comprehensive 10. B, operates
11. relatively 12. punctual 13. fares 14. directories
15. comprehensive 16. remote 17. operate 18. remainder
19. duration 20. deluxe 21. offset 22. entitle 23. C 24. A
25. B 26. D 27. D 28. D 29. C

Lesson 39 Hotels 1. C 2. B 3. D 4. C 5. A 6. B
7. A, reservations 8. D, precluded 9. B, expect
10. D, notified 11. preclude 12. rates 13. reservations
14. advance 15. notify 16. confirm 17. quoted 18. service
19. expect 20. housekeeper 21. chains 22. check in 23. C
24. B 25. A 26. B 27. D 28. A 29. B

Lesson 40 Car Rentals 1. D 2. C 3. A 4. C 5. D 6. A
7. C, disappointed 8. D, nervous 9. A, confusing
10. B, tempt 11. tempted 12. nervous 13. coincided
14. disappointment 15. busy 16. contacted 17. license
18. confusing 19. intended 20. optional 21. tier 22. thrill
23. C 24. B 25. B 26. A 27. D 28. D 29. C

Word Review #8: 1. D 2. C 3. A 4. D 5. C 6. D 7. A 8. C
9. D 10. B 11. A, reserving 12. B, distinguish 13. B, validity
14. D, contact 15. A, economical 16. A, expectations
7. D, relatively 18. C, announcements 19. A, optional
20. D, delay

Lessons 41–45 Entertainment
Lesson 41 Movies 1. A 2. C 3. A 4. B 5. D 6. B
7. B, combines 8. A, influence 9. C, continued/continues
10. D, representing 11. continues 12. entertaining
13. disperse 14. influence 15. descriptions 16. represent
17. successive 18. range 19. combines 20. released
21. attain 22. separate 23. A 24. C 25. A 26. D 27. D
28. C 29. A

Lesson 42 Theater 1. B 2. A 3. D 4. C 5. A 6. B
7. A, creative 8. B, performance 9. C, occurs 10. D, reviews
11. created 12. elements 13. performance 14. occurs
15. approach 16. action 17. experiences 18. dialogue
19. rehearsal 20. audience 21. reviews 22. sell out 23. A
24. B 25. C 26. A 27. B 28. D 29. D

Lesson 43 Music 1. C 2. A 3. D 4. A 5. D 6. B
7. D, available 8. B, divided 9. C, preference 10. B, relax
11. reason 12. available 13. category 14. taste 15. divided
16. broad 17. disparate 18. urge 19. instinctive 20. prefer
21. favorite 22. relax 23. D 24. A 25. C 26. B 27. B 28. C
29. A

Lesson 44 Museums 1. C 2. C 3. A 4. C 5. D 6. B
7. C, express 8. B, acquired 9. D, collection 10. D, leisure
11. admire 12. spectrum 13. responded 14. expressing
15. significant 16. fashion 17. criticism 18. schedule
19. leisure 20. collected 21. specialize 22. acquire 23. B
24. C 25. C 26. C 27. D 28. A 29. B

Lesson 45 Media 1. C 2. D 3. B 4. B 5. B 6. A
7. A, decisive 8. D, constant 9. B, investigates
10. B, assigned 11. subscribes 12. chooses 13. thoroughly
14. constitutes 15. disseminated 16. investigative
17. assignments 18. decisions 19. impact 20. links
21. constant 22. in-depth 23. C 24. C 25. A 26. B 27. D
28. C 29. C

Word Review #9: 1. D 2. B 3. C 4. D 5. A 6. A 7. B 8. C
9. B 10. B 11. C, specialists 12. B, criticism 13. C, impact
14. D, preferences 15. C, investigative 16. A, reviews
17. C, leisure 18. D, response(s) 19. B, constant
20. B, constitutes

Lessons 46–50 Health
Lesson 46 Doctor's Office 1. D 2. A 3. D 4. A 5. B 6. A
7. C, assess 8. B, diagnosis 9. A, effective
10. B, recommends 11. annually 12. effective
13. diagnosing 14. preventing 15. appointment 16. record
17. assessment 18. instruments 19. manage
20. recommend 21. refer 22. serious 23. A 24. C 25. B
26. D 27. C 28. B 29. A

Lesson 47 Dentist's Office 1. D 2. C 3. A 4. B 5. C 6. B
7. B, encouraging 8. D, restore 9. B, distract 10. C, irritating
11. aware 12. catch up 13. regularly 14. encourage
15. habit 16. position 17. irritates 18. illuminates
19. overview 20. evident 21. restores 22. distraction 23. B
24. C 25. A 26. D 27. A 28. B 29. C

Lesson 48 Health Insurance 1. A 2. C 3. C 4. B 5. D
6. B 7. B, emphasis 8. B, incurring 9. C, suitable
10. D, concerned 11. concerns 12. personnel 13. policy
14. portion 15. salary 16. allow 17. suitable 18. emphasize
19. alternatives 20. regardless 21. aspect 22. incurs 23. A
24. C 25. C 26. D 27. C 28. A 29. B

Lesson 49 Hospitals 1. B 2. A 3. B 4. D 5. C 6. A
7. C, admit 8. B, usual 9. C, designate 10. D, authorization
11. mission 12. pertinent 13. results 14. authorization
15. identification 16. admitting 17. procedures 18. usually
19. escort 20. statement 21. permitted 22. designated
23. D 24. C 25. A 26. D 27. D 28. A 29. C

Lesson 50 Pharmacy 1. B 2. D 3. A 4. A 5. B 6. C
7. A, consulting 8. C, volunteered 9. B, convenient
10. C, interactions 11. consulting 12. control 13. samples
14. volunteers 15. limit 16. convenient 17. factors
18. sense 19. interactions 20. monitor 21. potential
22. detection 23. C 24. C 25. B 26. D 27. A 28. B 29. A

Word Review #10: 1. D 2. A 3. D 4. A 5. C 6. D 7. A 8. B
9. A 10. D 11. A, convenient 12. C, effectively 13. A, manage
14. A, admitted 15. C, result 16. C, referring 17. D, aware
18. B, allow 19. A, volunteer 20. A, Distracted

Word Index

The number indicates the lesson in which the word is taught.

Appendix

Tapescript for the Listening Comprehension Exercises

LESSON 1
Listening Comprehension

Part I: Picture

Number 23. Look at the picture marked Number 23.
- (A) The signers are having a party.
- (B) The men are signing an agreement.
- (C) The provisions are in the cabinet.
- (D) The cancelled flight is on the tarmac.

Part II: Question-Response

Number 24.

You were engaged when you bought the car, right?
- (A) Yes, it's in the cage by the cart.
- (B) No, my fiancé can't drive.
- (C) We bought the car in March.

Number 25.

Haven't you resolved that problem yet?
- (A) We're working on it.
- (B) We have both letters.
- (C) You have my assurance.

Part III: Short Conversations

Number 26.

[M] Do you think we will ever resolve our difficulties with the computer company?

[W] I'm beginning to think that we should cancel our service and find another provider.

[M] Do we have any obligation to continue to pay them if we cancel our service?

Number 27.

[W] Now that the new contract has been negotiated, we will have to abide by it very closely.

[M] I'm not sure yet that this was a good agreement for us.

[W] Nevertheless, we gave our assurance we would fulfill the requirements.

Part IV: Short Talks

Questions 28 and 29 relate to the following recording. The last provision in the contract states that if either party determines it is in his best interest to cancel the contract, he is obligated to inform the other immediately of his intention. If you both agree, we can specify that the canceling party must communicate his intent at least 30 days prior to the cancellation.

Now read question 28 in your text book and answer it.

Now read question 29 in your text book and answer it.

LESSON 2
Listening Comprehension

Part I: Picture

Number 23. Look at the picture marked Number 23.
(A)   The clerk is competing with others.
(B)   The shoppers are comparing prices.
(C)   The man is not attracting a crowd.
(D)   The consumer is convincing the sales person.

Part II: Question-Response

Number 24.

Aren't pop-up ads on the Internet just a fad?
(A)   No, they're here to stay.
(B)   I put up with a lot.
(C)   She's not fat.

Number 25.

Was the customer satisfied with our work?
(A)   Satisfaction is guaranteed.
(B)   Very.
(C)   I found a new customer today.

Part III: Short Conversations

Number 26.

[M] We need to attract new customers to the business.

[W] How can we convince them to buy our products?

[M] Perhaps our ads could feature some of our satisfied customers.

Number 27.

[M] With a new store opening across the street, we must work harder to compete in our market.

[W] How can we be more productive?

[M] Once customers compare us to the other stores, they will see that we offer a better deal.

Part IV: Short Talks

Questions 28 and 29 relate to the following recording. To attract new customers, we first must convince them that we offer something worthwhile. We need to inspire them to try our services, just once, so that they can make their own comparison. Their experience will persuade them that we are better than the competition. But what is it that we offer that makes us unique? What do you think we offer, that the competition does not?

Now read question 28 in your text book and answer it.

Now read question 29 in your text book and answer it.

LESSON 3
Listening Comprehension

Part I: Picture

Number 23. Look at the picture marked Number 23.
- (A) They're considering purchasing the bag.
- (B) They're protecting their dog.
- (C) They're covering the carpet.
- (D) They're checking the expiration date.

Part II: Question-Response

Number 24.

When does the warranty expire?
- (A) I always check the warranty.
- (B) Three years from date of purchase.
- (C) That's the implication.

Number 25.

What are the consequences of not registering your purchase?
- (A) If you don't register, you won't receive any recall notices.
- (B) Consequently, we quit the company.
- (C) Our company purchased more this year than last.

Part III: Short Conversations

Number 26.

[M] What are the important characteristics of this warranty?

[W] The product is completely covered for one year.

[M] It seems that one-year warranties are the type most frequently provided for this kind of appliance.

Number 27.

[M] In order to have full protection, you must have the car serviced by an approved mechanic.

[W] What are the consequences if I choose not to use an approved mechanic?

[M] By not following the guidelines, you cause the warranty to expire immediately.

Part IV: Short Talks

Questions 28 and 29 relate to the following recording. We frequently receive items that are still under warranty, but we don't automatically repair them. Don't forget: A warranty is only valid if the product has been used according to the manufacturer's directions. Oftentimes a buyer will drop a machine, or use it for something other than what it's intended for. Consequently, they're not covered. A common characteristic of this type of return is that it's cracked or smashed, or it shows an unusual pattern of wear.

Now read question 28 in your text book and answer it.

Now read question 29 in your text book and answer it.

LESSON 4
Listening Comprehension

Part I: Picture

Number 23. Look at the picture marked Number 23.
- (A)   The managers are planning a strategy.
- (B)   The president is dressing for dinner.
- (C)   The primary shape is round.
- (D)   The demonstrators are avoiding the meeting.

Part II: Question-Response

Number 24.

Have you addressed the cost of infrastructure in your business plan?
- (A)   Those costs are all factored in.
- (B)   No, we can't dress so casually.
- (C)   These structures are higher than we had planned.

Number 25.

In what ways has the restaurant grown or developed?
- (A)   Its own vegetables in the back gardens.
- (B)   It's now a national chain.
- (C)   It is taller and stronger.

Part III: Short Conversations

Number 26.

[W] Alexa is developing a business plan. I told her you might be able to help with the market research.

[M] I'm proud of her. Going into business for yourself can be risky, but very rewarding.

[W] I know she is very serious about careful planning to avoid making obvious mistakes.

Number 27.

[M] The first problem Athos encountered was how to evaluate his competitor's share of the market.

[W] Can't he gather information from trade journals and the local trade association?

[M] I don't know if those sources offered him enough hard data to analyze the competition's share of the market.

Part IV: Short Talks

Questions 28 and 29 relate to the following recording. Now let's turn to page 17 of the business plan. This section addresses our strategy for long-term development of the company. In order to minimize risk over the long haul, we hope to grow only as quickly as the company can support. In other words, we want to avoid more borrowing, so that the primary funding for growth comes from profits.

Now read question 28 in your text book and answer it.

Now read question 29 in your text book and answer it.

LESSON 5
Listening Comprehension

Part I: Plcture

Number 23. Look at the picture marked Number 23.
- (A)   The attendees are registering at the desk.
- (B)   The organizers are selecting a podium.
- (C)   The banquet room is overcrowded.
- (D)   The participants are attending a session.

Part II: Question-Response

Number 24.

How many will attend the conference?
- (A)   On Thursday.
- (B)   At least 100 folks.
- (C)   We've made the arrangements.

Number 25.

Was the room overcrowded?
- (A)   No, the crowd waited.
- (B)   That, and hot, too.
- (C)   The room was number 212.

Part III: Short Conversations

Number 26.

[M] Has the committee selected a site for our conference next year?

[W] Not yet. It's been difficult to find a site that can accommodate a group of our size.

[M] With so many conference facilities available in this area, I would think we could find one that could hold the event.

Number 27.

[M] We'll tour the hotel about a month before our association has its conference.

[W] I'll want to see that all the arrangements for meeting rooms and audio equipment are taken care of.

[M] While we are there, we'll get in touch with thc manager to check on all the details.

Part IV: Short Talks

Questions 28 and 29 relate to the following recording. All conference facilities need to provide reasonable accommodation for people with disabilities. Disabled individuals need to be able to take part in every session that is being offered. In case a session is held in an off-site location, we are not responsible for providing accommodation. But for any event held at our facility, we need to make the necessary arrangements for disabled participants.

Now read question 28 in your text book and answer it.

Now read question 29 in your text book and answer it.

LESSON 6
Listening Comprehension

Part I: Picture

Number 23. Look at the picture marked Number 23.
- (A)   The workers are searching for a way to work.
- (B)   The store display is very attractive.
- (C)   Space is allocated on every desk for a computer.
- (D)   The warning lights are flashing.

Part II: Question-Response

Number 24.

Have you shut down your computer yet?
- (A)   It's still on.
- (B)   I just got my computer last week.
- (C)   Here's the showdown.

Number 25.

Do you want to duplicate it, or delete it?
- (A)   Oh, I definitely need a copy.
- (B)   I'll do it double time.
- (C)   Deleted files go into the recycle bin.

Part III: Short Conversations

Number 26.

[W] I did a computer search to see how much was spent on education last year.

[M] I'm sure you discovered that more money was allocated to the military than to education.

[W] Unfortunately, yes. I fail to see why we ignore this tragic fact.

Number 27.

[M] I can't figure this out. When I tried to access my e-mail program, the monitor went black.

[W] Sounds like there's a problem with the display.

[M] Let me shut down the computer and then try one more time.

Part IV: Short Talks

Questions 28 and 29 relate to the following recording. I strongly urge you to read the manual before attempting to run this software program. You may be tempted to ignore this advice. But I'm warning you all: It is not likely that you will be able to figure out this program on your own. This is especially important for owners of our competitor's products that aren't compatible with this program. Your computer could crash or shut down without warning. In fact, when you start working with this program, make sure you have duplicate files, so in case of system failure, you will not lose your work.

Now read question 28 in your text book and answer it.

Now read question 29 in your text book and answer it.

LESSON 7
Listening Comprehension

Part I: Picture

Number 23. Look at the picture marked Number 23.
  (A) He's using the keyboard as needed.
  (B) He is reducing the size of his office.
  (C) He is sitting on top of his work.
  (D) He's signing his initials on the desk.

Part II: Question-Response

Number 24.

Do you think we can afford the additional support?
  (A) Office morale seems fine.
  (B) It's already in the budget.
  (C) They're in stock.

Number 25.

Who's in charge of the fax machine?
  (A) It has twice the capacity.
  (B) The warranty has expired.
  (C) The office manager stays on top of it.

Part III: Short Conversations

Number 26.

[W] The new office furniture store has some good price reductions.

[M] Yeah. They have a lot of furniture in stock. To take advantage of these reductions, though, you have to buy in quantity.

[W] Who needs a dozen desks. We'll just buy on an as-needed basis.

Number 27.

[M] As part of the company's cost-saving initiative, we must have approval on all new purchases.

[W] Who will be in charge of all the approvals?

[M] Each of the department heads has been ordered to stay on top of the purchases.

Part IV: Short Talks

Questions 28 and 29 relate to the following recording. We have had a few problems with ordering these units on an as-needed basis. The first problem is that nobody seems to take the initiative to place the order with the provider. That's because when they're ordering just one recorder, they feel that it isn't worth their time. So even though their need is recurring, they don't feel that the effort is justified. Here's where a more aggressive provider could help us out, by anticipating our needs and staying on top of them.

Now read question 28 in your text book and answer it.

Now read question 29 in your text book and answer it.

LESSON 8
Listening Comprehension

Part I: Picture

Number 23. Look at the picture marked Number 23.
- (A) The desks are made of glass.
- (B) The workers are not dressed casually.
- (C) The golfers are practicing their game.
- (D) The waiters are bringing in food.

Part II: Question-Response

Number 24.

Can young workers really appreciate what it meant to publish a book before computers were around?
- (A) They are thankful.
- (B) Our youngest employee is a published author.
- (C) Of course they can't.

Number 25.

What is silicon made of?
- (A) The sale is still on.
- (B) We're out of intercoms.
- (C) Sand.

Part III: Short Conversations

Number 26.

[M] I appreciate the fact that you have taken time out of your schedule to come and talk with me.

[W] I want to make sure that you understand the practices of the company.

[M] It seems difficult for other employees to give me a verbal explanation of the practices, although they definitely are familiar with them.

Number 27.

[M] Even though the new attorney is young, she has been exposed to many difficult situations.

[W] Well, then we'll see what she is made of at the contract negotiations next week.

[M] If she hasn't run out of energy, she'll be a definite asset.

Part IV: Short Talks

Questions 28 and 29 relate to the following recording. This training is designed to reinforce and strengthen your current computer skills. We really don't have the time to introduce these programs from the start, and we'll only have limited time for practice today. What we want to do is verbally cover the main functions of the program, and make sure that you're all exposed to some of the features of the newer version.

Now read question 28 in your text book and answer it.

Now read question 29 in your text book and answer it.

LESSON 9
Listening Comprehension

Part I: Picture

Number 23. Look at the picture marked Number 23.
- (A)   The calculators are stored in the closet.
- (B)   The computers are linked by a network.
- (C)   The technician is replacing a part.
- (D)   The worker is reading the software manual.

Part II: Question-Response

Number 24.

How long will it take to replace the hard drive?
- (A)   Hard drives are expensive.
- (B)   Our technicians have the skills, don't worry.
- (C)   A few hours.

Number 25.

Can you understand the technical section?
- (A)   That's good advice, thanks.
- (B)   I hope so—I'm the technician.
- (C)   On page 13.

Part III: Short Conversations

Number 26.

[M] When was the computer revolution?

[W] It was a slow process, but by the nineties, we had replaced every fax machine and typewriter in the office.

[M] Thanks. Your knowledge is sure facilitating my research.

Number 27.

[W] Unfortunately, I don't have the skills to retrieve this file.

[M] Are your files on the network?

[W] No, they're stored on the company ftp site.

Part IV: Short Talks

Questions 28 and 29 relate to the following recording. Downloading software is a simple process. You can download a file from a remote server or you can simply download it from the company network. Once you've done it, you'll see how easy the process is. It really takes no technical skills and, indeed, everyday folks do it every day.

Now read question 28 in your text book and answer it.

Now read question 29 in your text book and answer it.

LESSON 10
Listening Comprehension

Part I: Picture

Number 23. Look at the picture marked Number 23.
 (A)   He's assembling a car.
 (B)   He's folding the newspaper in half.
 (C)   He's reviewing his correspondence.
 (D)   He's petitioning for a raise.

Part II: Question-Response

Number 24.

Did you send the letter by registered mail?
 (A)   Registration fees are paid in advance.
 (B)   Yes, and I sent it express.
 (C)   Nobody revised it.

Number 25.

Have you ever worked in assembly before?
 (A)   The workers assembled outside.
 (B)   I worked in layout and design.
 (C)   I used to assemble electronic cards.

Part III: Short Conversations

Number 26.

[M] Here are the documents we need to assemble for the meeting.

[W] You should have asked me beforehand. I'm too busy now.

[M] I mentioned that I would need your help today.

Number 27.

[M] The layout of this pamphlet should be simpler. It's hard to read and it looks very unprofessional.

[W] It is too complicated, isn't it?

[M] And the size of the paper is wrong, too. We can't fold this sheet into three parts.

Part IV: Short Talks

Questions 28 and 29 relate to the following recording. Tired of waiting in line? Try our new express, self-service Courier Center. You can purchase stamps, weigh parcels, look up zip codes, even send registered mail. The Courier Center is located in the lobby at the Fourth Street entrance.

Now read question 28 in your text book and answer it.

Now read question 29 in your text book and answer it.

LESSON 11
Listening Comprehension

Part I: Picture

Number 23. Look at the picture marked Number 23.
- (A) The job profile is posted on the board.
- (B) The qualifications are listed on the wall.
- (C) The harvest this season is abundant.
- (D) The candidate is checking the job listings in the newspaper.

Part II: Question-Response

Number 24.

Which candidate mentioned her father's fish boat?
- (A) The first one.
- (B) She fishes for a living.
- (C) Her father sells oats.

Number 25.

What recent accomplishment are you most proud of?
- (A) I need to resend this package.
- (B) I won the employee-of-the-month award in May.
- (C) I found it most time-consuming.

Part III: Short Conversations

Number 26.

[M] Have you come up with any ideas for finishing your job search?

[W] It has been very time-consuming and draining, but I think it's coming to an end.

[M] Does that mean that you've found a job that's the perfect match?

Number 27.

[M] I've been looking at our company profile, and I don't know how we can get people interested in working here.

[W] Let's bring together some employees and see what they like about working here.

[M] That could help us find workers whose skills match our workplace.

Part IV: Short Talks

Questions 28 and 29 relate to the following recording. Candidates are asked to submit a current resume and letter of interest. Your resume should list your qualifications for the job you are applying for. It should also list specific accomplishments in past jobs or in school. Your letter of interest should also outline your long-term career goals. If you bring together a picture of your past, your current goals, and your future, your profile will be more cohesive to our hirers.

Now read question 28 in your text book and answer it.

Now read question 29 in your text book and answer it.

LESSON 12
Listening Comprehension

Part I: Picture

Number 23. Look at the picture marked Number 23.
- (A) The applicant is called in for an interview.
- (B) The expert is putting on his coat.
- (C) The sick cat is hiding its weakness.
- (D) The room is ready for a party.

Part II: Question-Response

Number 24.

Can I mail in this application?
- (A) Yes, the address is on the last page.
- (B) It's not applicable.
- (C) It doesn't apply here.

Number 25.

Are you ready for the written test?
- (A) The test is administered by computer.
- (B) My score was sent in the mail.
- (C) Not quite, I don't have a pencil.

Part III: Short Conversations

Number 26.

[M] Do you remember the first time you applied for a job?

[W] I remember, I had absolutely no confidence in myself.

[M] And look where you are now: an expert in the field of computer networks.

Number 27.

[M] The two top candidates have very different backgrounds.

[W] Yes, but they both demonstrate a great ability to get the job done.

[M] Let's see how well they present themselves in front of the group of directors.

Part IV: Short Talks

Questions 28 and 29 relate to the following recording.
Thank you for calling the Salvo Human Resources Department Job Hotline.
To request an application, press one.
To listen to job descriptions for current job openings, press two.
To follow up on your application status, press three.
To learn the location of a Salvo Employment Presentation in a city near you, press four.
Please have pen and paper by the phone and be ready to record the relevant information.

Now read question 28 in your text book and answer it.

Now read question 29 in your text book and answer it.

LESSON 13
Listening Comprehension

Part I: Picture

Number 23. Look at the picture marked Number 23.
- (A) The conductor is signaling the train.
- (B) The trainer is conducting a session.
- (C) The applicant is setting up an interview.
- (D) The employees are rejecting the contract.

Part II: Question-Response

Number 24.

You don't think this will generate a lot of extra paperwork, do you?
- (A) No. In fact, I think it will reduce paperwork.
- (B) Yes, the papers have arrived.
- (C) I already turned on the generator.

Number 25.

Do you think that Lena looks up to Virginia?
- (A) Lena's application was rejected.
- (B) Virginia was her mentor, so it's natural that she would.
- (C) The team will update us on Thursday.

Part III: Short Conversations

Number 26.

[M] How has the week of training gone so far?

[W] We have a large group, but we've been able to stay on track and get a lot accomplished.

[M] Everyone is commenting on the amount of excitement that your program has generated.

Number 27.

[M] Finally, all the new employees have been hired.

[W] It was difficult to keep up with their demands.

[M] They asked for a lot, but I'm confident that they will be very successful and be an asset to the company.

Part IV: Short Talks

Questions 28 and 29 relate to the following recording. Welcome to our first annual mentors training program. You have been selected by your coworkers for this program, because they look up to you. And that's an honor. So congratulations to all of you for being here. Today we're going to start by generating a list of features that make a successful mentor. So I want you all to think back to a mentor you've known or worked with.

Now read question 28 in your text book and answer it.

Now read question 29 in your text book and answer it.

LESSON 14
Listening Comprehension

Part I: Picture

Number 23. Look at the picture marked Number 23.
- (A) The woman is raising her salary.
- (B) The workers are negotiating their pay.
- (C) The retiree is being honored.
- (D) The lunch hour is flexible.

Part II: Question-Response

Number 24.

Who is eligible to participate in the retirement plan?
- (A) She has already retired.
- (B) Employees who've been with us for at least three months.
- (C) You need to be aware of these benefits.

Number 25.

When will I get a raise?
- (A) Your first salary review will be in 6 months.
- (B) Lift it a little bit higher, please.
- (C) Usually four to six percent of your current salary.

Part III: Short Conversations

Number 26.

[M] I don't quite understand when I will be eligible for vacation.

[W] The supervisor is pretty flexible about that. You should talk to her.

[M] I thought it was a very strict policy. I wasn't aware of that flexibility!

Number 27.

[M] We can't seem to make ends meet with my hourly wage.

[W] Maybe you should ask for a raise.

[M] But, I don't want to ask for too much compensation; the company just offered me health coverage.

Part IV: Short Talks

Questions 28 and 29 relate to the following recording. Please open your Employee Handbook to page seven. This section deals with your salary and salary increases. You will have an annual salary review. The average raise is 4.2% a year, just above the cost of living. Also, be aware that not all employees get a raise. Compensation is based solely on performance and your contribution to the company and, sure enough, each year we find that some employees are not eligible for a raise.

Now read question 28 in your text book and answer it.

Now read question 29 in your text book and answer it.

LESSON 15
Listening Comprehension

Part I: Picture

Number 23. Look at the picture marked Number 23.
- (A) The librarian is dedicating her novel to her boss.
- (B) The promoter is putting away a book.
- (C) The employee is receiving a book as an award.
- (D) The manager is recognizing his old workers.

Part II: Question-Response

Number 24.

Has she proven her loyalty?
- (A) She's been with us for 47 years.
- (B) Loyalty deserves praise.
- (C) No, she hasn't completed it.

Number 25.

Where is the dedication ceremony going to be held?
- (A) The ceremony was full of fanfare.
- (B) Nobody questions her dedication.
- (C) At the flag pole, in the parking lot.

Part III: Short Conversations

Number 26.

[M] I'm looking forward to the awards ceremony tonight!

[W] So am I. I hope Darrell finally gets some recognition for all the work that he has done.

[M] He certainly has been very productive in the last few months.

Number 27.

[M] Sometimes your assistant doesn't feel as though you value her work.

[W] I judge work by merit, not by the quantity of paper produced.

[M] But it's obvious that she's just trying to please you.

Part IV: Short Talks

Questions 28 and 29 relate to the following remarks. Everyone enjoys receiving recognition for the work that they do. Today, we will honor two employees who have been with the company since we opened our doors. Their loyalty to the company is an honor for us. No value can be placed on these employees; they are priceless to us. Since 1965, these individuals have been promoted to higher paying positions not for their connections or their degrees, but for what they have done for the company. In other words they have been promoted on their merit. These high achievers are a credit to our community.

Now read question 28 in your text book and answer it.

Now read question 29 in your text book and answer it.

LESSON 16
Listening Comprehension

Part I: Picture

Number 23. Look at the picture marked Number 23.
- (A)   They're putting the merchandise on the shelves.
- (B)   They're pushing their cart to the check-out.
- (C)   They're examining the items for sale.
- (D)   They're behaving in an unusual way.

Part II: Question-Response

Number 24.

I'll go wait in the checkout line.
- (A)   Check this out, it's really fancy.
- (B)   I'll be there in a minute.
- (C)   You always find good bargains.

Number 25.

Which items are you returning?
- (A)   The computer itemizes them.
- (B)   All of them.
- (C)   I'll come back.

Part III: Short Conversations

Number 26.

[M] If we hurry, we can get into the checkout aisle before the clerk takes his break.

[W] There is a mandatory limit of nine items. Do we meet that criterion?

[M] Oh dear, I didn't count. Do you think they are strict about enforcing that rule?

Number 27.

[M] For my class in consumer behavior, we are secretly watching what people buy.

[W] I'm sure you'll find that people hunt for bargains to save money.

[M] Actually, shoppers told us they bought brands they knew best and felt most comfortable with, regardless of price.

Part IV: Short Talks

Questions 28 and 29 relate to the following recording. Attention shoppers. If you're looking for a true bargain, check out our sale on winter boots in aisle seven. All footwear is marked 10 to 40 percent off. While you're at it, why don't you explore our other winter merchandise? We have coats, scarves, hats, and lots of other items to keep you toasty warm this winter.

Now read question 28 in your text book and answer it.

Now read question 29 in your text book and answer it.

LESSON 17
Listening Comprehension

Part I: Picture

Number 23. Look at the picture marked Number 23.
   (A)   She's obtaining supplies from the cabinet.
   (B)   She's polishing her desk smoothly.
   (C)   She's using office stationery for her correspondence.
   (D)   She's buying quality toys.

Part II: Question-Response

Number 24.

Is an order form essential?
   (A)   The essence is in there.
   (B)   You can order 24 hours a day.
   (C)   It's a prerequisite for all orders.

Number 25.

What is the function of this stamp?
   (A)   You need to obtain a signature.
   (B)   We need a one-dollar stamp.
   (C)   It shows that the order has been received.

Part III: Short Conversations

Number 26.

[M] Do you know of a wholesale source for glassware?

[W] As a matter of fact, I know of a supplier who sells top-quality wine glasses.

[M] Well, I'm looking for a diverse range of glassware, but I can check their web site to find out about their product line.

Number 27.

[W] What is the everyday dress code for your office?

[M] Since you're going to be maintaining inventory, casual slacks will be fine.

[W] I'm happy to hear that because one of my prerequisites for taking this job is being able to wear casual clothing.

Part IV: Short Talks

Questions 28 and 29 relate to the following recording. As you all know, we had a little slipup in our order with Margatel last week. Now, Margatel is one of our biggest clients—they order more than fifty thousand dollars worth of stationery alone each year. It is essential that we maintain a smooth relationship with Margatel, or some of us may end up out on the street. So, let's see if we can find the source of this mix-up, and then we'll go about setting it straight. First, according to our records, Carlita, you took the order, on January 19th.

Now read question 28 in your text book and answer it.

Now read question 29 in your text book and answer it.

LESSON 18
Listening Comprehension

Part I: Picture

Number 23. Look at the picture marked Number 23.
  (A)   The goods are scanned in the catalog.
  (B)   The supplies are being counted by hand.
  (C)   The trucks are loading at the shipping dock.
  (D)   The carriers are using bicycles for deliveries.

Part II: Question-Response

Number 24.

Are these numbers accurate?
  (A)   They've been checked and double-checked.
  (B)   The numbers were written down.
  (C)   The spillage was minimal.

Number 25.

How many items are listed in the catalog?
  (A)   About 350.
  (B)   It is sufficiently clear.
  (C)   To fulfill customer's wishes.

Part III: Short Conversations

Number 26.

[M] Is the price quoted here accurate?

[W] Yes, it is. The price printed in the catalog is incorrect.

[M] I hope the salesperson remembered to alert the customer about the discrepancy.

Number 27.

[M] We are completely out of packing supplies and cannot prepare any more boxes today.

[W] It's your job to make certain that you have sufficient packing materials.

[M] I thought we had enough boxes on hand, but I was wrong.

Part IV: Short Talks

Questions 28 and 29 relate to the following recording. A quick review of our catalog shows the variety and quality of our products, but it does nothing to draw attention to our competitive pricing. Competitive pricing is integral to our success. Customers want to minimize costs and maximize value. Remember our motto: We supply the best, you pay the least.

Now read question 28 in your text book and answer it.

Now read question 29 in your text book and answer it.

LESSON 19
Listening Comprehension

Part I: Picture

Number 23. Look at the picture marked Number 23.
- (A)   She's looking over the orders.
- (B)   She's talking to the customers.
- (C)   She's ordering more paper by phone.
- (D)   She's asking a clerk for a discount.

Part II: Question-Response

Number 24.

Why were there so many mistakes in yesterday's orders?
- (A)   We had two temps working here.
- (B)   Seven mistakes.
- (C)   Because we improved our system.

Number 25.

How much was the discount?
- (A)   I've compiled the data.
- (B)   They placed the order.
- (C)   Fifteen percent.

Part III: Short Conversations

Number 26.

[M] I have compiled a list of office supplies we need to order immediately.

[W] Don't worry, I'll deal with it promptly.

[M] Please also check the supply room before you send out the order, just to be sure I didn't make any mistakes.

Number 27.

[W] I had a computer expert estimate the cost of installing new order processing software on our office computers.

[M] What will they charge for doing that?

[W] It's going to cost us about five hundred dollars, but according to the terms of payment, there'll be a fifty dollar discount if we pay the full amount up front.

Part IV: Short Talks

Questions 28 and 29 relate to the following recording. According to the terms of payment, a customer is eligible for a discount only if the entire invoice is paid upon completion of the service. Up front payment is much more efficient, because we don't have to bill the customer. Also, as soon as we receive payment, it becomes capital. We estimate that up front payments save us about 15% per project.

Now read question 28 in your text book and answer it.

Now read question 29 in your text book and answer it.

LESSON 20
Listening Comprehension

Part I: Picture

Number 23. Look at the picture marked Number 23.
    (A)   He's verifying the number of items in stock.
    (B)   He's adjusting the height of the ladder.
    (C)   He's disturbing the order of the shelves.
    (D)   He's scanning the goods by computer.

Part II: Question-Response

Number 24.

Shall we set it to be done automatically, or shall we do them all by hand?
    (A)   Automatically.
    (B)   They were hand delivered.
    (C)   Set it on the counter, please.

Number 25.

Would you be able to verify these facts?
    (A)   It's a fair price.
    (B)   No, the fax was only three pages.
    (C)   I got them all from the newspaper article.

Part III: Short Conversations

Number 26.

[M] This platter is missing its price tag and bar code. I'll just scan in the price tag of something else that's the same price.

[W] Don't do that. Then the inventory won't reflect this sale accurately and the counts will be off.

[M] I didn't realize that such accuracy was so crucial.

Number 27.

[M] The computer says we have three of these bedspreads left. Can you go to the stockroom and verify that, please?

[W] If the computer says we have three, why would there be any discrepancy?

[M] Sometimes there are adjustments to the inventory and I don't want to tell this lady we have a bedspread if we are out of stock.

Part IV: Short Talks

Questions 28 and 29 relate to the following recording. We verify the computer's count with a physical inventory every year in January. It's a tedious process, but it's crucial to keeping our records straight. Even the physical counting leaves us with some discrepancies, but we feel that it more closely reflects our numbers. As well, the physical count puts us two steps closer figuring out any huge discrepancies. Remember, in the long run, any discrepancy is a liability.

Now read question 28 in your text book and answer it.

Now read question 29 in your text book and answer it.

LESSON 21
Listening Comprehension

Part I: Picture

Number 23. Look at the picture marked number 23.
  (A)   She's balancing a cup on his head.
  (B)   She's accepting a gift from him.
  (C)   She's borrowing money from a friend.
  (D)   She's going to make a transaction at an ATM.

Part II: Question-Response

Number 24.

How much money did you take out of your bank account?
  (A)   I took out only 100 dollars.
  (B)   That accountant charges a lot for his services.
  (C)   Yes, I took the money to the bank.

Number 25.

What do you want to borrow so much money for?
  (A)   It didn't cost so much money.
  (B)   I earned all that money myself.
  (C)   I want to buy a car.

Part III: Short Conversations

Number 26.

[M] I need to cash a check. What kinds of identification do you accept?

[W] If you have an account with this bank, a photo ID, like a driver's license, is enough.

[M] I've lost my driver's license, but my signature is on file. Is that enough?

Number 27.

[W] Here's the contract for your loan. It's several pages long.

[M] It says here that the bank can automatically deduct the monthly payment from my checking account.

[W] That's right. All you'll need to do is make certain that you always have enough in your balance to cover the automatic deduction.

Part IV: Short Talks

Questions 28 and 29 refer to the following talk.
To qualify for a mortgage, you have to be able to make a down payment of ten percent. You also have to show that you have been at your current job for at least one year and at your current address for three or more years. It's also a good idea to have some extra money in a savings account.

Now read question 28 in your text book and answer it.

Now read question 29 in your text book and answer it.

LESSON 22
Listening Comprehension

Part I: Picture

Number 23. Look at the picture marked number 23.
- (A) The auditor is looking over the books.
- (B) Snow is accumulating on the ground.
- (C) The employee turnover is high.
- (D) She is meeting her clients in her office.

Part II: Question-Response

Number 24.

Do you have any outstanding debts?
- (A) Yes, I understand all about debts.
- (B) Yes, I still owe money on my car.
- (C) Yes, he's a very upstanding citizen.

Number 25.

What assets do you have?
- (A) I own my house and I have some money in the bank.
- (B) I felt quite upset by the news.
- (C) I don't have an assistant.

Part III: Short Conversations

Number 26.

[M] Have you seen our budget for next year?

[W] How do they expect us to meet our goals with such a small budget?

[M] We'll have to come up with something to increase our assets, or else we'll be out of a job!

Number 27.

[W] I'm going to see my client today. I'll be back at 4:30.

[M] Is this the client you are trying to save from all of his debt?

[W] That's the one! How he accumulated so much debt, I'll never understand!

Part IV: Short Talks

Questions 28 and 29 refer to the following talk.
The most important factor in making your accounting firm profitable is to build up a solid list of clients. You want your clients to continue bringing their accounting business to you year after year and to avoid the problem of client turnover. Also, keep in mind that charging higher fees does not mean that you will make more money. If your clients feel that your fees are fair, they will recommend your services to their friends and colleagues.

Now read question 28 in your text book and answer it.

Now read question 29 in your text book and answer it.

LESSON 23
Listening Comprehension

Part I: Picture

Number 23. Look at the picture marked number 23.
- (A)   The brokers are committed to their work.
- (B)   They're returning the products to the store.
- (C)   The supplies are out of stock.
- (D)   They're pulling the phone out of the box.

Part II: Question-Response

Number 24.

Who can give me advice about my portfolio?
- (A)   My stockbroker can help you with your investments.
- (B)   It's a very nice portfolio.
- (C)   I think you made a wise choice.

Number 25.

Will I get a good return on this investment?
- (A)   Please return it to me when you've finished.
- (B)   I'm sorry, we don't accept returns.
- (C)   You should earn at least a 15% return.

Part III: Short Conversations

Number 26.

[M] In order to minimize risk, investors should maintain a diverse portfolio by putting their money in various industry investments.

[W] You mean, we should invest in natural resources as well as in manufacturing industries?

[M] Perhaps. Unless you are very aggressive, you don't want to put all your eggs in one basket.

Number 27.

[W] How did you make such wise and profitable investments?

[M] I never invested much at one time because I needed the money, so I felt less pressure.

[W] I hope my returns will be as good as yours some day.

Part IV: Short Talks

Questions 28 and 29 refer to the following talk.
Have you thought about how you will fund your children's college education? Don't wait until they are in high school. The time to begin saving is when your children are still small. A good way to start is by investing some of your income in the stock market. You will get a good return on your money there. Even after just two or three years, you should see your investment grow.

Now read question 28 in your text book and answer it.

Now read question 29 in your text book and answer it.

LESSON 24
Listening Comprehension

Part I: Picture

Number 23. Look at the picture marked number 23.
  (A)   She's filling out a form.
  (B)   She's preparing dinner.
  (C)   She's filing her nails.
  (D)   She's calculating the total.

Part II: Question-Response

Number 24.

How much do I owe?
  (A)   About 125 dollars.
  (B)   I own two cars.
  (C)   I paid what I owed.

Number 25.

When do I have to file my income taxes?
  (A)   It's only about a mile from here.
  (B)   We received an incoming fax.
  (C)   The deadline is April 15th.

Part III: Short Conversations

Number 26.

[M] When is the deadline for this project? Isn't it tomorrow?

[W] No, we don't have to file the forms until the beginning of next week.

[M] That's still soon. I'll have Jack start to prepare them this morning.

Number 27.

[W] Who files the taxes in your family?

[M] My spouse does all the calculations. I'm no good with numbers.

[W] Then you're lucky she does them. Does she keep all the family accounts, too?

Part IV: Short Talks

Questions 28 and 29 refer to the following talk.
You will be getting a refund of 460 dollars, and you can expect to receive it in eight to ten weeks. While I know it's nice to get a refund check, it's better for your finances to avoid overpaying taxes in the first place. If you'd like, I can do some calculations which will show exactly how much you should ask your employer to withhold from your check in the future, and I'd only charge a small fee for this service.

Now read question 28 in your text book and answer it.

Now read question 29 in your text book and answer it.

LESSON 25
Listening Comprehension

Part I: Picture

Number 23. Look at the picture marked number 23.
  (A)   This orchard yields a lot of fruit.
  (B)   The weather reporter is making a forecast.
  (C)   The crew is making the drive level.
  (D)   The arrow hit its target.

Part II: Question-Response

Number 24.

What is our projected income for next year?
  (A)   We expect several projects to come in.
  (B)   It can't be protected.
  (C)   It'll probably be slightly higher than this year.

Number 25.

Is this an accurate translation of the statement?
  (A)   Yes, the translator did an excellent job.
  (B)   No, we don't need eight translators.
  (C)   The transportation in this area is not adequate.

Part III: Short Conversations

Number 26.

[M] I can't believe our sales targets for this month. I can't make that many sales.

[W] I'm surprised at the level of sales activity our manager expects.

[M] Especially since we're a new company, and it requires more sales calls to translate into a sale.

Number 27.

[W] I'm developing a projected financial statement for my business.

[M] That's great. It'll help you forecast periods where you might have financial problems.

[W] I'll also use it to see what kind of profits we can expect to yield this quarter.

Part IV: Short Talks

Questions 28 and 29 refer to the following talk.
Many small businesses fail because of poor financial advice. Remember, a small business is no different from a large company in that financial planning is the key to success. It is realistic to expect your small business to become profitable during its first five years, but typically not during the first year. With this in mind, you can set reasonable targets and project expenses for the first year or two of your business.

Now read question 28 in your text book and answer it.

Now read question 29 in your text book and answer it.

LESSON 26
Listening Comprehension

Part I: Picture

Number 23. Look at the picture marked number 23.
- (A)   They're scrutinizing the drawings.
- (B)   They're moving up the ladder.
- (C)   They're concentrating on the pathway.
- (D)   They're working in the street.

Part II: Question-Response

Number 24.

Where is your new office?
- (A)   It's adjacent to the lobby.
- (B)   I moved up to a new position.
- (C)   I'm open to it.

Number 25.

Is your boss open to new ideas?
- (A)   Yes, I like to keep the window open.
- (B)   Yes, it opens early every day.
- (C)   Yes, she always listens to my proposals.

Part III: Short Conversations

Number 26.

[M] What do you think about the plans for the new office lobby?

[W] I've spent a lot of time scrutinizing them and I'm quite pleased.

[M] I hope they're more conducive to conversation than our current lobby is.

Number 27.

[W] It was so inconsiderate of the marketing department to have a party in the middle of the afternoon.

[M] Unfortunately, your meeting was the one most hampered by the noise.

[W] I was glad their director told them they were too disruptive and had to stop.

Part IV: Short Talks

Questions 28 and 29 refer to the following talk.
The design of an office can contribute a great deal to employee productivity. It is important to plan your office space so that it is conducive to collaboration, yet at the same time allows staff members to concentrate on their work. Many companies opt for a design that includes several smaller offices adjacent to a lobby rather than one large one, as they find that the level of activity in an open office is often disruptive to work.

Now read question 28 in your text book and answer it.

Now read question 29 in your text book and answer it.

LESSON 27
Listening Comprehension

Part I: Picture

Number 23. Look at the picture marked number 23.
  (A)   The periodicals are on the stand.
  (B)   The cars are going ahead.
  (C)   The waste basket is under the table.
  (D)   The meeting is adhering to an agenda.

Part II: Question-Response

Number 24.

Do your staff members meet periodically?
  (A)   They read several newspapers and magazines.
  (B)   I haven't seen him for quite a long period.
  (C)   We have a meeting every Friday.

Number 25.

How did the meeting go?
  (A)   It was right after lunch.
  (B)   It was in the boardroom.
  (C)   It was a real waste of time.

Part III: Short Conversations

Number 26.

[M] That meeting was such a waste of time.

[W] You're right. It was too lengthy and we didn't accomplish anything.

[M] We didn't even talk about the most important matters.

Number 27.

[W] What is on today's agenda?

[M] Well, the first thing is to cover next year's goals.

[W] I'm glad to hear that that is a priority.

Part IV: Short Talks

Questions 28 and 29 refer to the following talk.
In order to keep everyone from feeling that this meeting is a waste of time, I've developed the following guidelines. Please adhere to them. One: Please discuss only the items on the agenda. This is not the time to bring up irrelevant or personal matters. Two: Please do not make unnecessarily lengthy speeches. Make your point as quickly and clearly as possible.

Now read question 28 in your text book and answer it.

Now read question 29 in your text book and answer it.

LESSON 28
Listening Comprehension

Part I: Picture

Number 23. Look at the picture marked number 23.
  (A)   She's trying on a new garment.
  (B)   She's taking back damaged goods to the store.
  (C)   She's inspecting the products for defects.
  (D)   She's throwing out her uniform.

Part II: Question-Response

Number 24.

Which brand is better?
  (A)   I love the music that band plays.
  (B)   Most of our customers prefer this one.
  (C)   No, I don't understand this letter.

Number 25.

Is this coat water repellent?
  (A)   Yes, this water tastes excellent.
  (B)   Yes, it will keep you very dry.
  (C)   Yes, you can wash it with soap and water.

Part III: Short Conversations

Number 26.

[M] What does the company do with the garments that have defects in them?

[W] Sometimes we change the brand name and sell them in discount stores.

[M] That's certainly more profitable than throwing them out.

Number 27.

[W] In quality control, it's important to ensure uniform quality.

[M] But some of our best products have defects.

[W] That's why we have to inspect each item very carefully.

Part IV: Short Talks

Questions 28 and 29 refer to the following talk.
We assure you that all our products go through strict quality control. All defective products are thrown out before they leave the factory. You can be sure that all our products that reach the store have been thoroughly inspected to make sure they conform to our high quality standards. If for any reason, however, you are not completely satisfied with our product, you can take it back to the store for a 100 percent refund, no questions asked.

Now read question 28 in your text book and answer it.

Now read question 29 in your text book and answer it.

LESSON 29
Listening Comprehension

Part I: Picture

Number 23. Look at the picture marked number 23.
- (A) She's ascertaining the time of the flight.
- (B) She's examining the contents of the test tube.
- (C) She's experimenting with a new way home.
- (D) She's solving a crossword puzzle.

Part II: Question-Response

Number 24.

How long have you worked as a supervisor?
- (A) I like it very much.
- (B) He doesn't have an advisor.
- (C) For almost a decade.

Number 25.

What kind of responsibilities does Jim have at his new job?
- (A) He supervises the entire department.
- (B) He's a fairly responsive person.
- (C) He's responding very well.

Part III: Short Conversations

Number 26.

[M] How did your team ascertain that the market needed another stuffed toy?

[W] Product Development started with the assumption that stuffed toys have a successful history.

[M] Just because they have been popular for the last four or five decades doesn't mean that they will last forever.

Number 27.

[W] We need to examine the data for our Binky doll sales before we decide how to modify it.

[M] Several companies have successfully experimented with modifications such as bright colors and noisemakers.

[W] Consumers today are anxious about inflation, so our next modification should be to make the doll cheaper.

Part IV: Short Talks

Questions 28 and 29 refer to the following talk.
This product has been on the market for over two decades and it continues to sell well. Researchers aren't sure of the reason for this. They have examined hundreds of pages of market data but haven't ascertained an exact reason for the product's popularity. Is it the low price or the wide availability? Perhaps it is the consumers' familiarity with it. Researchers don't know which factors are responsible, but consumers continue to buy the product as it enters its 22nd year on the market.

Now read question 28 in your text book and answer it.

Now read question 29 in your text book and answer it.

LESSON 30
Listening Comprehension

Part I: Picture

Number 23. Look at the picture marked number 23.
(A)   The woman is apprehensive about signing the lease.
(B)   The couple is due to arrive any minute.
(C)   The man is trying to get out of the building.
(D)   The occupancy rate for this room is 450.

Part II: Question-Response

Number 24.

Who are the occupants on the second floor?
(A)   They'll take occupancy next week.
(B)   Two lawyer's offices.
(C)   No, we only occupy the first floor.

Number 25.

Is the building in good condition?
(A)   Yes, the landlord keeps it in good repair.
(B)   Yes, it's near all the bus routes.
(C)   Yes, all the tenants are very nice.

Part III: Short Conversations

Number 26.

[M] I understand that we may be able to get out of our unfortunate situation.

[W] Yes, under certain conditions, a clause in your contract may not be valid.

[M] I just don't want to be subjected to any lawsuit.

Number 27.

[W] According to all the indicators, now is the time to buy.

[M] You're not apprehensive about making such a large commitment now?

[W] I'm telling you, interest rates may start to fluctuate if we don't buy now.

Part IV: Short Talks

Questions 28 and 29 refer to the following talk.
Before you sign a lease on a space for your business, make sure you have chosen the best location. Look for the indicators of a neighborhood that is good for business. Are there other, successful businesses nearby? Is there access to public transportation? Is the area attractive to customers and clients? If the conditions don't look right for your business, look into other options. Don't lock yourself into a long-term lease on a space that isn't right for you.

Now read question 28 in your text book and answer it.

Now read question 29 in your text book and answer it.

LESSON 31
Listening Comprehension

Part I: Picture

Number 23. Look at the picture marked number 23.
- (A) They're relying on the waiter's suggestions.
- (B) They're guiding the man through the mall.
- (C) They're arriving at an empty restaurant.
- (D) They're securing the cloth to the table.

Part II: Question-Response

Number 24.

How can I secure reservations at such a popular restaurant?
- (A) Call early in the day.
- (B) You can feel secure at that restaurant.
- (C) I can recommend a popular restaurant.

Number 25.

How can I choose a good restaurant?
- (A) Look in the restaurant guide.
- (B) I never refuse food at a restaurant.
- (C) Yes, it's a very good restaurant.

Part III: Short Conversations

Number 26.

[M] Did you look in the guide for suggestions for a restaurant for this weekend?

[W] No, but the majority of the people at my office like that new seafood restaurant.

[M] Do you think we can rely on their opinion?

Number 27.

[W] The woman who writes the weekly restaurant reviews for the newspaper has published a guide to local restaurants.

[M] That won't be too helpful. I don't think the same food appeals to her as appeals to me.

[W] I know what you mean. There's a lot of subjectivity in reviewing restaurants.

Part IV: Short Talks

Questions 28 and 29 refer to the following talk.
I have secured a reservation for you for 8:30 p.m. tomorrow evening. Please arrive on time. We have a bar where you can enjoy appetizers and drinks before dinner. If that idea appeals to you, I suggest arriving at 7:30 or 8 o'clock. We have a parking lot in the back. Are you familiar with our location, or will you need directions?

Now read question 28 in your text book and answer it.

Now read question 29 in your text book and answer it.

LESSON 32
Listening Comprehension

Part I: Picture

Number 23. Look at the picture marked number 23.
(A)   The chef is adding ingredients to his list.
(B)   The patron is waiting to be served.
(C)   The forecaster is making a prediction.
(D)   The judge is consulting with the lawyers.

Part II: Question-Response

Number 24.

What kinds of flavors does the chef use?
(A)   I don't like this kind of food.
(B)   She uses a blend of Asian spices.
(C)   Yes, the food is very flavorful.

Number 25.

Can you judge a restaurant just by looking at the menu?
(A)   No, the judge didn't like that restaurant.
(B)   No, I haven't looked at the menu yet.
(C)   No, I think you have to eat there first.

Part III: Short Conversations

Number 26.

[M] This restaurant reminds me of one we visited last year on vacation.

[W] I think they use many of the same ingredients in the dishes.

[M] Yes, the flavor of the dishes is similar.

Number 27.

[W] The waiter forgot to offer us water.

[M] He didn't even complete our order.

[W] Don't get excited. I predict he'll come back.

Part IV: Short Talks

Questions 28 and 29 refer to the following talk.
I'm sorry for the delay. I'm sure you thought I'd forgotten your order. The problem is, we have a new assistant chef and he's mixed up everything in the kitchen. It will take a while longer for your meal to be ready, but we want to keep all our patrons happy so I'd be happy to bring you some free appetizers to enjoy while you wait. And I predict that when you finally get your meal, you'll judge that our chef's cooking is worth the wait.

Now read question 28 in your text book and answer it.

Now read question 29 in your text book and answer it.

LESSON 33
Listening Comprehension

Part I: Picture

Number 23. Look at the picture marked number 23.
- (A)   The customer is settling the bill.
- (B)   The waiter is picking up the glass.
- (C)   The individual is ordering his lunch.
- (D)   The patron is making a list.

Part II: Question-Response

Number 24.

Does your restaurant have free delivery?
- (A)   Yes, deliveries are free on orders of ten dollars or more.
- (B)   Yes, we charge a fee for that service.
- (C)   Yes, we make deliveries after three.

Number 25.

Would you like that order delivered, or will you pick it up?
- (A)   Yes, please pick it up.
- (B)   I'll pick it up in half an hour.
- (C)   Pick up after yourself.

Part III: Short Conversations

Number 26.

[M] Will you please arrange for an elegant lunch to be delivered to the office during the regional manager's visit?

[W] That's such an annoying burden. Why don't you just go to a restaurant?

[M] I need to show our impressive sales data during lunch and can't show slides at a restaurant.

Number 27.

[W] Here's a list of 12 restaurants in the area.

[M] Let's narrow this list to two or three then ask the staff to make a final selection.

[W] First, let's double-check that they all offer free delivery to this building.

Part IV: Short Talks

Questions 28 and 29 refer to the following advertisement.
Don't settle for uninteresting food and slow service. Order your next lunch from the Parkside Cafe, where speedy service is guaranteed. It's easy. Make your selection from our list of made-to-order sandwiches and salads, then call in your order and it will be ready to be picked up in ten minutes, guaranteed. Or have your meal delivered directly to your office. Our delivery fee is just 15% of the price of your order. We handle both individual and group orders.

Now read question 28 in your text book and answer it.

Now read question 29 in your text book and answer it.

LESSON 34
Listening Comprehension

Part I: Picture

Number 23. Look at the picture marked number 23.
- (A) The chef is instructing the apprentices.
- (B) The professionals are chopping the food.
- (C) The customers are demanding menus.
- (D) The designers are incorporating fish motifs into the décor.

Part II: Question-Response

Number 24.

How did you decide to enter the cooking profession?
- (A) Yes, I'm still looking for a profession.
- (B) The kitchen door is to your right.
- (C) I've always wanted to work in a restaurant.

Number 25.

How do you plan to draw new customers to the restaurant?
- (A) Yes, I'm accustomed to eating here.
- (B) We will expand the menu and offer new specials.
- (C) We saw several new customers there.

Part III: Short Conversations

Number 26.

[M] This soup is delicious. What culinary secret have you discovered?

[W] It's fennel, an herb I've become accustomed to using lately.

[M] I also like how it's incorporated into the squash casserole.

Number 27.

[W] There's been a large influx of new chefs recently.

[M] I've noticed that, also. They're demanding large salaries, too.

[W] Good chefs manage to draw customers into restaurants.

Part IV: Short Talks

Questions 28 and 29 refer to the following talk.
Are you trying to decide on a profession? Don't forget to consider a career in the culinary arts. Many people find professional cooking to be an excellent outlet for their creativity. It's a demanding but exciting career with numerous opportunities. Graduates of culinary schools become chefs, caterers, cooking instructors, and more. Join the many creative people who have been drawn to the cooking profession. You'll never be bored!

Now read question 28 in your text book and answer it.

Now read question 29 in your text book and answer it.

LESSON 35
Listening Comprehension

Part I: Picture

Number 23. Look at the picture marked number 23.
(A)   The exact number of guests is ten.
(B)   The location is ideal for a playground.
(C)   The regulations limit parking at night.
(D)   The banquet is staged in the ballroom.

Part II: Question-Response

Number 24.

Can you give me a general idea of the number of guests you expect?
(A)   That's the ideal number.
(B)   About 150 people will attend.
(C)   Generally, I have good expectations.

Number 25.

How much lead time will we need?
(A)   The event should last about three or four hours.
(B)   I was the leader last time.
(C)   The hall has to be reserved a month in advance.

Part III: Short Conversations

Number 26.

[M] I've found the ideal site for our wedding reception.

[W] Will we be able to coordinate all the details?

[M] It's exactly what we wanted, and the manager will help us with the details.

Number 27.

[W] We have very strict regulations about serving food and alcohol at the museum.

[M] I'm sure you do. In fact, I'm surprised you'll let us stage a reception here.

[W] We are the only museum in town that will allow parties.

Part IV: Short Talks

Questions 28 and 29 refer to the following talk.
I am coordinating the plans for the office party with the assistance of Tom. The event isn't until next month, so we've given ourselves plenty of lead time. We're looking for a site that is in close proximity to the office and isn't too small to stage our event. We have a general idea of how many will attend, but we'll need an exact count by the end of next week, so please let us know soon if you plan to attend.

Now read question 28 in your text book and answer it.

Now read question 29 in your text book and answer it.

LESSON 36
Listening Comprehension

Part I: Picture

Number 23. Look at the picture marked number 23.
- (A) The passengers are waiting for an announcement.
- (B) The travel agents are issuing the tickets.
- (C) The travelers are claiming their bags.
- (D) The flight crew is boarding the plane.

Part II: Question-Response

Number 24.

When does the train depart?
- (A) In fifteen minutes.
- (B) From Gate 15.
- (C) In another part of the station.

Number 25.

Will a meal be served during the flight?
- (A) Yes, I reserved your flight.
- (B) No, just beverages and a snack.
- (C) Their service is all right.

Part III: Short Conversations

Number 26.

[M] The travel agent said that you will need a visa for your trip next week.

[W] Oh, dear. I don't have a valid passport. I'll have to get it renewed.

[M] I'm afraid that will force you to delay your trip and you'll have to change your ticket.

Number 27.

[W] Would you care for another beverage?

[M] Is there time? According to my itinerary, we should be landing soon.

[W] We've been delayed. Would you like a blanket so you can take a nap?

Part IV: Short Talks

Questions 28 and 29 refer to the following announcement.
Welcome to Flight 115. We will begin embarkation in five minutes. Please have a valid passport and ticket ready to show the flight attendant as you board. The itinerary for our trip today includes a 30 minute stop in Chicago before we continue on to Los Angeles. We are scheduled for take off in twenty minutes and since the captain has announced that he expects no delays in our trip, we should be departing on time.

Now read question 28 in your text book and answer it.

Now read question 29 in your text book and answer it.

LESSON 37
Listening Comprehension

Part I: Picture

Number 23. Look at the picture marked number 23.
(A)   The airline system is on strike.
(B)   The tourists are looking for an excursion ticket.
(C)   The passengers are arriving at their destination.
(D)   The expensive business class section is not crowded.

Part II: Question-Response

Number 24.

How can we keep expenses down?
(A)   You're right, it's too expensive to keep.
(B)   We can use the elevator.
(C)   We can fly in economy class.

Number 25.

How long can you extend your stay?
(A)   It's a long way away.
(B)   I can't spend any more money.
(C)   I can stay three more days.

Part III: Short Conversations

Number 26.

[M] If you are willing to be flexible about your excursion dates, I can get you a lower airfare.

[W] We have to reach our destination by noon on Sunday.

[M] I didn't realize your situation was so structured.

Number 27.

[W] The airfares to Hong Kong are too expensive.

[M] I know you need to economize. Let's see if we can find you a better airfare.

[W] I'll really need a substantial discount to make my trip possible.

Part IV: Short Talks

Questions 28 and 29 refer to the following message. Thank you for calling Travel Time Travel Agency, your place for economically-priced airline tickets. If your destination is within this country, press one. If your destination is in another country, press two. If you would like to make hotel reservations or travel arrangements other than purchasing airline tickets, press three. We're sorry, information on special excursion rates is not currently available because our computer system is down. Please call back later to find out if the situation has changed.

Now read question 28 in your text book and answer it.

Now read question 29 in your text book and answer it.

LESSON 38
Listening Comprehension

Part I: Picture

Number 23. Look at the picture marked number 23.
(A)   They're checking the directory.
(B)   They're paying their fare.
(C)   They're promptly boarding the train.
(D)   They're using the remainder of their ticket.

Part II: Question-Response

Number 24.

Why is the fare to London so high?
(A)   Because this is a deluxe train.
(B)   The weather in London is unusually fair.
(C)   We already said good-bye.

Number 25.

Do you think the train will be punctual?
(A)   Yes, it's always fun to ride the train.
(B)   No, it will be several minutes late.
(C)   Everything functions well.

Part III: Short Conversations

Number 26.

[M] I can't believe this train is so crowded! We'll be standing for the duration of the trip.

[W] I always thought that buying a fare entitled me to a seat.

[M] They should operate more trains on busy holidays like today.

Number 27.

[W] Take a look at the directory to see exactly when the next train to New York leaves.

[M] Do you think it will leave punctually?

[W] I think so. The trains have to operate on time or people won't want to ride them.

Part IV: Short Talks

Questions 28 and 29 refer to the following talk.
People often ask if the higher fares charged on the new high-speed trains are offset by the savings in time. The answer is yes. In fact, the duration of a high-speed train trip in some cases is not much more than a plane trip, and the fare is always cheaper than a plane ticket. Unfortunately, these trains operate out of far fewer cities than do planes and the traditional slower trains.

Now read question 28 in your text book and answer it.

Now read question 29 in your text book and answer it.

LESSON 39
Listening Comprehension

Part I: Picture

Number 23. Look at the picture marked number 23.
- (A) The guests are checking into the hotel.
- (B) The housekeeper is cleaning the room.
- (C) This room has been serviced and is ready for occupancy.
- (D) The reservations agent is quoting a high rate.

Part II: Question-Response

Number 24.

What rate do you charge for a double room?
- (A) Yes, you could change to a double room.
- (B) It costs eighty-five dollars a night.
- (C) This hotel has great rooms.

Number 25.

What time should we check in?
- (A) Before nine o'clock.
- (B) We only take credit cards.
- (C) At the registration desk.

Part III: Short Conversations

Number 26.

[M] Mrs. Kim called today to confirm her stay this weekend.

[W] She made a reservation several weeks ago.

[M] Yes, she took advantage of the special rate we advertised for the winter holidays.

Number 27.

[W] What is our hotel chain's policy on canceling reservations?

[M] If we are notified of a cancellation at least 24 hours in advance, we refund the deposit.

[W] That's good news because the customer expects to have his deposit returned.

Part IV: Short Talks

Questions 28 and 29 refer to the following talk.
Welcome to the Palm Garden Hotel chain. As one of our employees, many opportunities await you. You may be starting out as housekeepers, but any one of you could advance to manager as you gain experience. Our goal at the Palm Tree Hotels is to provide the highest level of service possible. Our customers pay high rates to stay at our hotels and they expect an advanced level of service in return.

Now read question 28 in your text book and answer it.

Now read question 29 in your text book and answer it.

LESSON 40
Listening Comprehension

Part I: Picture

Number 23. Look at the picture marked number 23.
- (A) He's disappointed in the movie.
- (B) He's showing his driver's license.
- (C) He's contacting the agency to rent a car.
- (D) He's tempted to have more cake.

Part II: Question-Response

Number 24.

Is collision insurance optional with a rental car?
- (A) No, we haven't yet made a decision.
- (B) Yes, but we recommend you get it.
- (C) We hope to rent a luxury car.

Number 25.

How many car rental agencies have you contacted?
- (A) We asked for a compact car.
- (B) I've only called two or three.
- (C) Each agency has its own contract.

Part III: Short Conversations

Number 26.

[M] I'm sorry to disappoint you, but we don't have any rental cars available.

[W] I didn't realize that a holiday coincided with our vacation.

[M] This holiday weekend has been especially busy.

Number 27.

[W] Would you like collision insurance on the rental car? It's optional.

[M] I doubt that we'll have an accident, but I'd feel less nervous with the insurance.

[W] No one ever intends to have an accident, of course, but most customers opt for the insurance when they rent from us.

Part IV: Short Talks

Questions 28 and 29 refer to the following talk.
If you are traveling to another country and intend to rent a car while there, there are several things to do before you leave. First, get an international driver's license. Then, contact your local car rental agency to find out if they have offices abroad. If so, you can arrange to rent your car through them and avoid the confusion of signing a contract in a foreign language. This way, when you arrive and pick up your car, you won't be disappointed.

Now read question 28 in your text book and answer it.

Now read question 29 in your text book and answer it.

LESSON 41
Listening Comprehension

Part I: Picture

Number 23. Look at the picture marked number 23.
  (A)   There are four separate movie posters on the wall.
  (B)   The film description is read to the moviegoers.
  (C)   The pedestrians are being entertained.
  (D)   The fans are continuing to buy tickets.

Part II: Question-Response

Number 24.

When will the movie be released?
  (A)   It'll be reviewed in next Friday's paper.
  (B)   It'll be over in about 30 minutes.
  (C)   It'll be in theaters next month.

Number 25.

How would you describe that movie?
  (A)   It was the most romantic film I've ever seen.
  (B)   I'd move it over here.
  (C)   We decided it together.

Part III: Short Conversations

Number 26.

[M] I was amazed to see how the film represented good and evil through symbols.

[W] The descriptions were much more graphic on film than in the novel.

[M] The film was certainly able to attain a high degree of suspense.

Number 27.

[W] Did you find the latest movie as entertaining as the previous ones?

[M] Oh, yes. I can see how the actress has been influenced by light situation comedies on television.

[W] She certainly has developed a broader range of styles in the past two years.

Part IV: Short Talks

Questions 28 and 29 refer to the following announcement.
On next week's show we'll interview a big name in the entertainment industry, Maria Moreno. She's attained worldwide fame over the last several years through her outstanding performances in several hit movies. Her impressive acting abilities range from the comedic to the dramatic. We'll talk about her latest movie, which has recently finished production and will be released next month, and about the directors and fellow actors who have influenced her career.

Now read question 28 in your text book and answer it.

Now read question 29 in your text book and answer it.

LESSON 42
Listening Comprehension

Part I: Picture

Number 23. Look at the picture marked number 23.
- (A) The dancer is rehearsing for a performance.
- (B) The audience is entering the theater.
- (C) The reviewer is watching the action.
- (D) The actor is approaching the musician.

Part II: Question-Response

Number 24.

Do you think tickets will sell out quickly?
- (A) Yes, they'll sell them at the box office.
- (B) Yes, it's a very popular play.
- (C) Yes, I'll tell them about the tickets.

Number 25.

How long did the performance last?
- (A) No, it was first.
- (B) It was very well-done.
- (C) About an hour and a half.

Part III: Short Conversations

Number 26.

[M] Did you read the review of the new musical comedy in yesterday's paper?

[W] I can't believe the tickets are already sold out for the entire run.

[M] I hear the charming dialogue among the characters is very funny.

Number 27.

[W] The meaning of the play can be approached from many different levels.

[M] There was so much action, I think I missed the meaning. I'll have to think about it for a while.

[W] That's all part of the theater experience.

Part IV: Short Talks

Questions 28 and 29 refer to the following advertisement.
Audiences can't stop talking about the Shakespeare Theater's production of *Romeo and Juliet*. Shouldn't you see it too? Performances are at eight o'clock Thursday through Sunday evenings and at two o'clock on Saturday and Sunday afternoons. Order your tickets by e-mail: *tickets@shakespeare.org*. Call 656-9025 for prices and other information or visit our web site at *www.shakespeare.org* to read play reviews. Tickets are expected to sell out quickly so order yours today. See *Romeo and Juliet* and experience the magic of live theater.

Now read question 28 in your text book and answer it.

Now read question 29 in your text book and answer it.

LESSON 43
Listening Comprehension

Part I: Picture

Number 23. Look at the picture marked number 23.
- (A)   The critic is tasting the new dish.
- (B)   The fans are urging the team to win.
- (C)   The nurse is recommending relaxation.
- (D)   The orchestra is playing the conductor's favorite music.

Part II: Question-Response

Number 24.

Is there a reason that you don't like opera?
- (A)   Yes, I find it really boring.
- (B)   The opera season begins in December.
- (C)   No, I don't.

Number 25.

What are your musical preferences?
- (A)   The musical instruments are in the next room.
- (B)   The library has a good reference collection.
- (C)   I like jazz and classical music.

Part III: Short Conversations

Number 26.

[M] I looked for the music I favor at the store, but they were out of stock. Everything available was pretty uninteresting.

[W] With all the disparate music out there, how could everything in the store be boring?

[M] I guess my tastes don't match those of the majority of the people.

Number 27.

[W] Please don't adjust the preset button on my radio.

[M] Sorry. I'm just trying to find some relaxing music.

[W] OK, but that button is set to the station that plays the music I prefer.

Part IV: Short Talks

Questions 28 and 29 refer to the following talk. Welcome to the Music Appreciation class. I know you are all here to broaden your tastes in music. We'll do that by looking at several categories of music and disparate composers' styles. We will also look at the development of musical instruments throughout history. The text book for this class is available at the college bookstore and I urge you to buy it and start reading it right away.

Now read question 28 in your text book and answer it.

Now read question 29 in your text book and answer it.

LESSON 44
Listening Comprehension

Part I: Picture

Number 23. Look at the picture marked number 23.
  (A)   The secretary is keeping a schedule.
  (B)   The artist is expressing himself by drawing.
  (C)   The carpenter is working leisurely.
  (D)   The critic is admiring her collection.

Part II: Question-Response

Number 24.

Which artist do you admire most?
  (A)   Painting is the hardest to do.
  (B)   We hired a photographer.
  (C)   Picasso is my favorite.

Number 25.

Have you seen the museum's sculpture collection?
  (A)   Yes, your coats are over there.
  (B)   Yes, I can give you directions to the museum.
  (C)   Yes, they have some amazing pieces of sculpture.

Part III: Short Conversations

Number 26.

[M] Art historians say that this painting is a significant contribution to the field. Do you like it?

[W] I'm drawn to it, but I'm never sure if I can tell what abstract art is trying to express.

[M] Neither can I, but I still think it's a beautiful painting. I admire the use of color.

Number 27.

[W] How will the museum staff respond to the charges that they have an insufficient number of works by minority artists in the collection?

[M] They are certainly embarrassed by the criticism.

[W] I think they should acquire a more diverse range of works for their collection.

Part IV: Short Talks

Questions 28 and 29 refer to the following message. Thank you for calling the National Museum of Art. Our collection of newly-acquired paintings is on view this month in the main gallery. Next month begins our winter weekly lecture series. The series this year includes specialists in African sculpture, 19th century painting, and several well-known art critics. To hear the lecture series schedule, press one. To hear the schedule of guided tours, press two. To speak with an operator, please stay on the line.

Now read question 28 in your text book and answer it.

Now read question 29 in your text book and answer it.

LESSON 45
Listening Comprehension

Part I: Picture

Number 23. Look at the picture marked number 23.
- (A)   The magazine reader is subscribing to a journal.
- (B)   The newspaper journalist is choosing a story.
- (C)   The TV reporter is covering an assignment.
- (D)   The e-columnist is adding a link on line.

Part II: Question-Response

Number 24.

Why do you subscribe to that newspaper?
- (A)   I decided to buy the newspaper.
- (B)   Yes, I write for that newspaper.
- (C)   Because it's the best newspaper around.

Number 25.

Who did you assign that story to?
- (A)   I gave the assignment to Mr. Lee.
- (B)   I've already signed the papers.
- (C)   I didn't see the signs.

Part III: Short Conversations

Number 26.

[M] Would you choose to work for television instead of a newspaper?

[W] No way! Newspapers can cover a story much more thoroughly than TV news.

[M] That's certainly a decisive answer.

Number 27.

[W] Does the Internet constitute a legitimate media vehicle?

[M] If an organization disseminates news to the public, it is considered a news outlet.

[W] I think many people find it convenient to link the news right from their computers.

Part IV: Short Talks

Questions 28 and 29 refer to the following announcement.
Coming up next on the six o'clock news we'll bring you in-depth coverage of the investigation into the fraud allegedly committed by the president of the National Industrial Company over the past twelve months. We'll have commentary on whether or not the president's alleged actions constitute a crime which should be prosecuted in court, then we'll look at the impact this controversy could have on our national economy. Remember, you heard it first on the Channel 5 six o'clock news, your link to what's happening in the world.

Now read question 28 in your text book and answer it.

Now read question 29 in your text book and answer it.

LESSON 46
Listening Comprehension

Part I: Picture

Number 23. Look at the picture marked number 23.
- (A)   He's diagnosing a patient.
- (B)   He's making an appointment to play golf.
- (C)   He's recommending a restaurant.
- (D)   He's playing a musical instrument.

Part II: Question-Response

Number 24.

What is the most effective way to prevent heart disease?
- (A)   Yes, I feel at ease.
- (B)   He was born with a heart defect.
- (C)   Diet and exercise are the best way.

Number 25.

What is that instrument for?
- (A)   No, I only use three instruments.
- (B)   It's for listening to your heart.
- (C)   Yes, I used it before.

Part III: Short Conversations

Number 26.

[M] I'm glad that you remember to schedule your physical annually.

[W] I was surprised that it took so long to get an appointment this year.

[M] Sometimes I can manage to see patients sooner if the really need to be seen.

Number 27.

[W] I'm recommending that you see a specialist at the university hospital for another test.

[M] That sounds serious. Am I OK?

[W] I often refer patients with your condition to specialists who have more experience than I do in the latest treatment options.

Part IV: Short Talks

Questions 28 and 29 refer to the following advertisement.

Dr. Sato's office has an opening for an experienced office manager. Responsibilities include keeping track of the doctor's appointments, managing patients' medical and billing records, and overseeing the work of two office assistants who answer the phones and make appointments. The successful candidate will be an effective organizer and have a serious attitude. Previous experience in a doctor's office is required. Please send a resume and two letters of recommendation to Dr. Sato.

Now read question 28 in your text book and answer it.

Now read question 29 in your text book and answer it.

LESSON 47
Listening Comprehension

Part I: Picture

Number 23. Look at the picture marked number 23.
- (A) The neighbors are catching up on the news.
- (B) The dental technician is restoring the whiteness to his teeth.
- (C) The plumber checks the drains regularly.
- (D) The dietician is encouraging good eating habits.

Part II: Question-Response

Number 24.

Can you restore my broken tooth?
- (A) Yes, I'll remove it.
- (B) Yes, the store is open tonight.
- (C) Yes, I can fix it.

Number 25.

Can you adjust the position of the chair?
- (A) I can change it if you're uncomfortable.
- (B) The chair belongs to me.
- (C) I think the air feels fine.

Part III: Short Conversations

Number 26.

[M] One of my teeth has a rough edge that is irritating the inside of my cheek.

[W] You need to call your dentist and make him aware of your problem.

[M] I have a regular appointment soon so I don't think I need to schedule an emergency appointment.

Number 27.

[W] A quick overview of your dental records shows that there's cause for concern.

[M] I don't care about cavities. I just want you to restore the shine to my teeth.

[W] Your best chance is to kick the habits of smoking and drinking coffee. They both dull the teeth.

Part IV: Short Talks

Questions 28 and 29 refer to the following advertisement.
Are you aware that restoring the whiteness to your teeth can be easy and inexpensive too? That's right! Our product can be used at home without the need to visit the dentist. Just apply the product to your teeth every night after your regular tooth brushing. It's that simple. Maintain your usual cleaning habits and after just a few days your teeth will start to look whiter. Unlike similar products, ours is guaranteed not to irritate sensitive gums.

Now read question 28 in your text book and answer it.

Now read question 29 in your text book and answer it.

LESSON 48
Listening Comprehension

Part I: Picture

Number 23. Look at the picture marked number 23.
(A)   Specialized personnel give a CAT scan.
(B)   The woman is signing a health insurance policy.
(C)   The pay clerk is preparing the salary checks.
(D)   Administrators emphasize the importance of rest.

Part II: Question-Response

Number 24.

Will my insurance policy cover my elective surgery?
(A)   Yes, it covers emergencies.
(B)   You can select any surgeon on the list.
(C)   No, you have to pay for that yourself.

Number 25.

Who was in charge of choosing an insurance policy for our company?
(A)   It's charged against your monthly salary.
(B)   The Director of Personnel chose it.
(C)   We can't make any changes.

Part III: Short Conversations

Number 26.

[M] Does the health plan allow me to see a specialist immediately, or do I have to see my primary care provider first?

[W] If you go without your primary provider's referral, you will incur a higher percentage of the total cost.

[M] So, I would pay an increased portion of the bill.

Number 27.

[W] I'm not happy about having to change to an alternative health plan. I like the traditional plan even if it is more expensive.

[M] Come on, some of the benefits of the new policy are great. It covers a portion of the cost of membership at a health club.

[W] I have to admit I like that aspect of the plan.

Part IV: Short Talks

Questions 28 and 29 refer to the following talk.
In response to the concerns many of our personnel have expressed about the cost of our current health plan, we have decided to make an alternative plan available to anyone who is interested. This plan offers fewer benefits, but those who opt for it will incur fewer costs. I would like to emphasize that even though we have chosen this alternative to help people save money, it is available to everyone regardless of what your salary is or how long you have worked at the company.

Now read question 28 in your text book and answer it.

Now read question 29 in your text book and answer it.

LESSON 49
Listening Comprehension

Part I: Picture

Number 23. Look at the picture marked number 23.
  (A)   The escorts are leading the group.
  (B)   The guards are authorizing the visitors.
  (C)   The musicians are following the procedures.
  (D)   The nurses are identifying the medicine.

Part II: Question-Response

Number 24.

When will I be permitted to go home?
  (A)   Because you're in good health now.
  (B)   You'll be admitted to the hospital next week.
  (C)   You can leave tomorrow morning.

Number 25.

When will I find out my test results?
  (A)   Some time next week.
  (B)   They look very good.
  (C)   I found them in the drawer.

Part III: Short Conversations

Number 26.

[M] Your mother needs a surgical procedure to treat her condition.

[W] Will she need to be admitted to the hospital for an overnight stay?

[M] Not at all. We usually perform this type of surgery on an outpatient basis.

Number 27.

[W] I'm not at all happy with the care my husband received here. Is there someone designated to handle complaints?

[M] Our mission is to deliver complete satisfaction. What is your problem?

[W] The hospital identified my husband incorrectly in the computer system and now all his records are mixed up.

Part IV: Short Talks

Questions 28 and 29 refer to the following talk.
I've gotten the lab results from the tests we did last week and, as I expected, you'll have to be admitted to the hospital for surgery. I've already sent the form to the insurance company. It's not unusual for it to take 7 or 8 days to receive their authorization, so I'd like to schedule the procedure for 10 days from now. You should expect a hospital stay of 2 or 3 days. I'll prepare the pertinent paperwork for you to give to the admitting nurse.

Now read question 28 in your text book and answer it.

Now read question 29 in your text book and answer it.

LESSON 50
Listening Comprehension

Part I: Picture

Number 23. Look at the picture marked number 23.
- (A)   The consultant is greeting the doctor.
- (B)   The volunteers are cleaning the shelves.
- (C)   The pharmacist is checking the samples.
- (D)   The patient is limiting his activity.

Part II: Question-Response

Number 24.

Is there a limited number of refills I can have on this prescription?
- (A)   Yes, I can fill it before three o'clock.
- (B)   Yes, you can have this prescription.
- (C)   Yes, you only get two.

Number 25.

What are the potential side effects of this medication?
- (A)   It's one of the most effective medications I've seen.
- (B)   It can cause sleepiness in some people.
- (C)   No, it isn't essential.

Part III: Short Conversations

Number 26.

[M] Will this pill control my runny nose?

[W] You should be able to detect a change within two days.

[M] I'll try the samples and, if they work, I'll fill the prescription you wrote.

Number 27.

[W] The doctor has volunteered to call in a prescription for you. What pharmacy do you use?

[M] The one near my house is convenient, but my wife will be picking up the prescription for me. Can I ask her which one she'd prefer?

[W] Sure. Why don't you consult with her and let me know.

Part IV: Short Talks

Questions 28 and 29 refer to the following talk.
The medication I'd like to prescribe for you is one of the most effective drugs for controlling sleeping problems and should also help alleviate your headaches. It's very convenient to use. You just take it once a day, about 30 minutes before you go to bed. I'll give you a few free samples. Call me in four or five days to let me know how it's working. The only potential side effect it has is stomachaches and it shouldn't have any interactions with your other medications.

Now read question 28 in your text book and answer it.

Now read question 29 in your text book and answer it.

NOTES